DESTINY

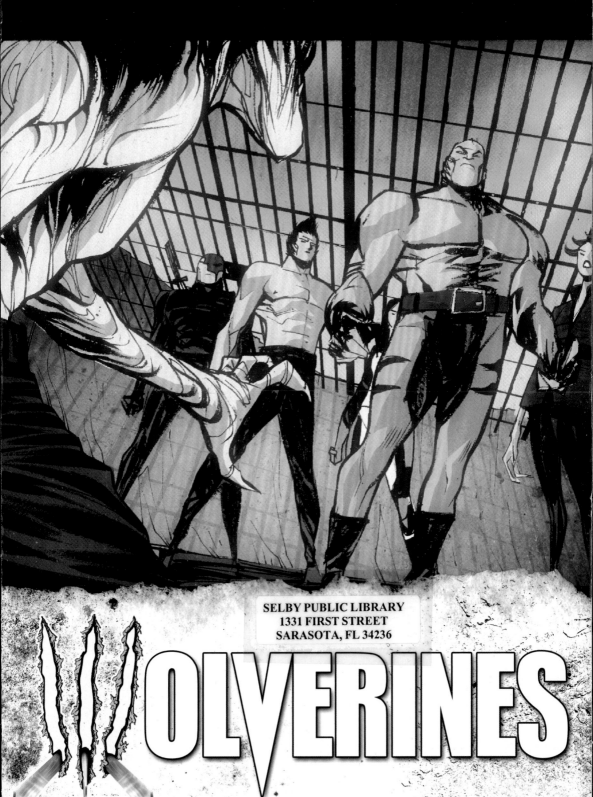

WOLVERINES

WRITERS
CHARLES SOULE (#16, #19-20) & RAY FAWKES (#17-18)

ARTISTS
ARIO ANINDITO (#16), JUAN CABAL (#17), JONATHAN MARKS (#18),
ARIELA KRISTANTINA (#19) AND JUAN DOE (#10)

COLORISTS
SONIA OBACK (#16 & #19), ANTONIO FABELA (#17)
AND LEE LOUGHRIDGE (#18)

COVER ART
GUILLEM MARCH (#16), JUAN DOE (#17-19)
AND ZACH HOWARD & NELSON DÁNIEL (#20)

LETTERER
VC's CORY PETIT

ASSISTANT EDITOR
CHRISTINA HARRINGTON

EDITORS
KATIE KUBERT
& MIKE MARTS

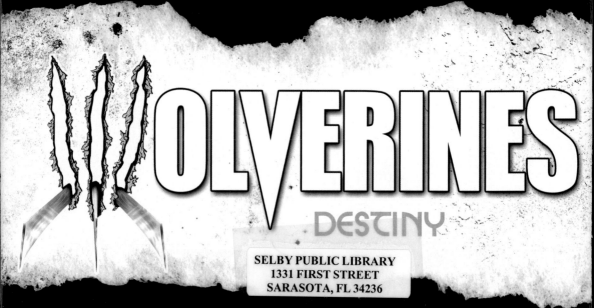

COLLECTION EDITOR: **SARAH BRUNSTAD**
ASSOCIATE MANAGING EDITOR: **ALEX STARBUCK**
EDITORS, SPECIAL PROJECTS: **JENNIFER GRÜNWALD & MARK D. BEAZLEY**
SENIOR EDITOR, SPECIAL PROJECTS: **JEFF YOUNGQUIST**
SVP PRINT, SALES & MARKETING: **DAVID GABRIEL**

EDITOR IN CHIEF: **AXEL ALONSO**
CHIEF CREATIVE OFFICER: **JOE QUESADA**
PUBLISHER: **DAN BUCKLEY**
EXECUTIVE PRODUCER: **ALAN FINE**

WOLVERINES VOL. 4: DESTINY. Contains material originally published in magazine form as WOLVERINES #16-20. First printing 2015. ISBN# 978-0-7851-9767-6. Published by MARVEL WORLDWIDE, INC., a subsidiary of MARVEL ENTERTAINMENT, LLC. OFFICE OF PUBLICATION: 135 West 50th Street, New York, NY 10020. Copyright © 2015 MARVEL No similarity between any of the names, characters, persons, and/or institutions in this magazine with those of any living or dead person or institution is intended, and any such similarity which may exist is purely coincidental. **Printed in Canada.** ALAN FINE, President, Marvel Entertainment; DAN BUCKLEY, President, TV, Publishing and Brand Management; JOE QUESADA, Chief Creative Officer; TOM BREVOORT, SVP of Publishing; DAVID BOGART, SVP of Operations & Procurement, Publishing; C.B. CEBULSKI, VP of International Development & Brand Management; DAVID GABRIEL, SVP Print, Sales & Marketing; JIM O'KEEFE, VP of Operations & Logistics; DAN CARR, Executive Director of Publishing Technology; SUSAN CRESPI, Editorial Operations Manager; ALEX MORALES, Publishing Operations Manager; STAN LEE, Chairman Emeritus. For information regarding advertising in Marvel Comics or on Marvel.com, please contact Jonathan Rheingold, VP of Custom Solutions & Ad Sales, at jrheingold@marvel.com. For Marvel subscription inquiries, please call 800-217-9158. **Manufactured between 7/3/2015 and 8/10/2015 by SOLISCO PRINTERS, SCOTT, QC, CANADA.**

10 9 8 7 6 5 4 3 2 1

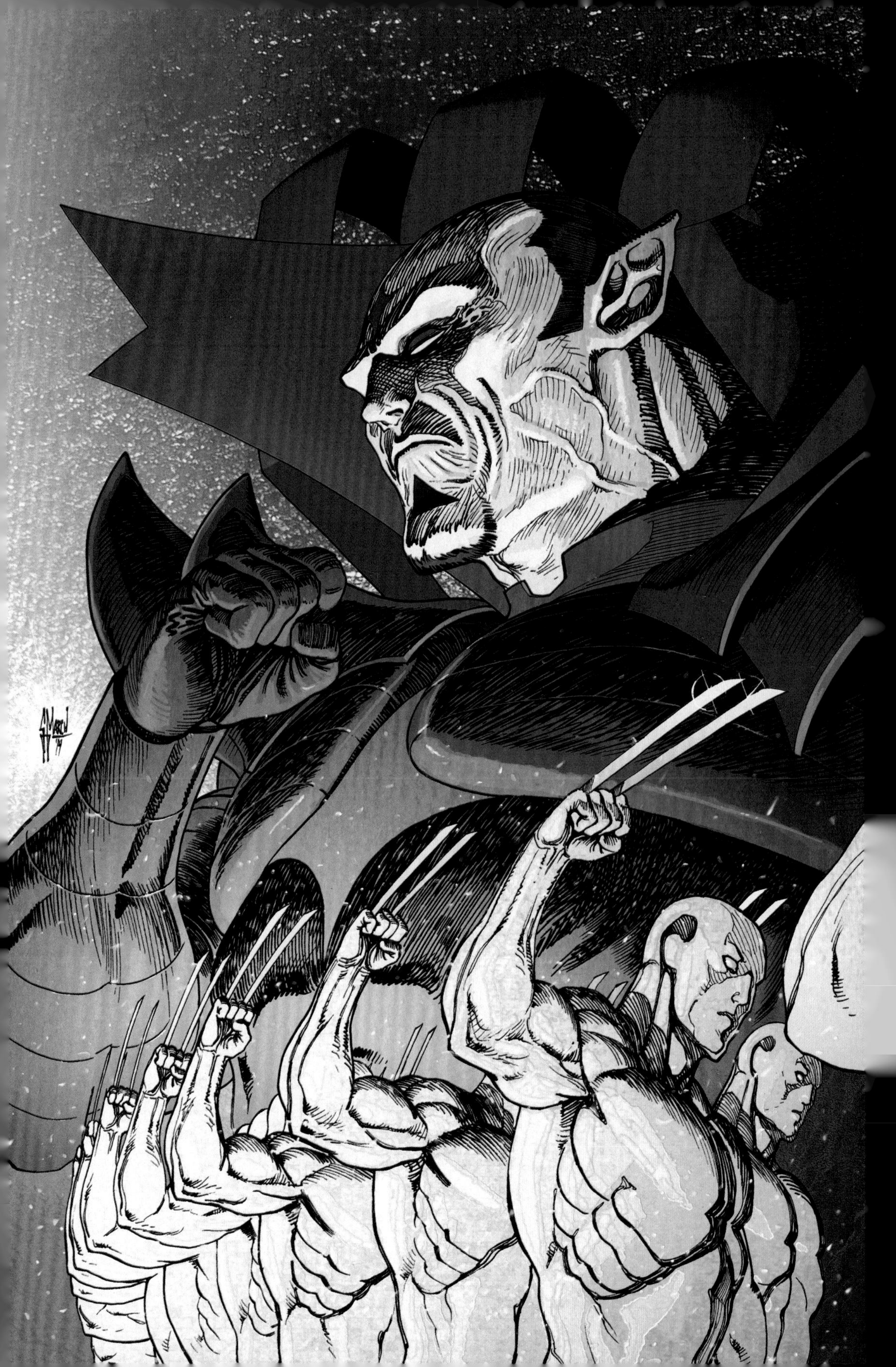

the wolverine is dead.
His legacy remains.

PARADISE

SHOGUN   NEURO   ENDO   SKEL   JUNK   FANTOMELLE

THE WOLVERINES

MYSTIQUE   SABRETOOTH   LADY DEATHSTRIKE   DAKEN   X-23

Logan met his end while destroying a revamped version of the Weapon X project located in a facility known as Paradise. Dr. Abraham Cornelius — the man responsible for Wolverine's Adamantium skeleton — was employed by the Arcadians, an organization devoted to creating individuals with super-powers — but his experiments were not a total loss.

Logan could not escape his death, but others did: Five test subjects, all granted strange new powers, became known as the Paradise Group. None were ever intended to survive outside the program, and all have been infused with a ticking clock in their DNA that will kill them unless it can be deactivated.

These lost weapons kidnapped five of Wolverine's deadliest associates in the hope that their healing factors might hold the answer to saving the test subjects' lives. The refugees from Paradise hold significant leverage over the five killers — secret "control words" that can manipulate, sedate or even kill each of them.

However, the Paradise patients split — Shogun and Junk remained with the Wolverines, while Neuro, Skel and Endo abandoned them for Mr. Sinister! Siphon, the creature responsible for the loss of Daken's healing factor, has been apprehended; Portal, a teleporter with a grudge against Mystique, has been captured, and both are being held captive on the Wolverines' ship, the *Changeling*.

Presiding over all of these players is none other than Mystique — whose motive continues to be a mystery.

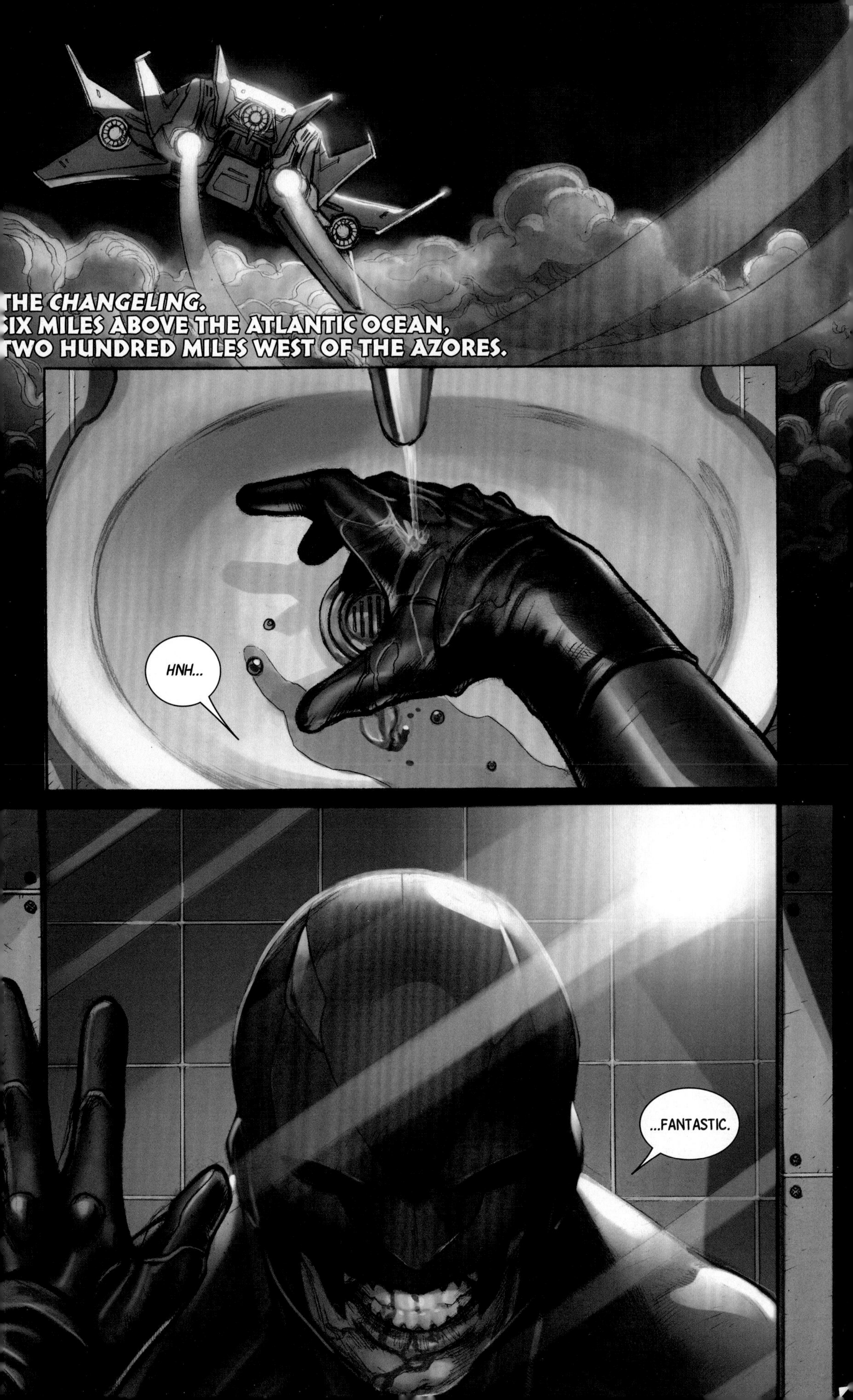
THE CHANGELING.
SIX MILES ABOVE THE ATLANTIC OCEAN,
TWO HUNDRED MILES WEST OF THE AZORES.
HNH...
...FANTASTIC.

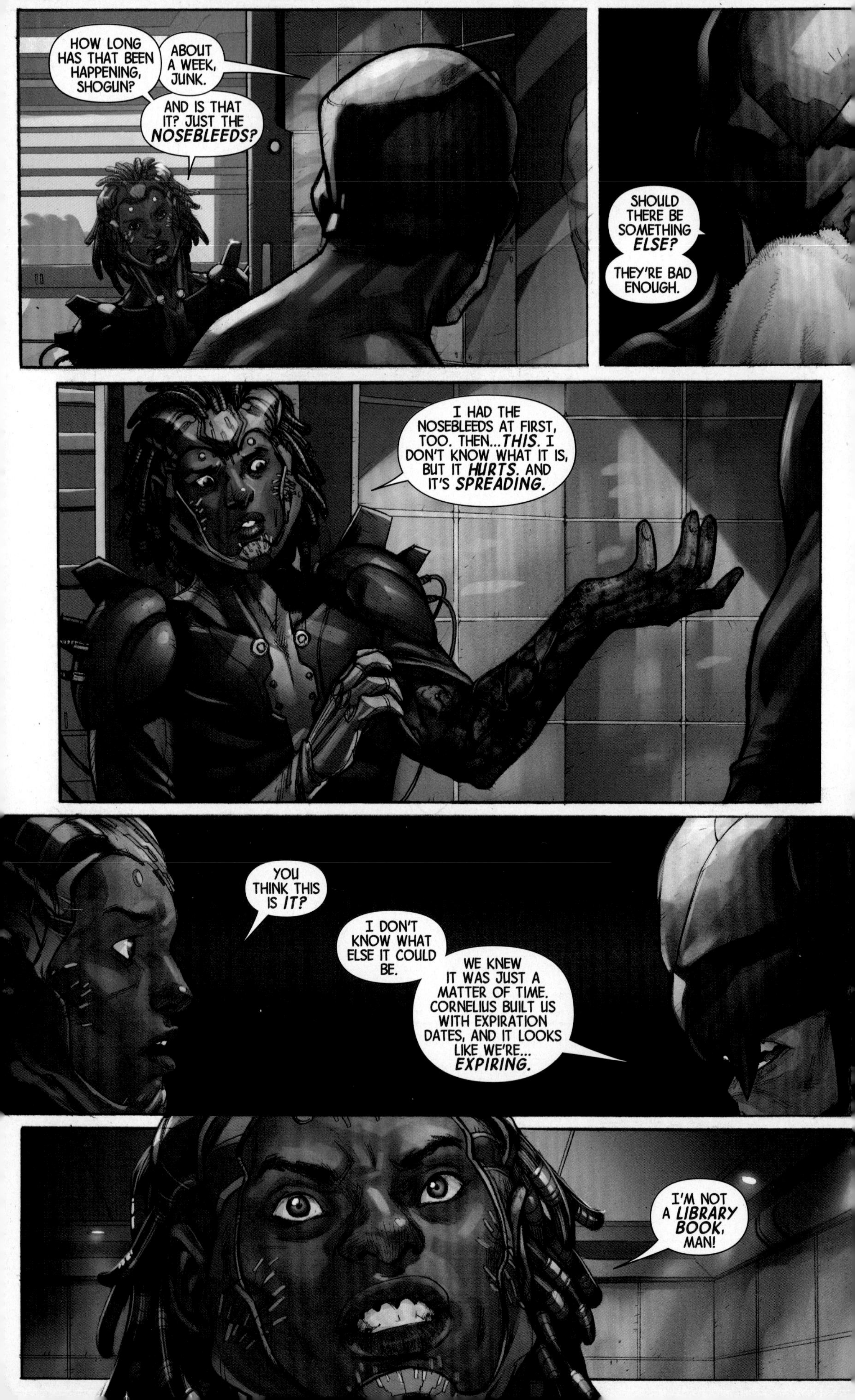
HOW LONG HAS THAT BEEN HAPPENING, SHOGUN?
ABOUT A WEEK, JUNK.
AND IS THAT IT? JUST THE NOSEBLEEDS?
SHOULD THERE BE SOMETHING ELSE?
THEY'RE BAD ENOUGH.
I HAD THE NOSEBLEEDS AT FIRST, TOO. THEN...THIS. I DON'T KNOW WHAT IT IS, BUT IT HURTS. AND IT'S SPREADING.
YOU THINK THIS IS IT?
I DON'T KNOW WHAT ELSE IT COULD BE.
WE KNEW IT WAS JUST A MATTER OF TIME. CORNELIUS BUILT US WITH EXPIRATION DATES, AND IT LOOKS LIKE WE'RE... EXPIRING.
I'M NOT A LIBRARY BOOK, MAN!

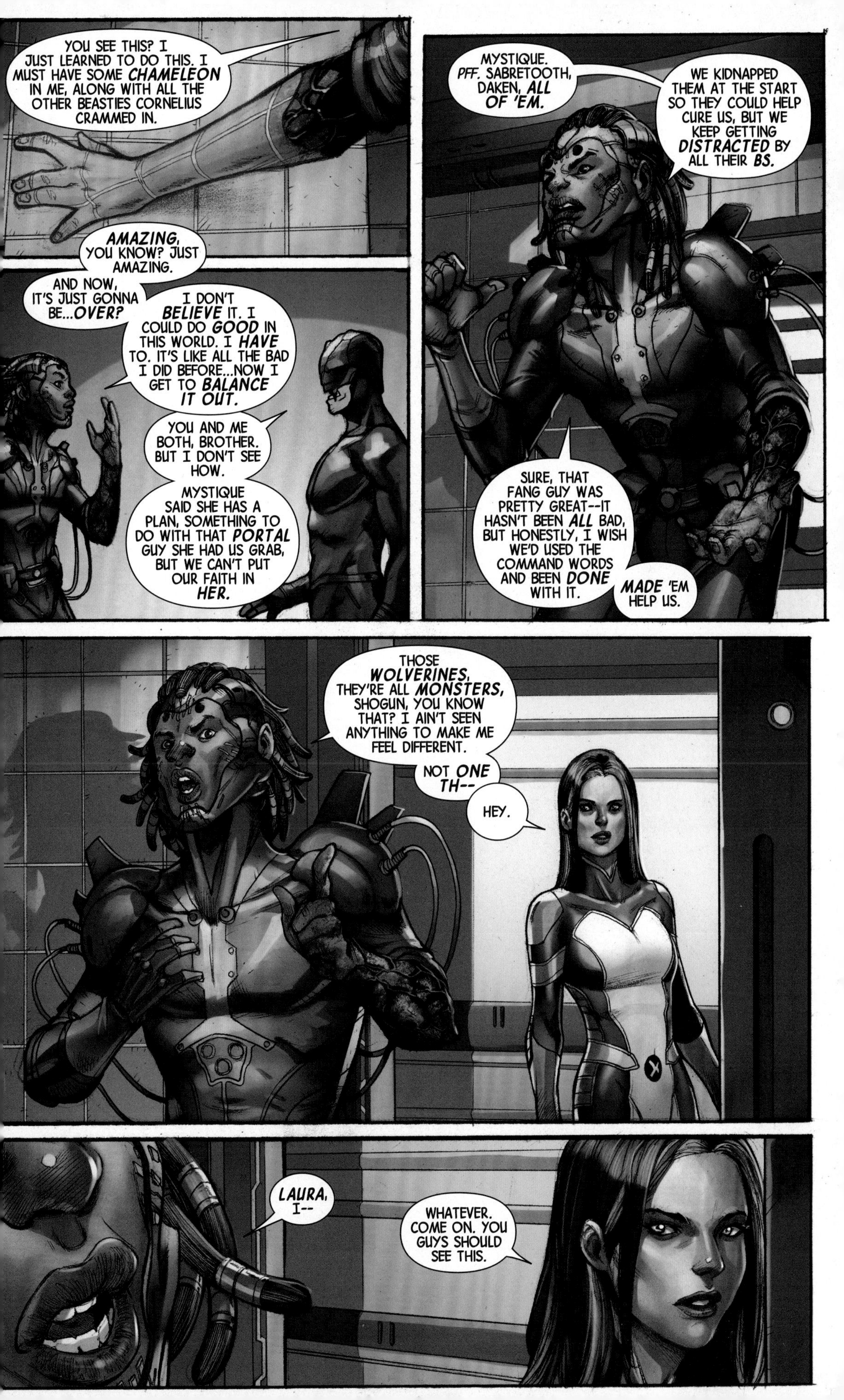
YOU SEE THIS? I JUST LEARNED TO DO THIS. I MUST HAVE SOME CHAMELEON IN ME, ALONG WITH ALL THE OTHER BEASTIES CORNELIUS CRAMMED IN.
AMAZING, YOU KNOW? JUST AMAZING.
AND NOW, IT'S JUST GONNA BE...OVER?
I DON'T BELIEVE IT. I COULD DO GOOD IN THIS WORLD. I HAVE TO. IT'S LIKE ALL THE BAD I DID BEFORE...NOW I GET TO BALANCE IT OUT.
YOU AND ME BOTH, BROTHER. BUT I DON'T SEE HOW.
MYSTIQUE SAID SHE HAS A PLAN, SOMETHING TO DO WITH THAT PORTAL GUY SHE HAD US GRAB, BUT WE CAN'T PUT OUR FAITH IN HER.
MYSTIQUE. PFF. SABRETOOTH, DAKEN, ALL OF 'EM.
WE KIDNAPPED THEM AT THE START SO THEY COULD HELP CURE US, BUT WE KEEP GETTING DISTRACTED BY ALL THEIR BS.
SURE, THAT FANG GUY WAS PRETTY GREAT--IT HASN'T BEEN ALL BAD, BUT HONESTLY, I WISH WE'D USED THE COMMAND WORDS AND BEEN DONE WITH IT.
MADE 'EM HELP US.
THOSE WOLVERINES, THEY'RE ALL MONSTERS, SHOGUN, YOU KNOW THAT? I AIN'T SEEN ANYTHING TO MAKE ME FEEL DIFFERENT.
NOT ONE TH--
HEY.
LAURA, I--
WHATEVER. COME ON. YOU GUYS SHOULD SEE THIS.

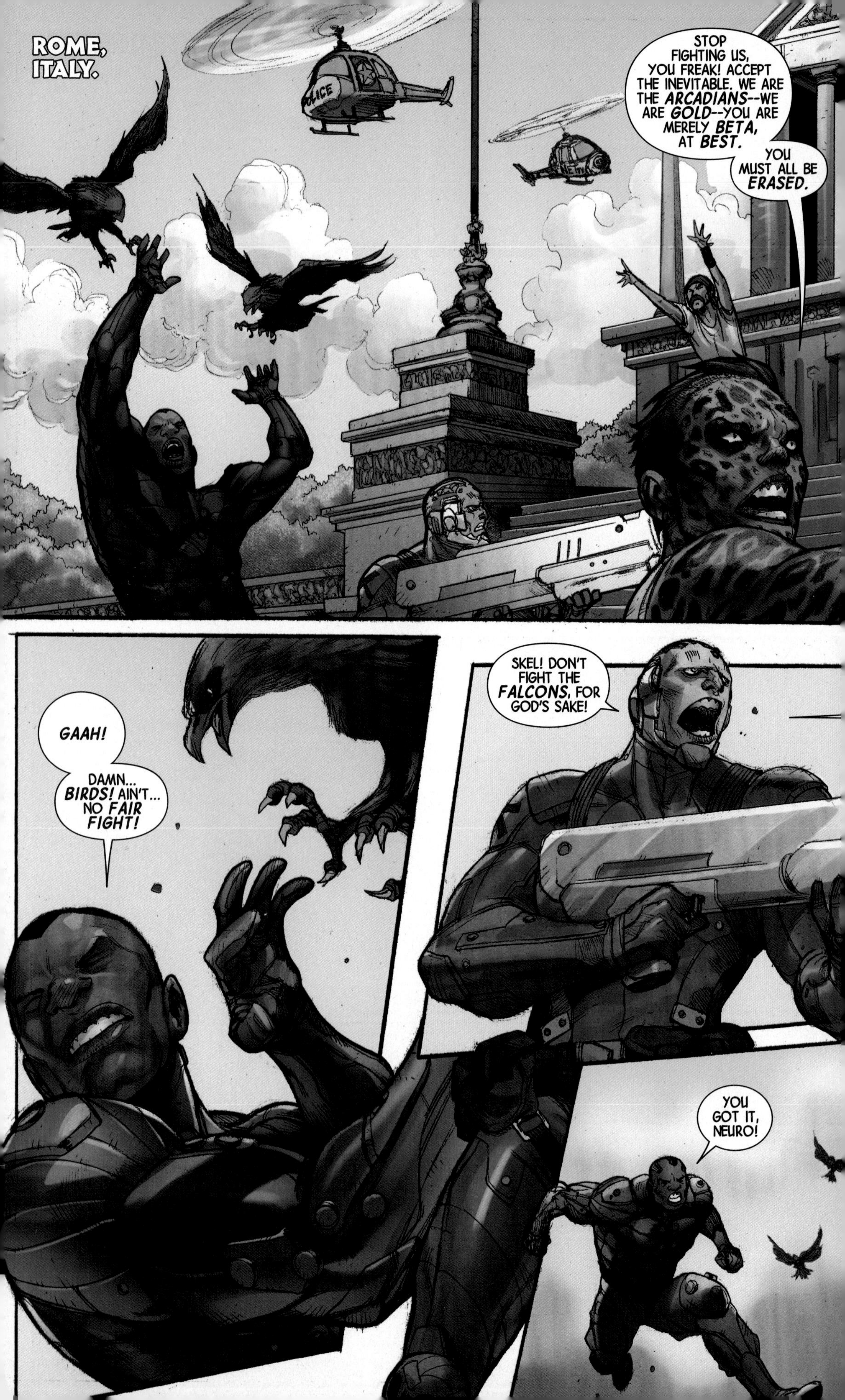

ROME, ITALY.
POLICE
STOP FIGHTING US, YOU FREAK! ACCEPT THE INEVITABLE. WE ARE THE ARCADIANS--WE ARE GOLD--YOU ARE MERELY BETA, AT BEST.
YOU MUST ALL BE ERASED.
GAAH!
DAMN... BIRDS! AIN'T... NO FAIR FIGHT!
SKEL! DON'T FIGHT THE FALCONS, FOR GOD'S SAKE!
YOU GOT IT, NEURO!

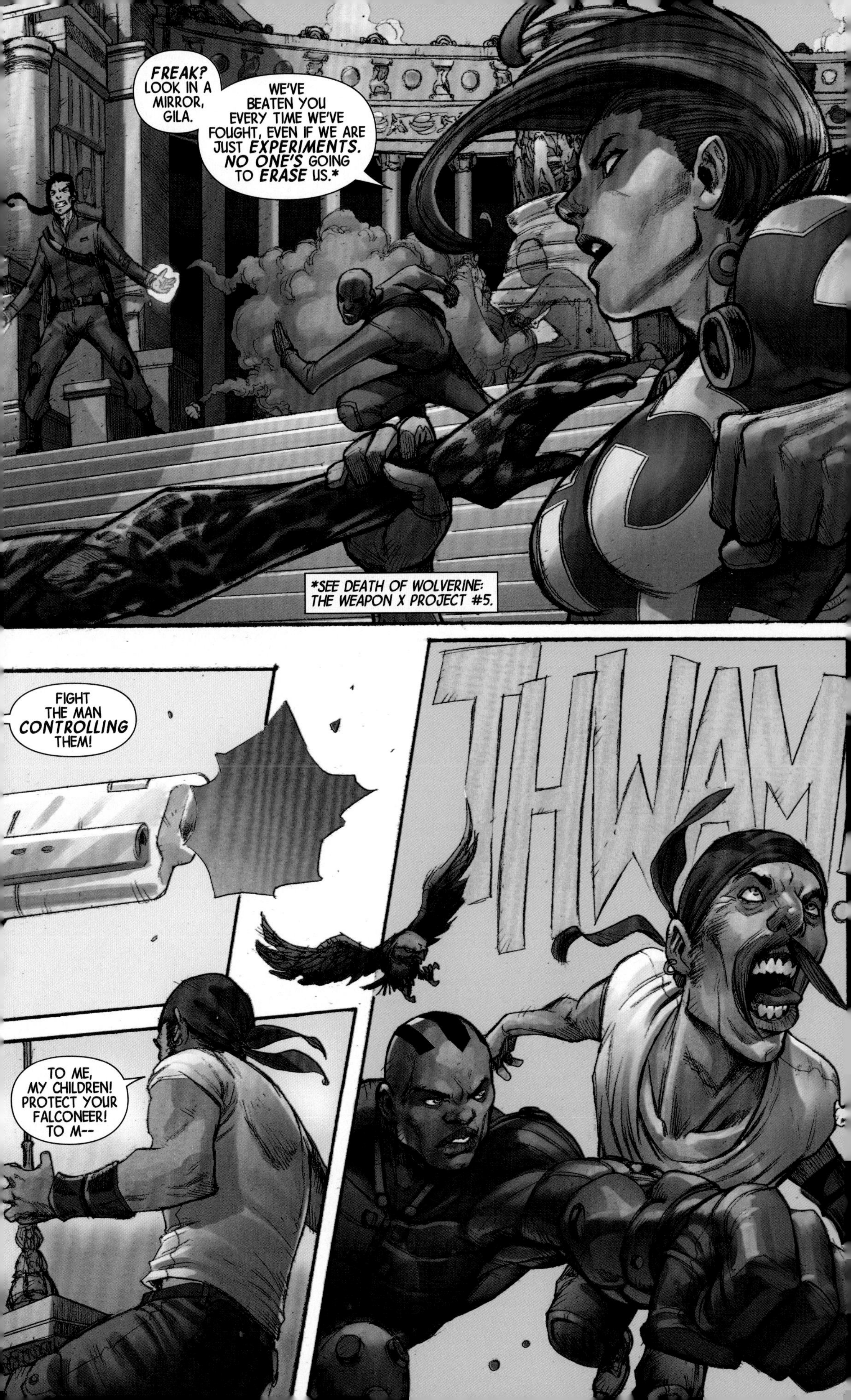
FREAK? LOOK IN A MIRROR, GILA.
WE'VE BEATEN YOU EVERY TIME WE'VE FOUGHT, EVEN IF WE ARE JUST EXPERIMENTS. NO ONE'S GOING TO ERASE US.*
*SEE DEATH OF WOLVERINE: THE WEAPON X PROJECT #5.
FIGHT THE MAN CONTROLLING THEM!
THWAM!
TO ME, MY CHILDREN! PROTECT YOUR FALCONEER! TO M--

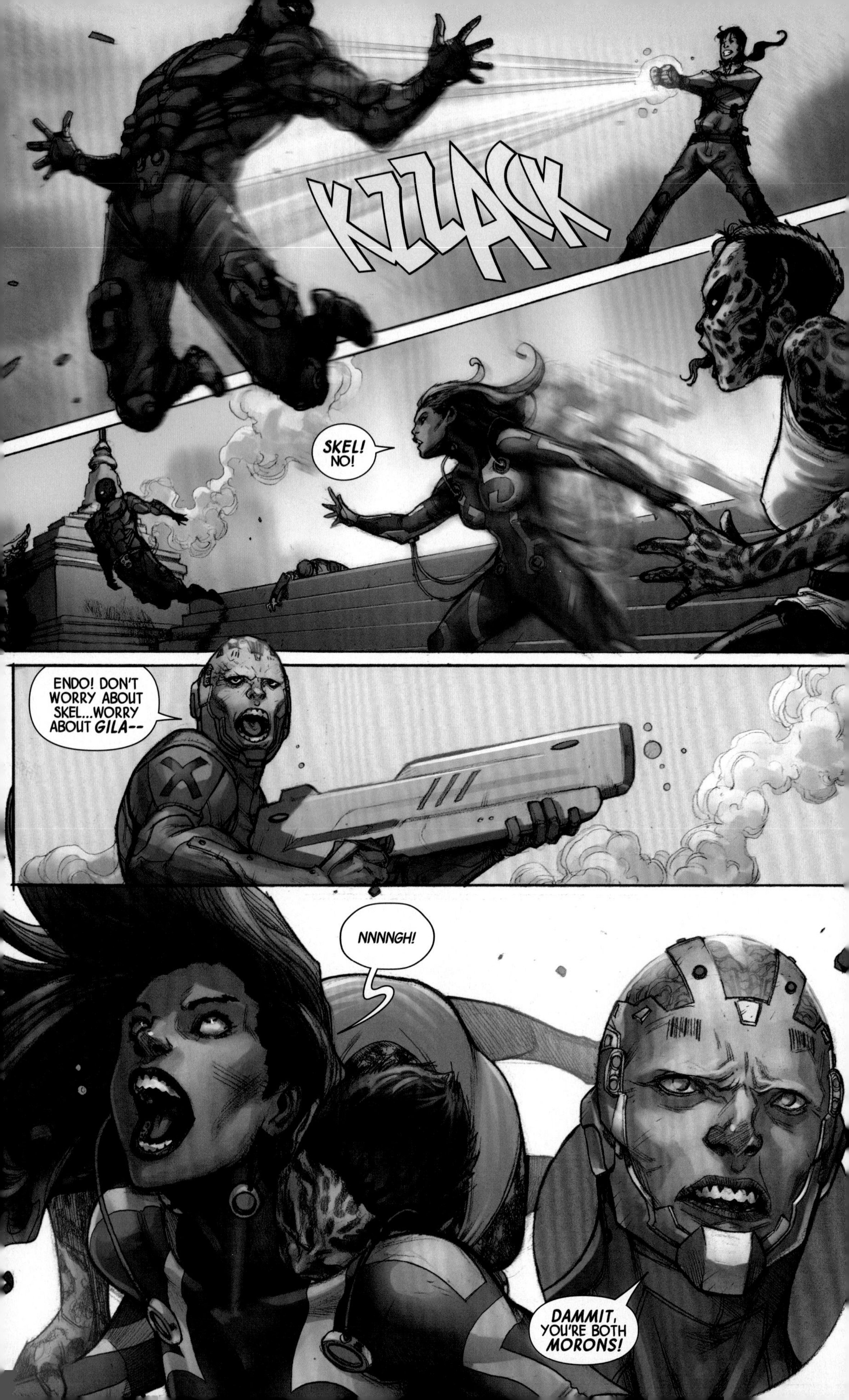
KZZLACK
SKEL! NO!
ENDO! DON'T WORRY ABOUT SKEL...WORRY ABOUT GILA--
NNNNGH!
DAMMIT, YOU'RE BOTH MORONS!

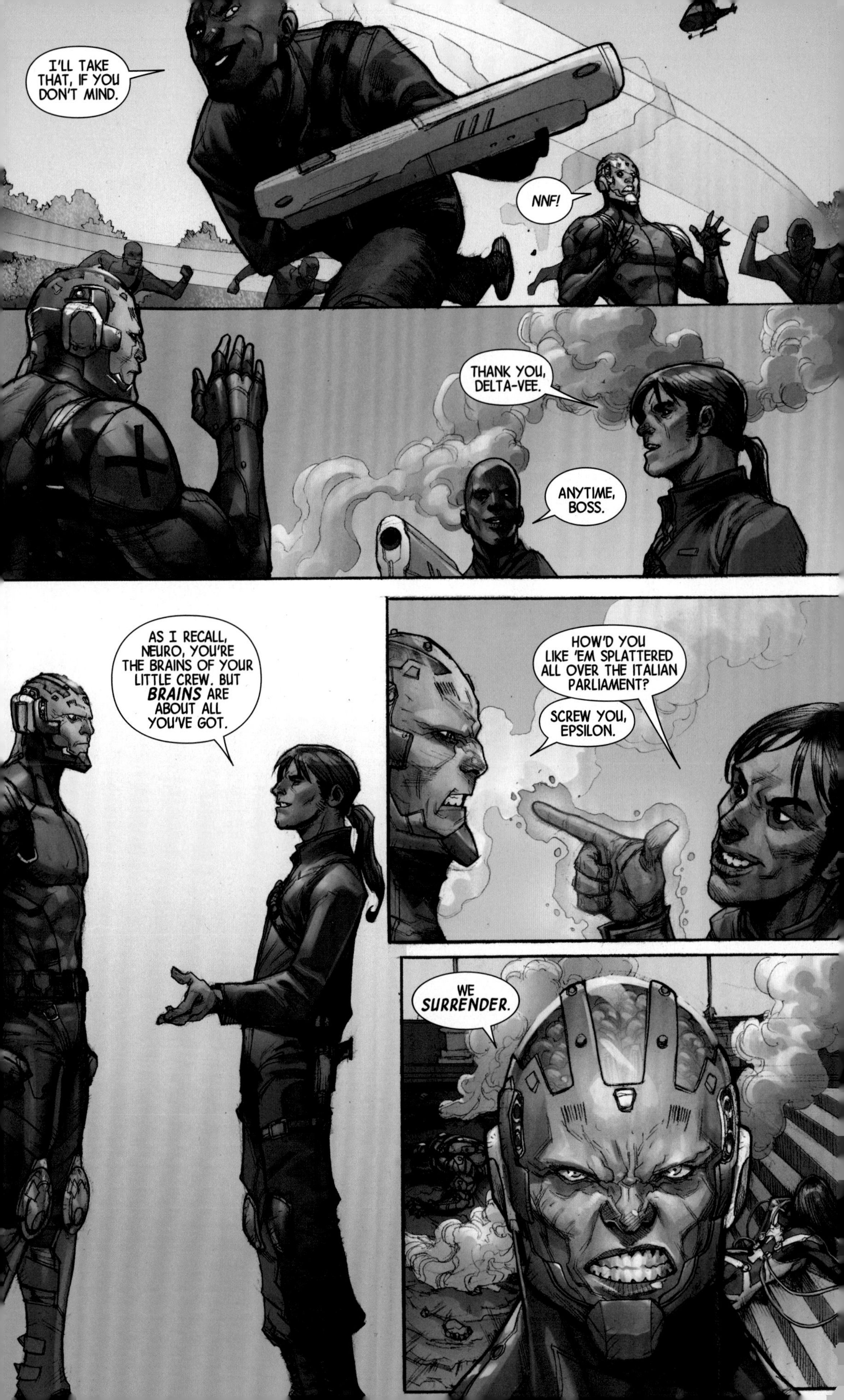
I'LL TAKE THAT, IF YOU DON'T MIND.
NNF!
THANK YOU, DELTA-VEE.
ANYTIME, BOSS.
AS I RECALL, NEURO, YOU'RE THE BRAINS OF YOUR LITTLE CREW. BUT BRAINS ARE ABOUT ALL YOU'VE GOT.
HOW'D YOU LIKE 'EM SPLATTERED ALL OVER THE ITALIAN PARLIAMENT?
SCREW YOU, EPSILON.
WE SURRENDER.

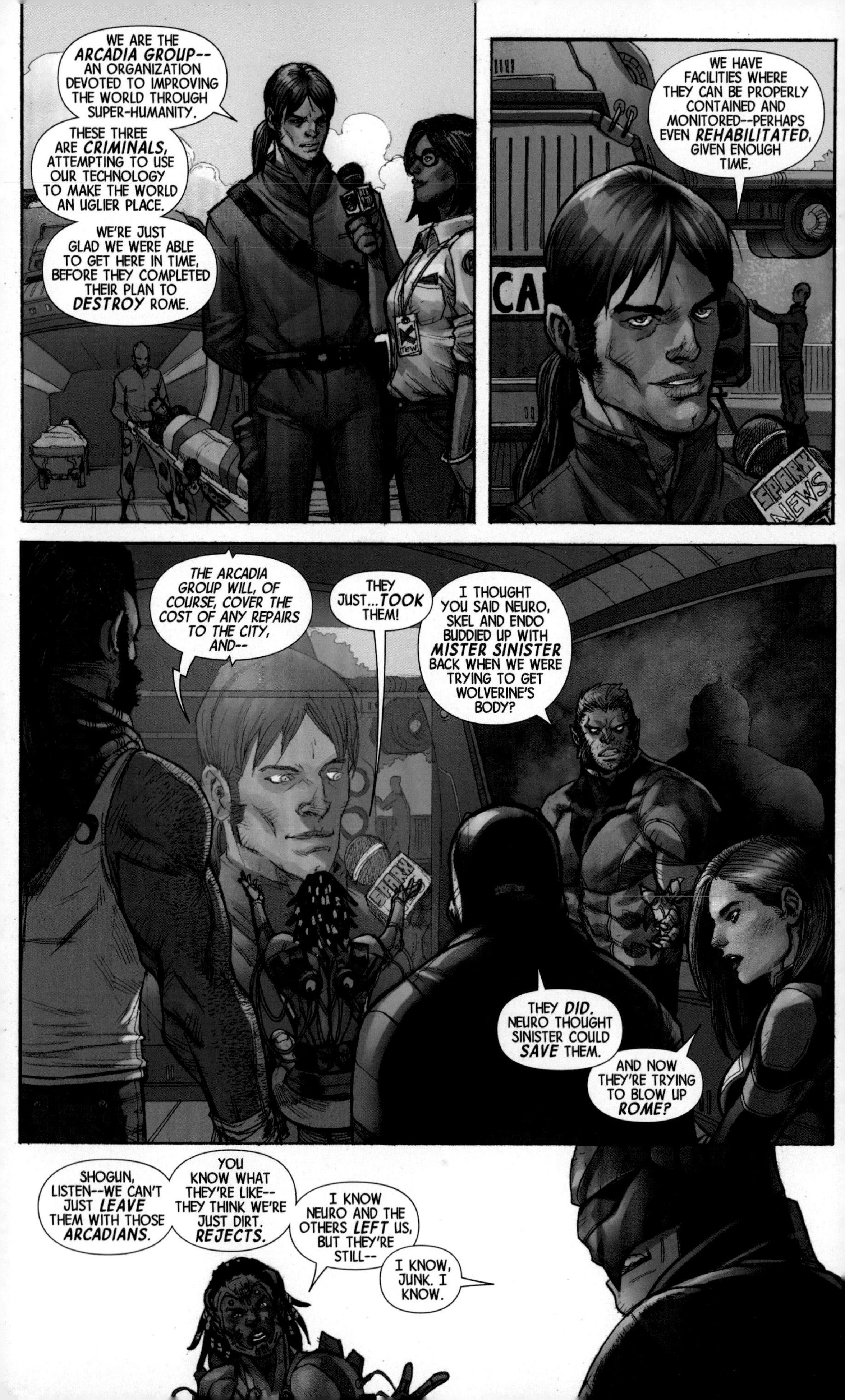
WE ARE THE ARCADIA GROUP-- AN ORGANIZATION DEVOTED TO IMPROVING THE WORLD THROUGH SUPER-HUMANITY.
THESE THREE ARE CRIMINALS, ATTEMPTING TO USE OUR TECHNOLOGY TO MAKE THE WORLD AN UGLIER PLACE.
WE'RE JUST GLAD WE WERE ABLE TO GET HERE IN TIME, BEFORE THEY COMPLETED THEIR PLAN TO DESTROY ROME.
WE HAVE FACILITIES WHERE THEY CAN BE PROPERLY CONTAINED AND MONITORED--PERHAPS EVEN REHABILITATED, GIVEN ENOUGH TIME.
SPARK NEWS
THE ARCADIA GROUP WILL, OF COURSE, COVER THE COST OF ANY REPAIRS TO THE CITY, AND--
THEY JUST...TOOK THEM!
I THOUGHT YOU SAID NEURO, SKEL AND ENDO BUDDIED UP WITH MISTER SINISTER BACK WHEN WE WERE TRYING TO GET WOLVERINE'S BODY?
THEY DID. NEURO THOUGHT SINISTER COULD SAVE THEM.
AND NOW THEY'RE TRYING TO BLOW UP ROME?
SHOGUN, LISTEN--WE CAN'T JUST LEAVE THEM WITH THOSE ARCADIANS.
YOU KNOW WHAT THEY'RE LIKE-- THEY THINK WE'RE JUST DIRT. REJECTS.
I KNOW NEURO AND THE OTHERS LEFT US, BUT THEY'RE STILL--
I KNOW, JUNK. I KNOW.

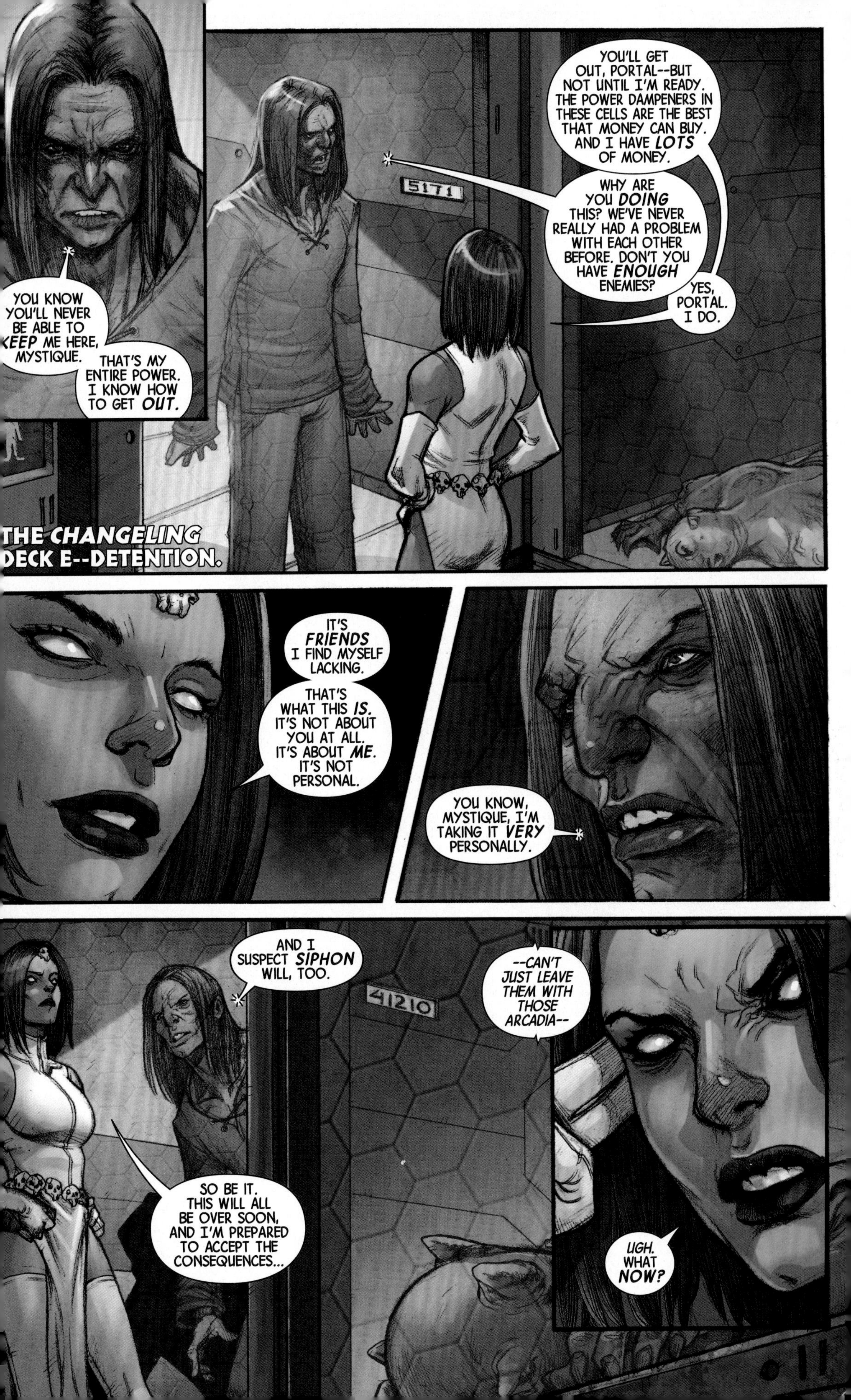
THE CHANGELING DECK E--DETENTION.
YOU KNOW YOU'LL NEVER BE ABLE TO KEEP ME HERE, MYSTIQUE.
THAT'S MY ENTIRE POWER. I KNOW HOW TO GET OUT.
YOU'LL GET OUT, PORTAL--BUT NOT UNTIL I'M READY. THE POWER DAMPENERS IN THESE CELLS ARE THE BEST THAT MONEY CAN BUY. AND I HAVE LOTS OF MONEY.
WHY ARE YOU DOING THIS? WE'VE NEVER REALLY HAD A PROBLEM WITH EACH OTHER BEFORE. DON'T YOU HAVE ENOUGH ENEMIES?
YES, PORTAL. I DO.
5171
IT'S FRIENDS I FIND MYSELF LACKING.
THAT'S WHAT THIS IS. IT'S NOT ABOUT YOU AT ALL. IT'S ABOUT ME. IT'S NOT PERSONAL.
YOU KNOW, MYSTIQUE, I'M TAKING IT VERY PERSONALLY.
AND I SUSPECT SIPHON WILL, TOO.
41210
SO BE IT. THIS WILL ALL BE OVER SOON, AND I'M PREPARED TO ACCEPT THE CONSEQUENCES...
--CAN'T JUST LEAVE THEM WITH THOSE ARCADIA--
UGH. WHAT NOW?

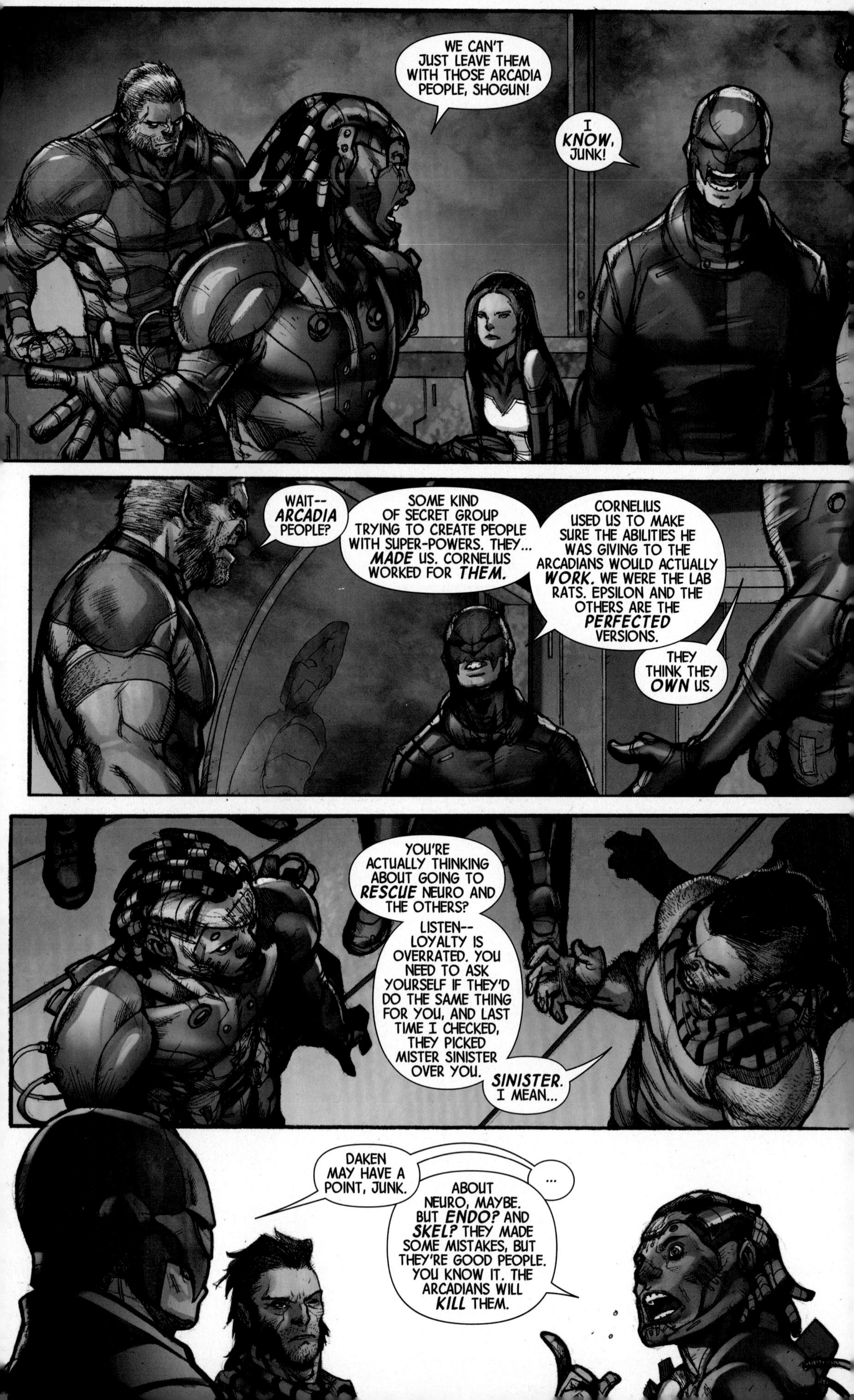
WE CAN'T JUST LEAVE THEM WITH THOSE ARCADIA PEOPLE, SHOGUN!
I KNOW, JUNK!
WAIT-- ARCADIA PEOPLE?
SOME KIND OF SECRET GROUP TRYING TO CREATE PEOPLE WITH SUPER-POWERS. THEY... MADE US. CORNELIUS WORKED FOR THEM.
CORNELIUS USED US TO MAKE SURE THE ABILITIES HE WAS GIVING TO THE ARCADIANS WOULD ACTUALLY WORK. WE WERE THE LAB RATS. EPSILON AND THE OTHERS ARE THE PERFECTED VERSIONS.
THEY THINK THEY OWN US.
YOU'RE ACTUALLY THINKING ABOUT GOING TO RESCUE NEURO AND THE OTHERS?
LISTEN-- LOYALTY IS OVERRATED. YOU NEED TO ASK YOURSELF IF THEY'D DO THE SAME THING FOR YOU, AND LAST TIME I CHECKED, THEY PICKED MISTER SINISTER OVER YOU.
SINISTER. I MEAN...
DAKEN MAY HAVE A POINT, JUNK.
...
ABOUT NEURO, MAYBE. BUT ENDO? AND SKEL? THEY MADE SOME MISTAKES, BUT THEY'RE GOOD PEOPLE. YOU KNOW IT. THE ARCADIANS WILL KILL THEM.

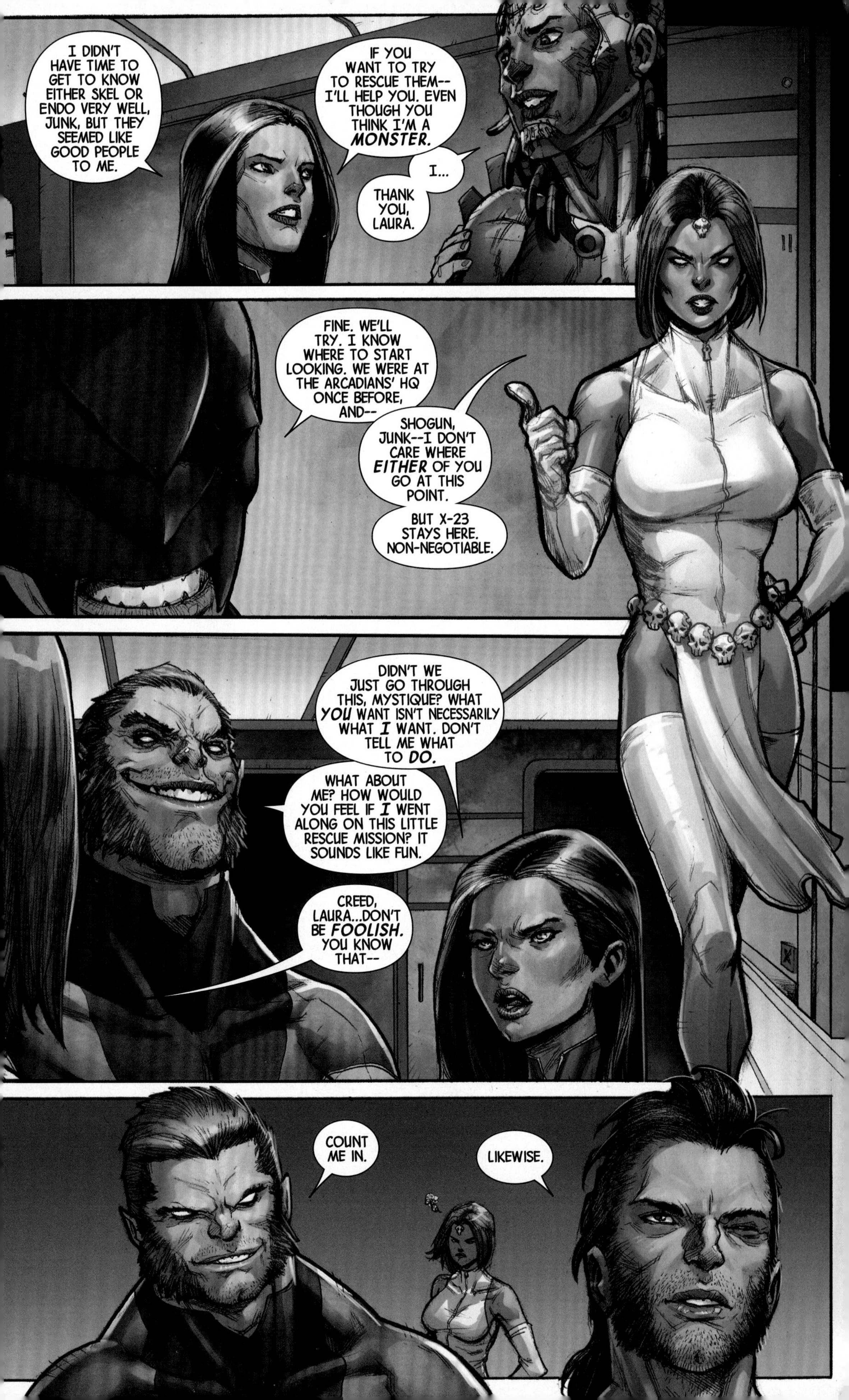
I DIDN'T HAVE TIME TO GET TO KNOW EITHER SKEL OR ENDO VERY WELL, JUNK, BUT THEY SEEMED LIKE GOOD PEOPLE TO ME.
IF YOU WANT TO TRY TO RESCUE THEM-- I'LL HELP YOU. EVEN THOUGH YOU THINK I'M A MONSTER.
I...
THANK YOU, LAURA.
FINE. WE'LL TRY. I KNOW WHERE TO START LOOKING. WE WERE AT THE ARCADIANS' HQ ONCE BEFORE, AND--
SHOGUN, JUNK--I DON'T CARE WHERE EITHER OF YOU GO AT THIS POINT.
BUT X-23 STAYS HERE. NON-NEGOTIABLE.
DIDN'T WE JUST GO THROUGH THIS, MYSTIQUE? WHAT YOU WANT ISN'T NECESSARILY WHAT I WANT. DON'T TELL ME WHAT TO DO.
WHAT ABOUT ME? HOW WOULD YOU FEEL IF I WENT ALONG ON THIS LITTLE RESCUE MISSION? IT SOUNDS LIKE FUN.
CREED, LAURA...DON'T BE FOOLISH. YOU KNOW THAT--
COUNT ME IN.
LIKEWISE.

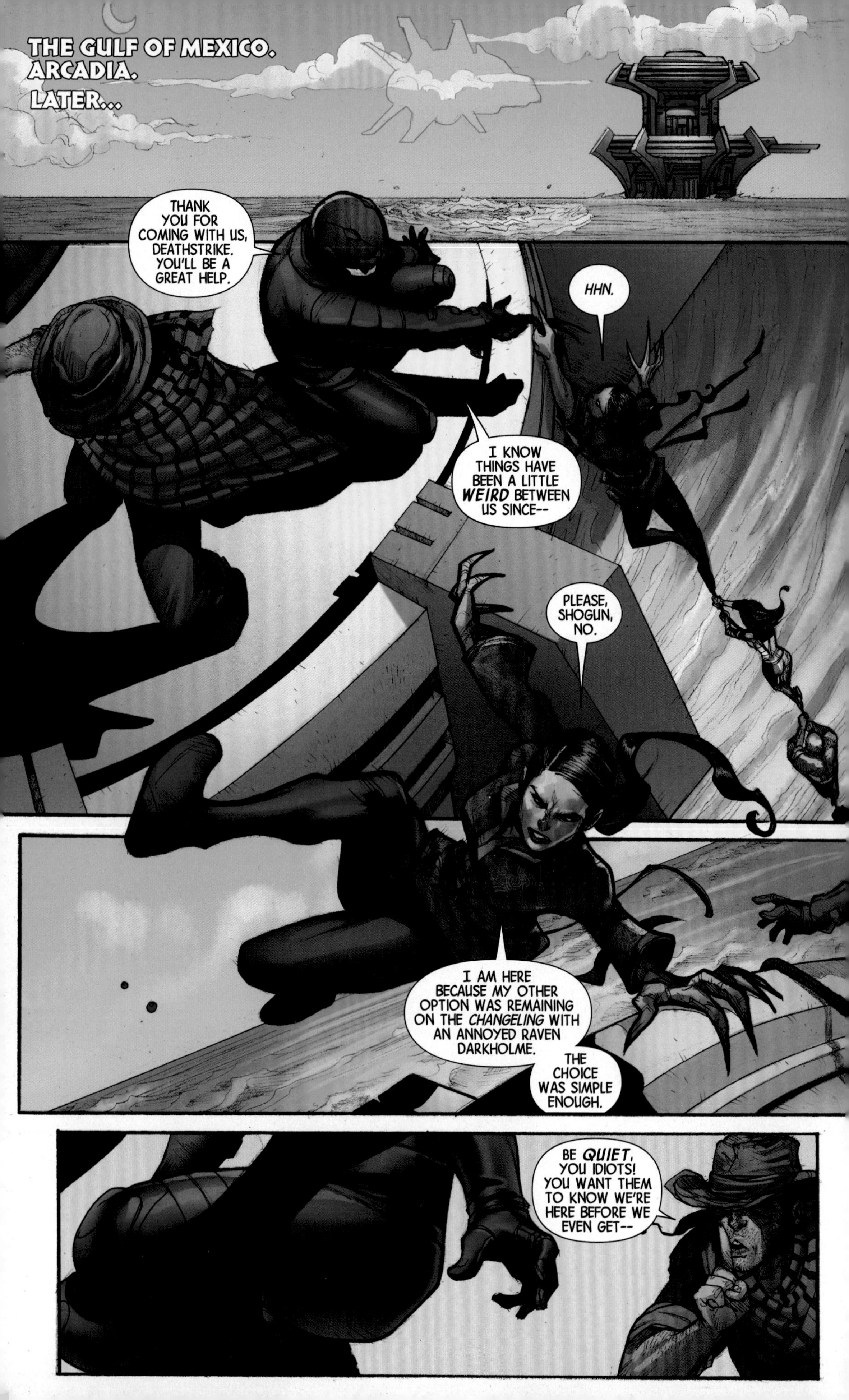
THE GULF OF MEXICO.
ARCADIA.
LATER...
THANK YOU FOR COMING WITH US, DEATHSTRIKE. YOU'LL BE A GREAT HELP.
HHN.
I KNOW THINGS HAVE BEEN A LITTLE WEIRD BETWEEN US SINCE--
PLEASE, SHOGUN, NO.
I AM HERE BECAUSE MY OTHER OPTION WAS REMAINING ON THE CHANGELING WITH AN ANNOYED RAVEN DARKHOLME.
THE CHOICE WAS SIMPLE ENOUGH.
BE QUIET, YOU IDIOTS! YOU WANT THEM TO KNOW WE'RE HERE BEFORE WE EVEN GET--

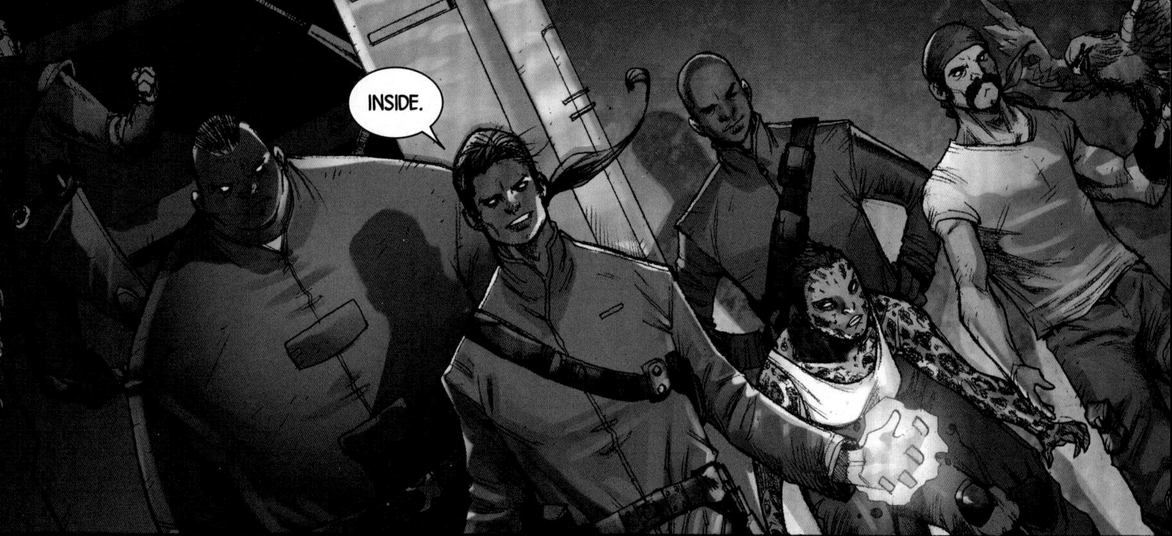
INSIDE.

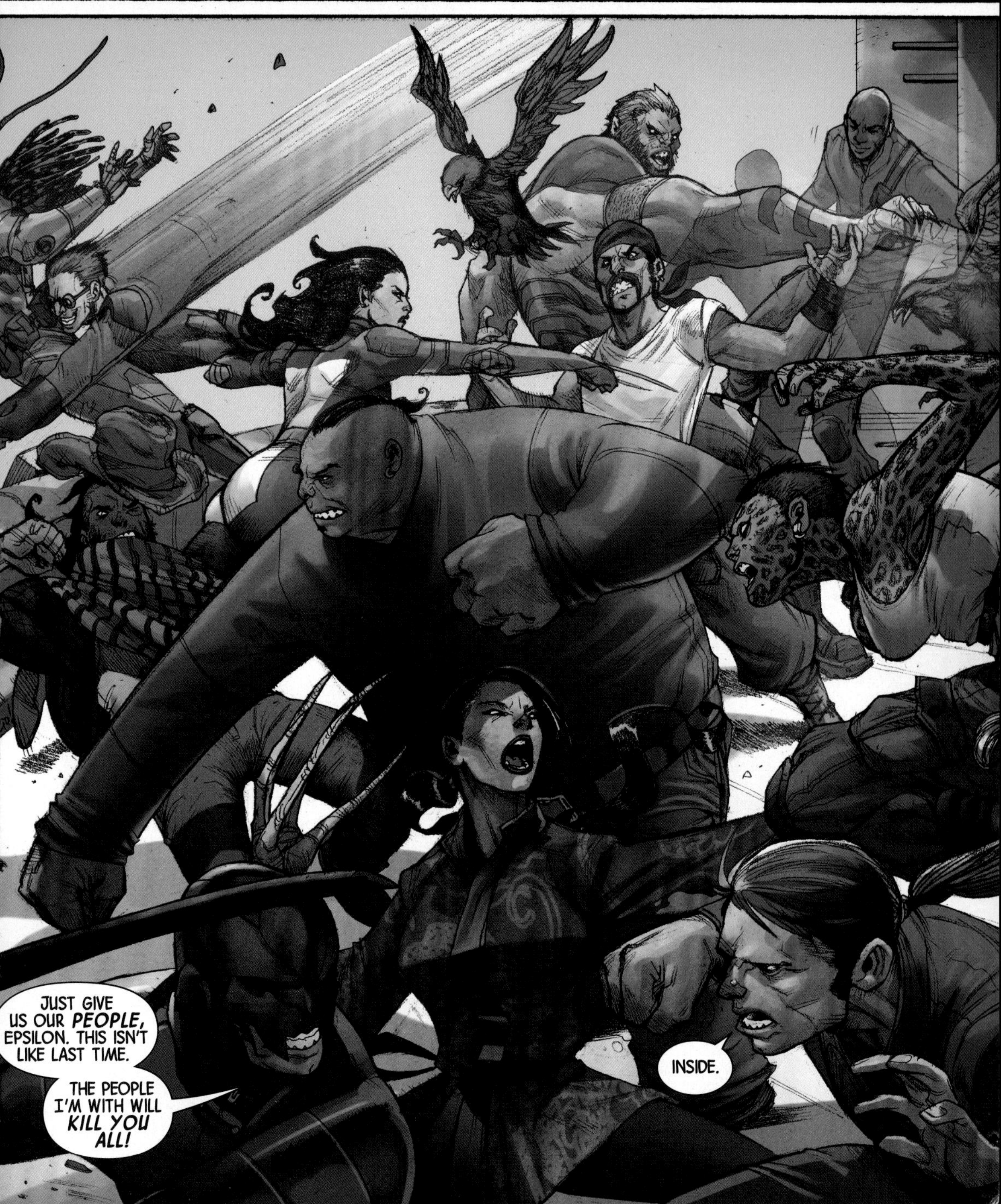
JUST GIVE US OUR PEOPLE, EPSILON. THIS ISN'T LIKE LAST TIME.
THE PEOPLE I'M WITH WILL KILL YOU ALL!
INSIDE.

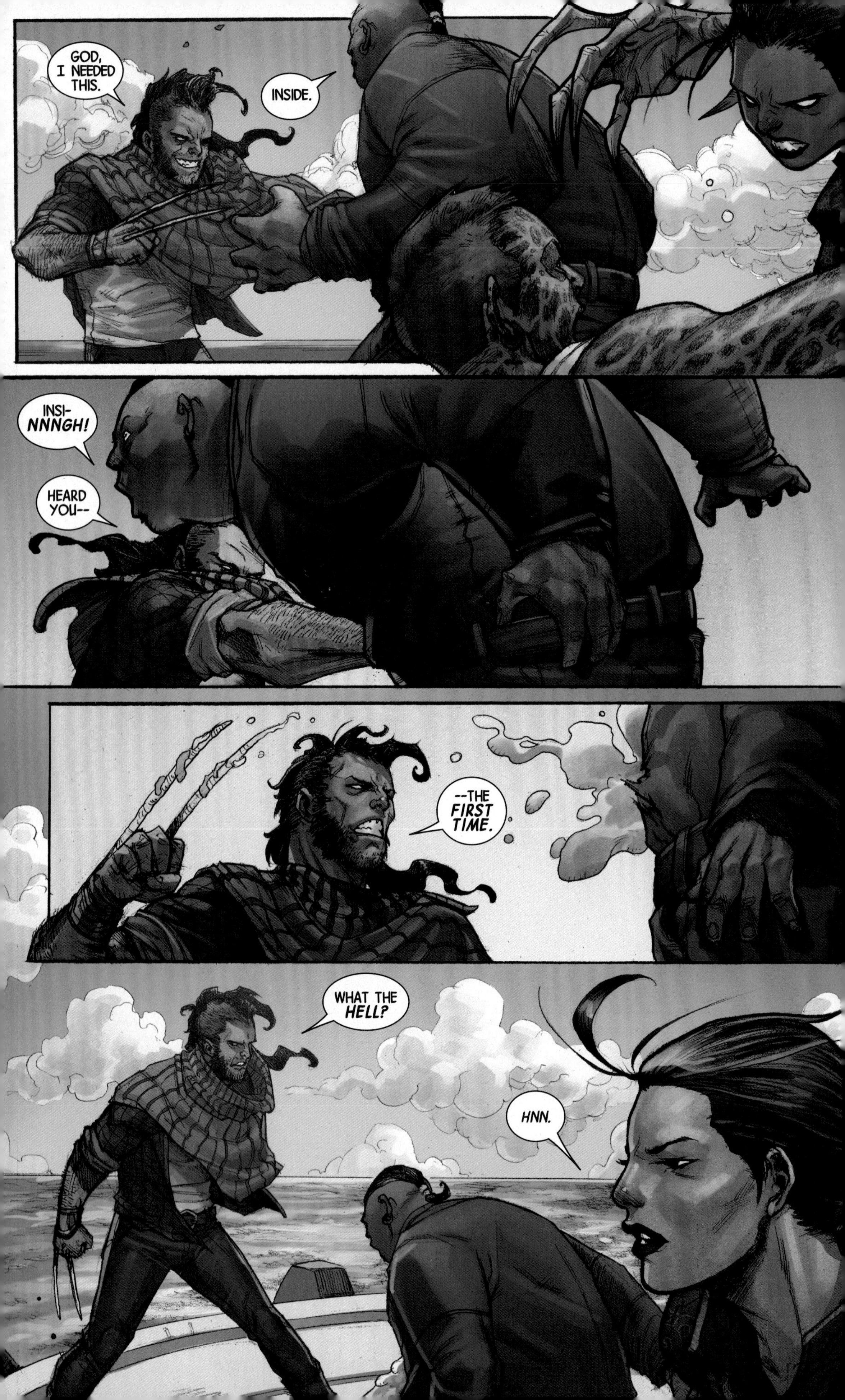
GOD, I NEEDED THIS.
INSIDE.
INSI- NNNGH!
HEARD YOU--
--THE FIRST TIME.
WHAT THE HELL?
HNN.

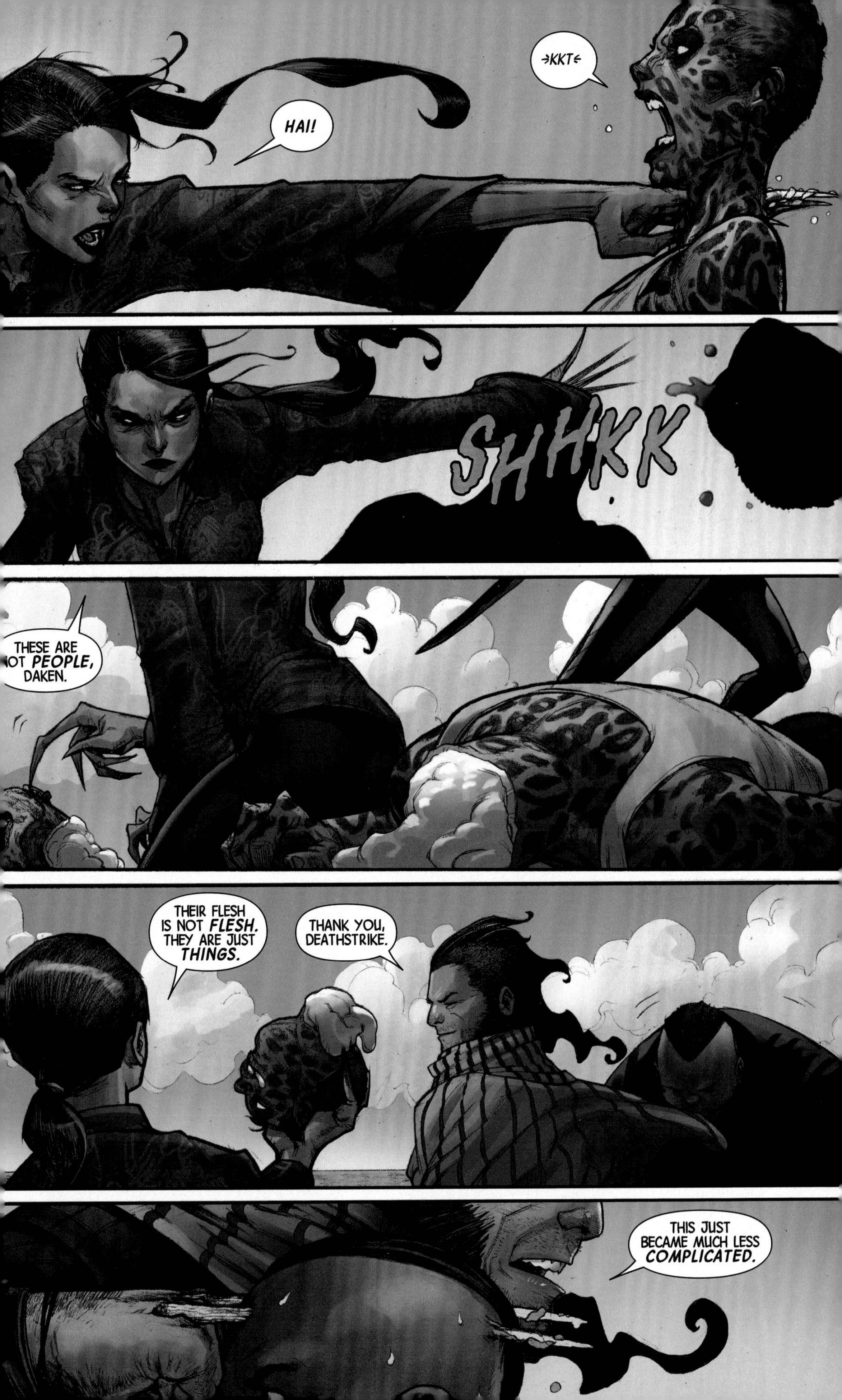

HAI!
→KKT←
SHHKK
THESE ARE NOT PEOPLE, DAKEN.
THEIR FLESH IS NOT FLESH. THEY ARE JUST THINGS.
THANK YOU, DEATHSTRIKE.
THIS JUST BECAME MUCH LESS COMPLICATED.

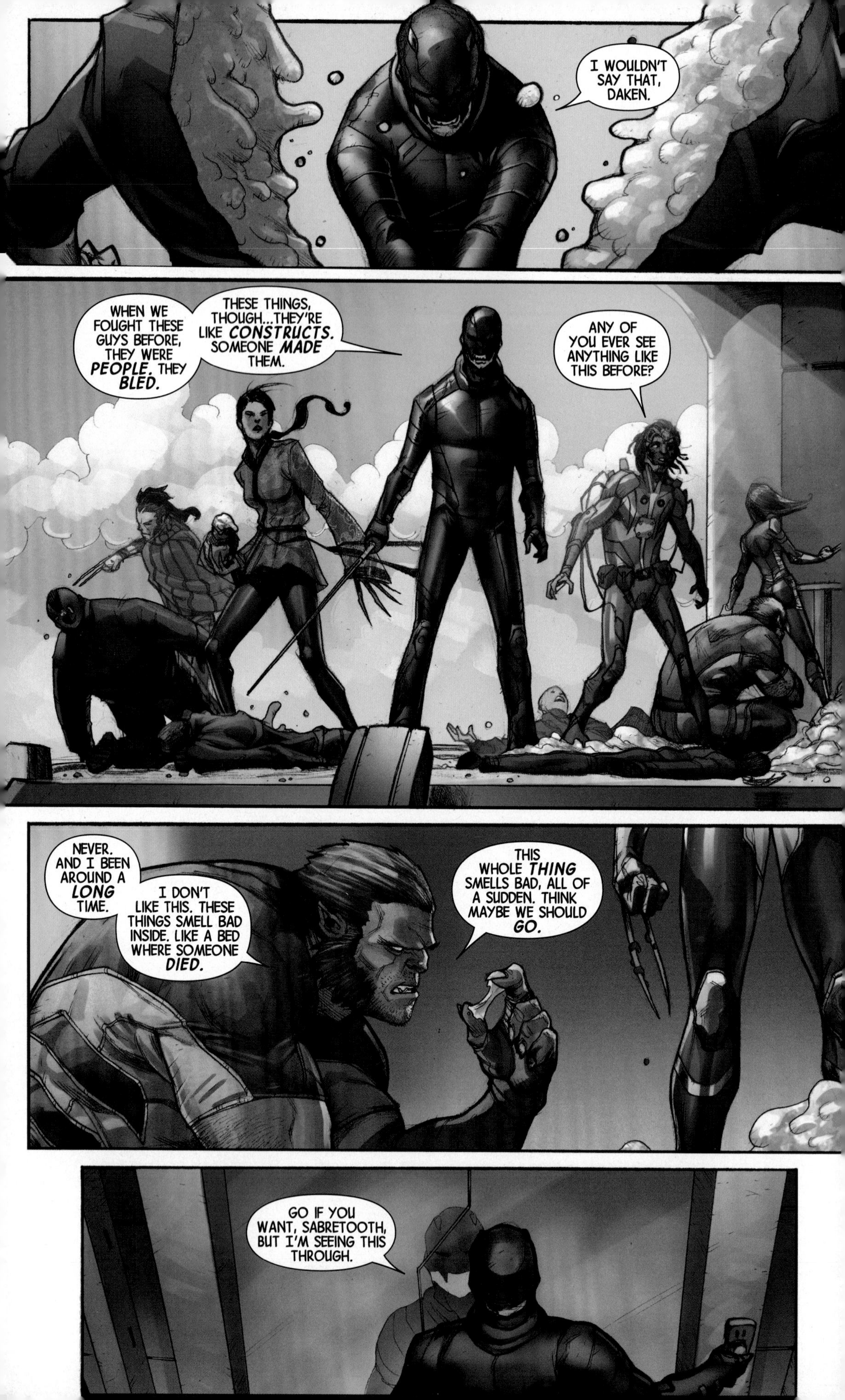
I WOULDN'T SAY THAT, DAKEN.
WHEN WE FOUGHT THESE GUYS BEFORE, THEY WERE PEOPLE. THEY BLED.
THESE THINGS, THOUGH...THEY'RE LIKE CONSTRUCTS. SOMEONE MADE THEM.
ANY OF YOU EVER SEE ANYTHING LIKE THIS BEFORE?
NEVER. AND I BEEN AROUND A LONG TIME.
I DON'T LIKE THIS. THESE THINGS SMELL BAD INSIDE. LIKE A BED WHERE SOMEONE DIED.
THIS WHOLE THING SMELLS BAD, ALL OF A SUDDEN. THINK MAYBE WE SHOULD GO.
GO IF YOU WANT, SABRETOOTH, BUT I'M SEEING THIS THROUGH.

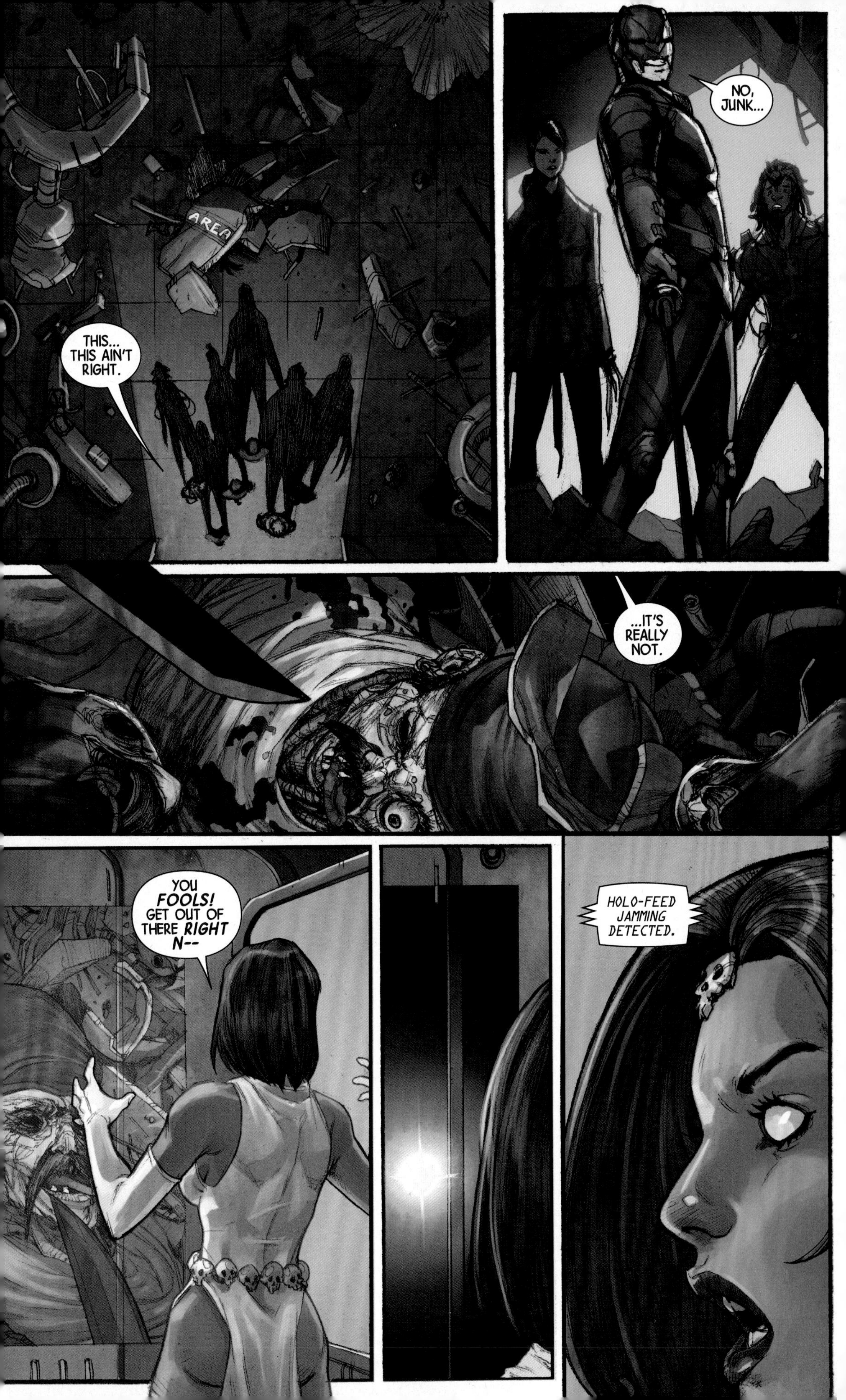
THIS... THIS AIN'T RIGHT.
NO, JUNK...
...IT'S REALLY NOT.
YOU *FOOLS!* GET OUT OF THERE *RIGHT* N--
HOLO-FEED JAMMING DETECTED.

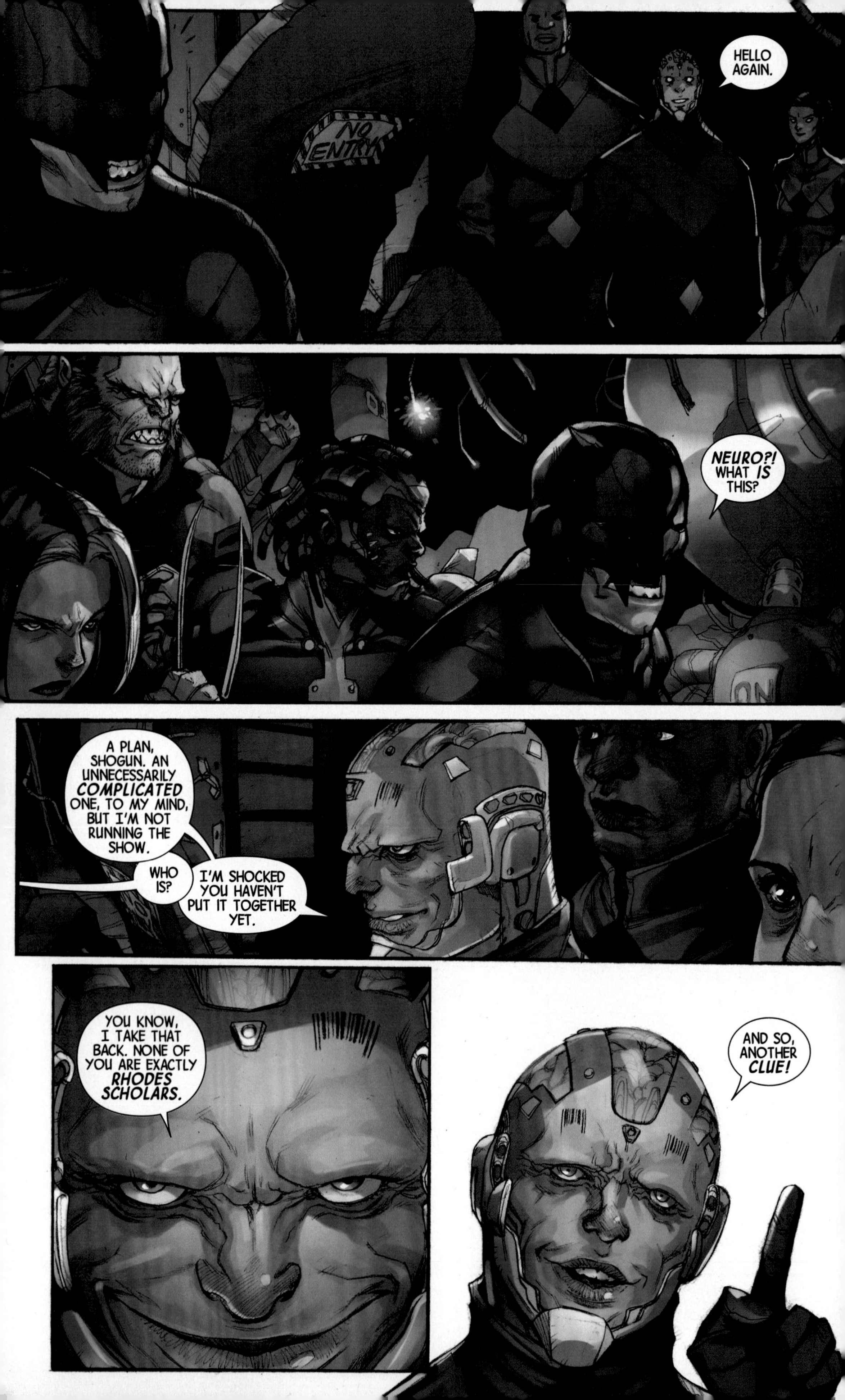

HELLO AGAIN.
NO ENTRY
NEURO?! WHAT IS THIS?
A PLAN, SHOGUN. AN UNNECESSARILY COMPLICATED ONE, TO MY MIND, BUT I'M NOT RUNNING THE SHOW.
WHO IS?
I'M SHOCKED YOU HAVEN'T PUT IT TOGETHER YET.
YOU KNOW, I TAKE THAT BACK. NONE OF YOU ARE EXACTLY RHODES SCHOLARS.
AND SO, ANOTHER CLUE!

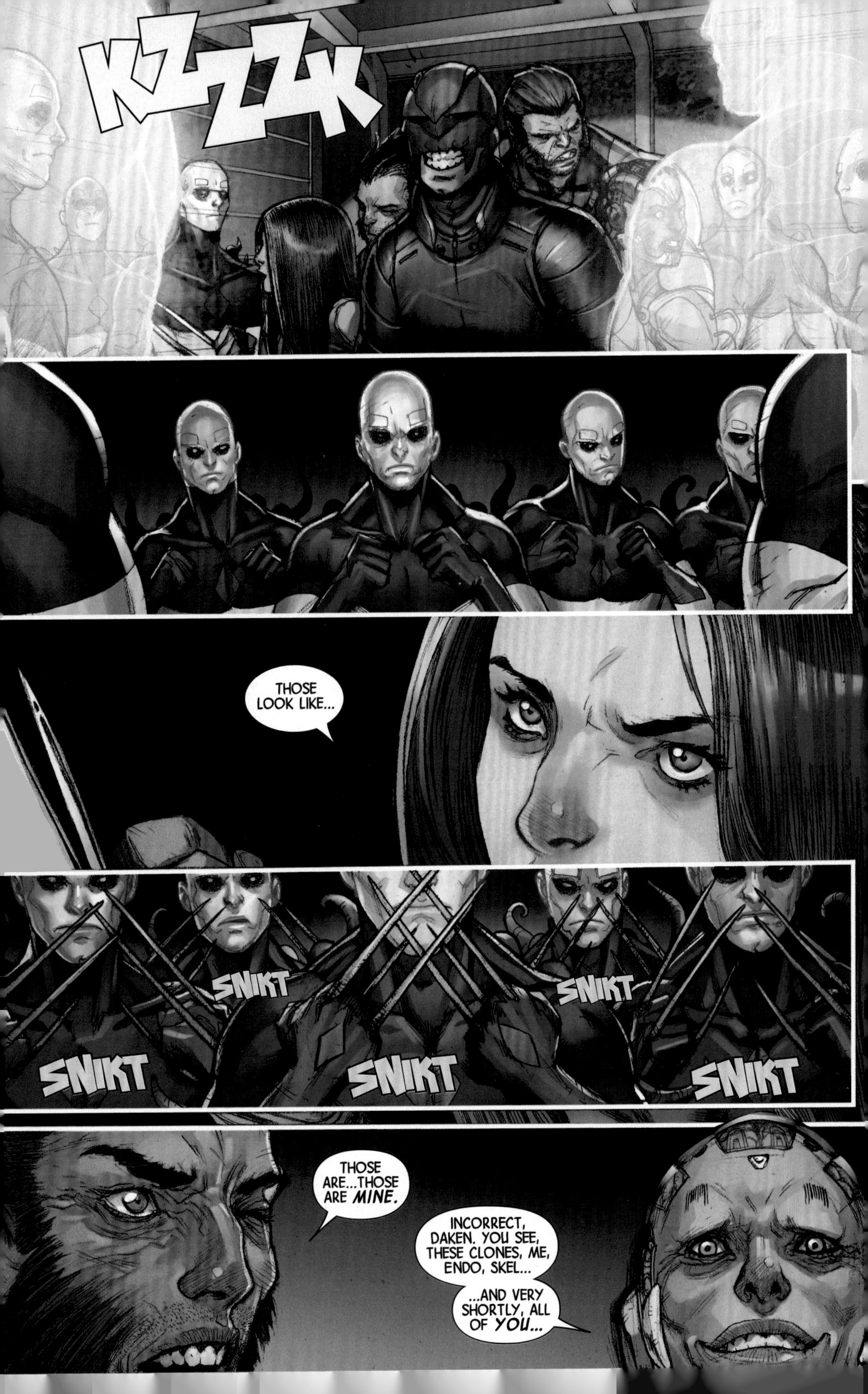
KZZZK
THOSE LOOK LIKE...
SNIKT
SNIKT
SNIKT
SNIKT
SNIKT
THOSE ARE...THOSE ARE MINE.
INCORRECT, DAKEN. YOU SEE, THESE CLONES, ME, ENDO, SKEL...
...AND VERY SHORTLY, ALL OF YOU...

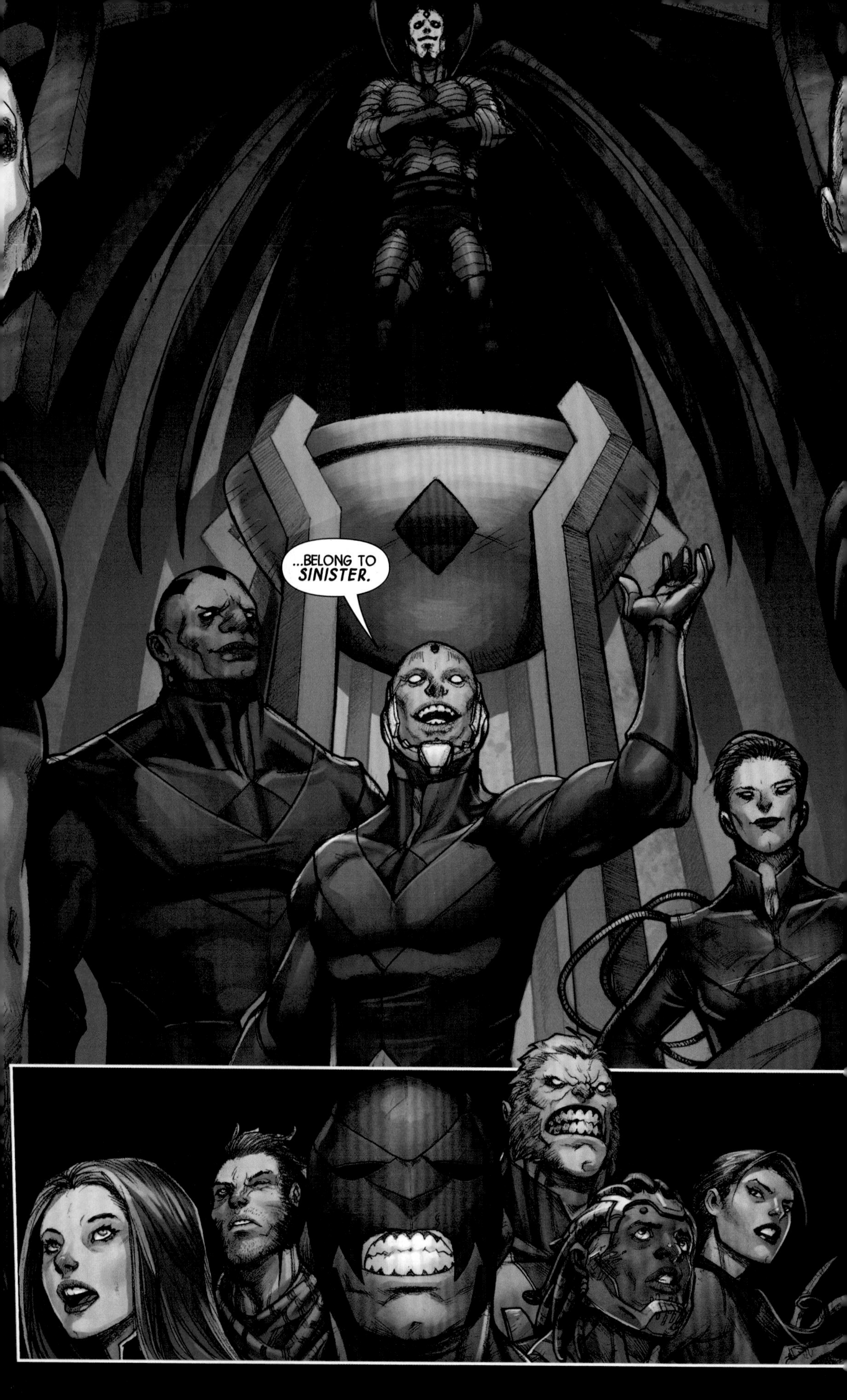
...BELONG TO SINISTER.

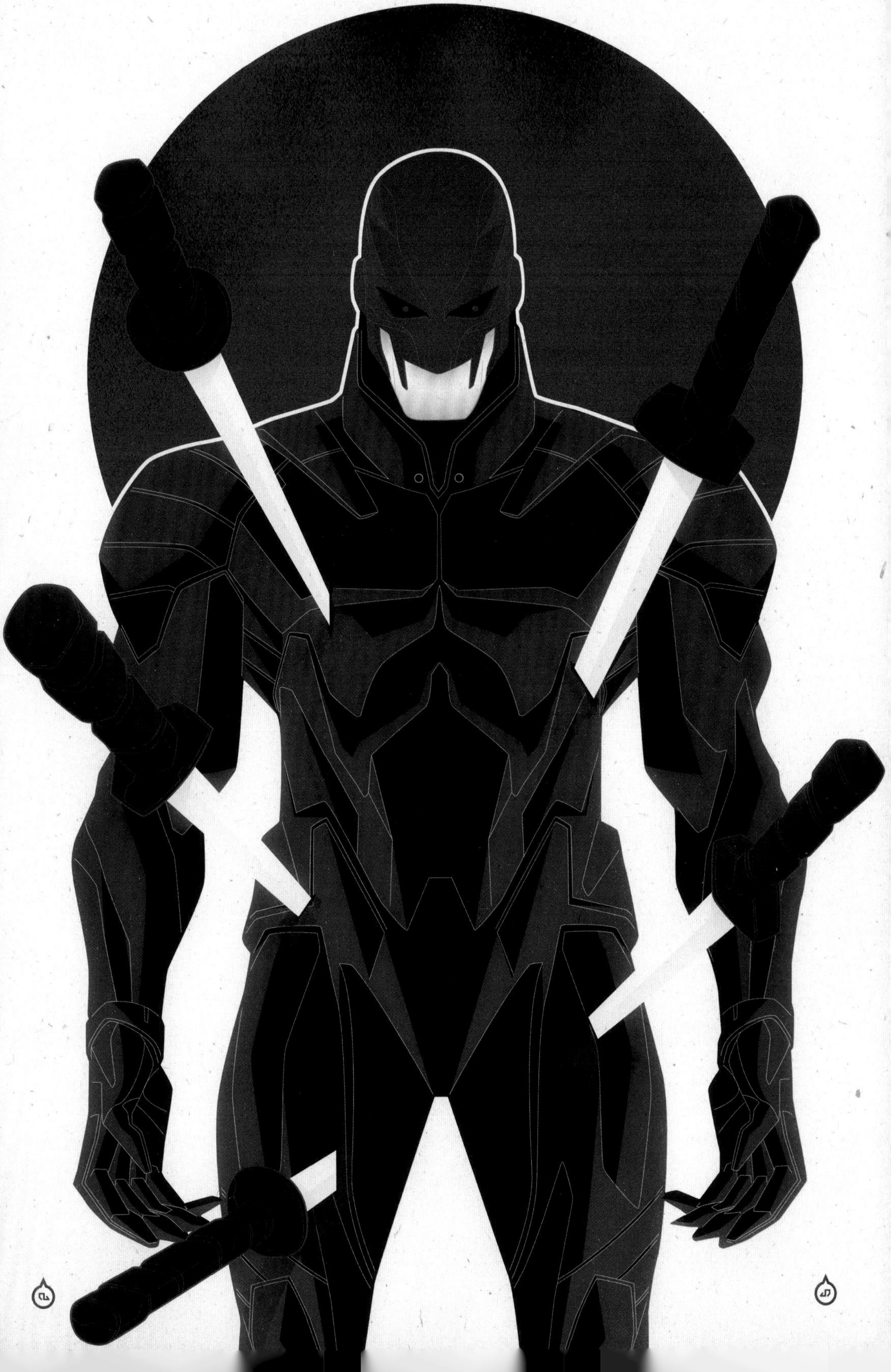

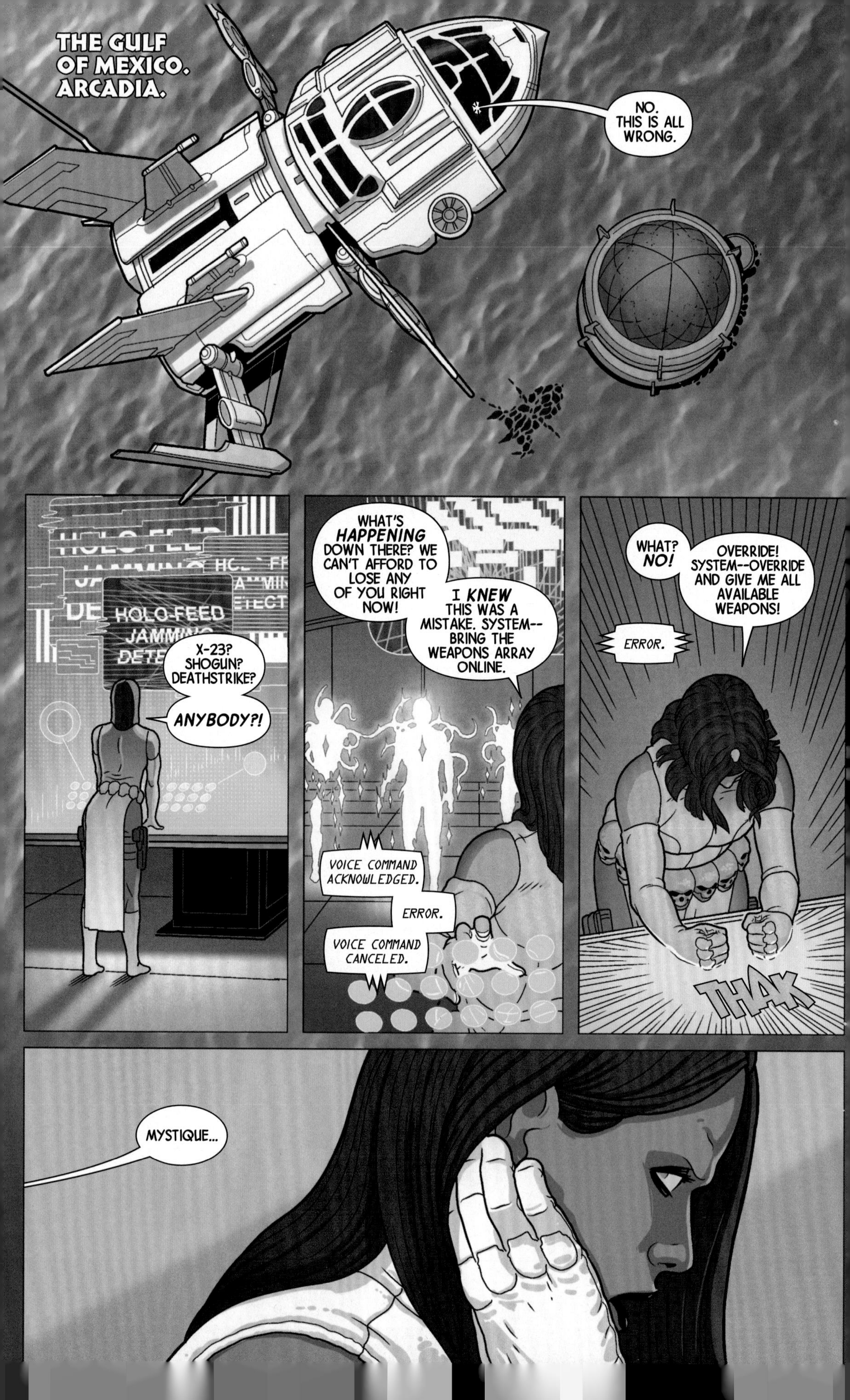
THE GULF OF MEXICO. ARCADIA.
NO. THIS IS ALL WRONG.
HOLO-FEED JAMMING DETE
X-23? SHOGUN? DEATHSTRIKE?
ANYBODY?!
WHAT'S HAPPENING DOWN THERE? WE CAN'T AFFORD TO LOSE ANY OF YOU RIGHT NOW!
I KNEW THIS WAS A MISTAKE. SYSTEM-- BRING THE WEAPONS ARRAY ONLINE.
VOICE COMMAND ACKNOWLEDGED.
ERROR.
VOICE COMMAND CANCELED.
WHAT? NO!
OVERRIDE! SYSTEM--OVERRIDE AND GIVE ME ALL AVAILABLE WEAPONS!
ERROR.
THAK
MYSTIQUE...

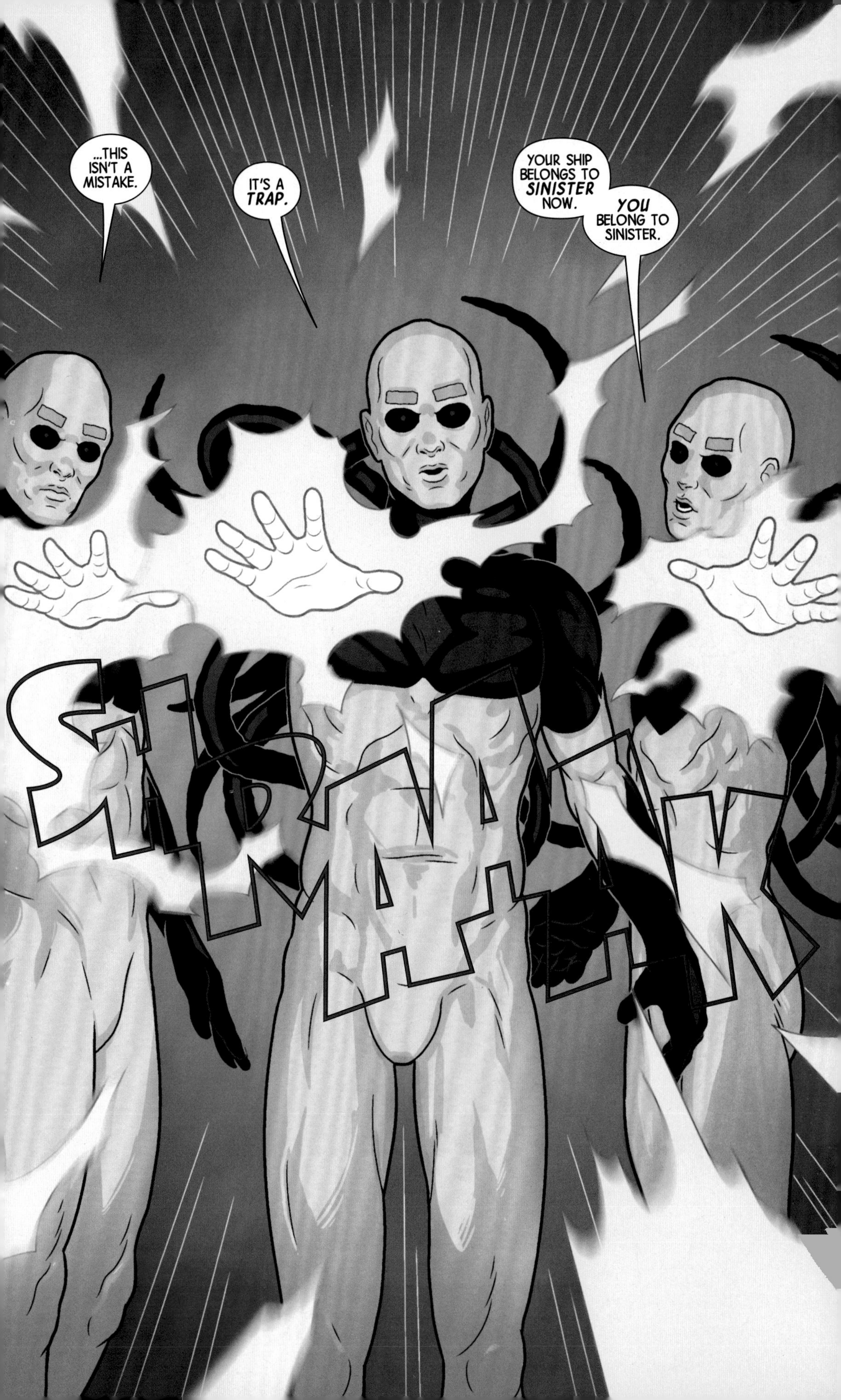
...THIS ISN'T A MISTAKE.
IT'S A TRAP.
YOUR SHIP BELONGS TO SINISTER NOW.
YOU BELONG TO SINISTER.

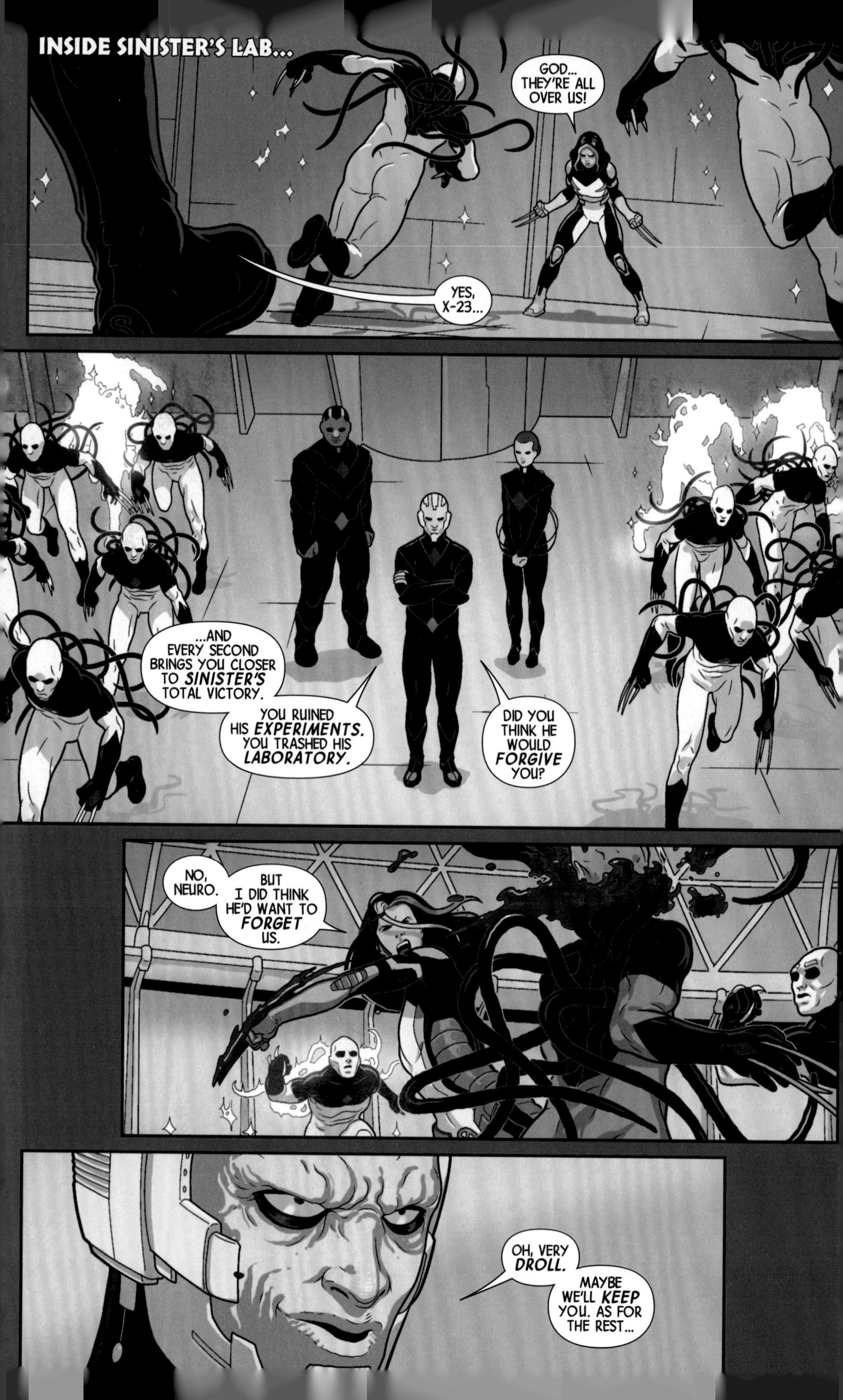
INSIDE SINISTER'S LAB...
GOD... THEY'RE ALL OVER US!
YES, X-23...
...AND EVERY SECOND BRINGS YOU CLOSER TO SINISTER'S TOTAL VICTORY.
YOU RUINED HIS EXPERIMENTS. YOU TRASHED HIS LABORATORY.
DID YOU THINK HE WOULD FORGIVE YOU?
NO, NEURO.
BUT I DID THINK HE'D WANT TO FORGET US.
OH, VERY DROLL.
MAYBE WE'LL KEEP YOU. AS FOR THE REST...

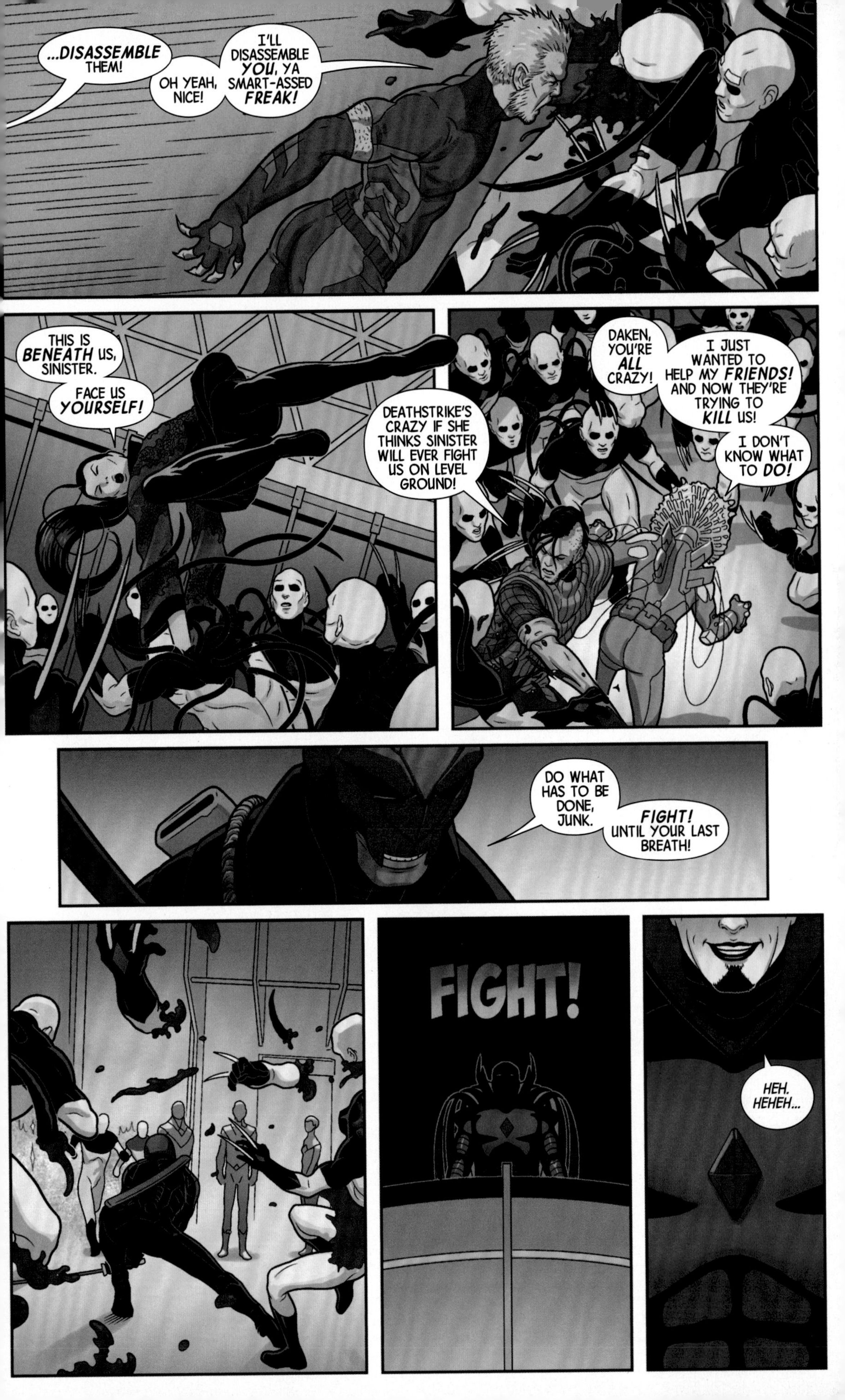
...DISASSEMBLE THEM!
OH YEAH, NICE!
I'LL DISASSEMBLE YOU, YA SMART-ASSED FREAK!
THIS IS BENEATH US, SINISTER.
FACE US YOURSELF!
DEATHSTRIKE'S CRAZY IF SHE THINKS SINISTER WILL EVER FIGHT US ON LEVEL GROUND!
DAKEN, YOU'RE ALL CRAZY!
I JUST WANTED TO HELP MY FRIENDS! AND NOW THEY'RE TRYING TO KILL US!
I DON'T KNOW WHAT TO DO!
DO WHAT HAS TO BE DONE, JUNK.
FIGHT! UNTIL YOUR LAST BREATH!
FIGHT!
HEH. HEHEH...

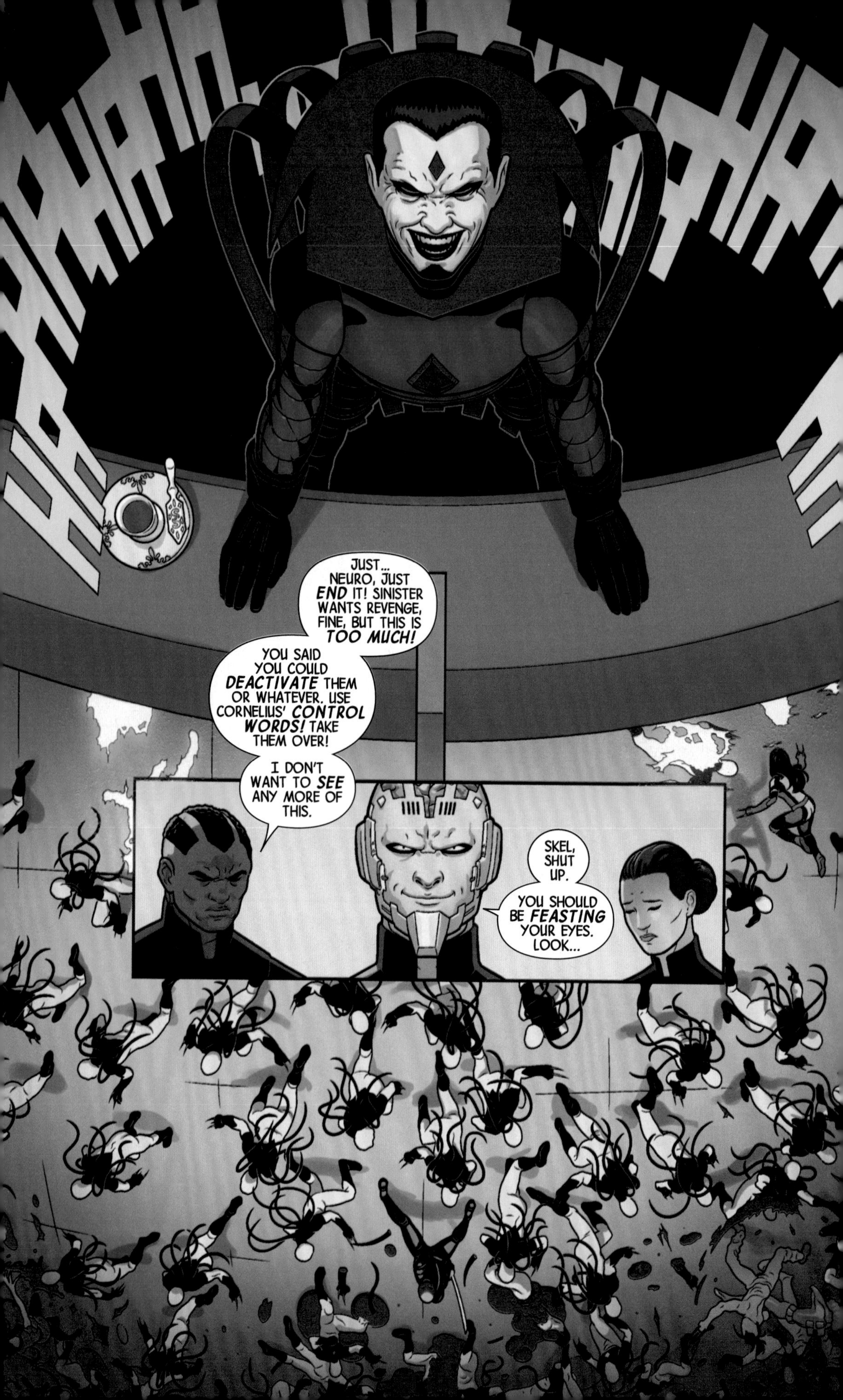
HAHAHA HAHAHA
JUST... NEURO, JUST END IT! SINISTER WANTS REVENGE, FINE, BUT THIS IS TOO MUCH!
YOU SAID YOU COULD DEACTIVATE THEM OR WHATEVER. USE CORNELIUS' CONTROL WORDS! TAKE THEM OVER!
I DON'T WANT TO SEE ANY MORE OF THIS.
SKEL, SHUT UP.
YOU SHOULD BE FEASTING YOUR EYES. LOOK...

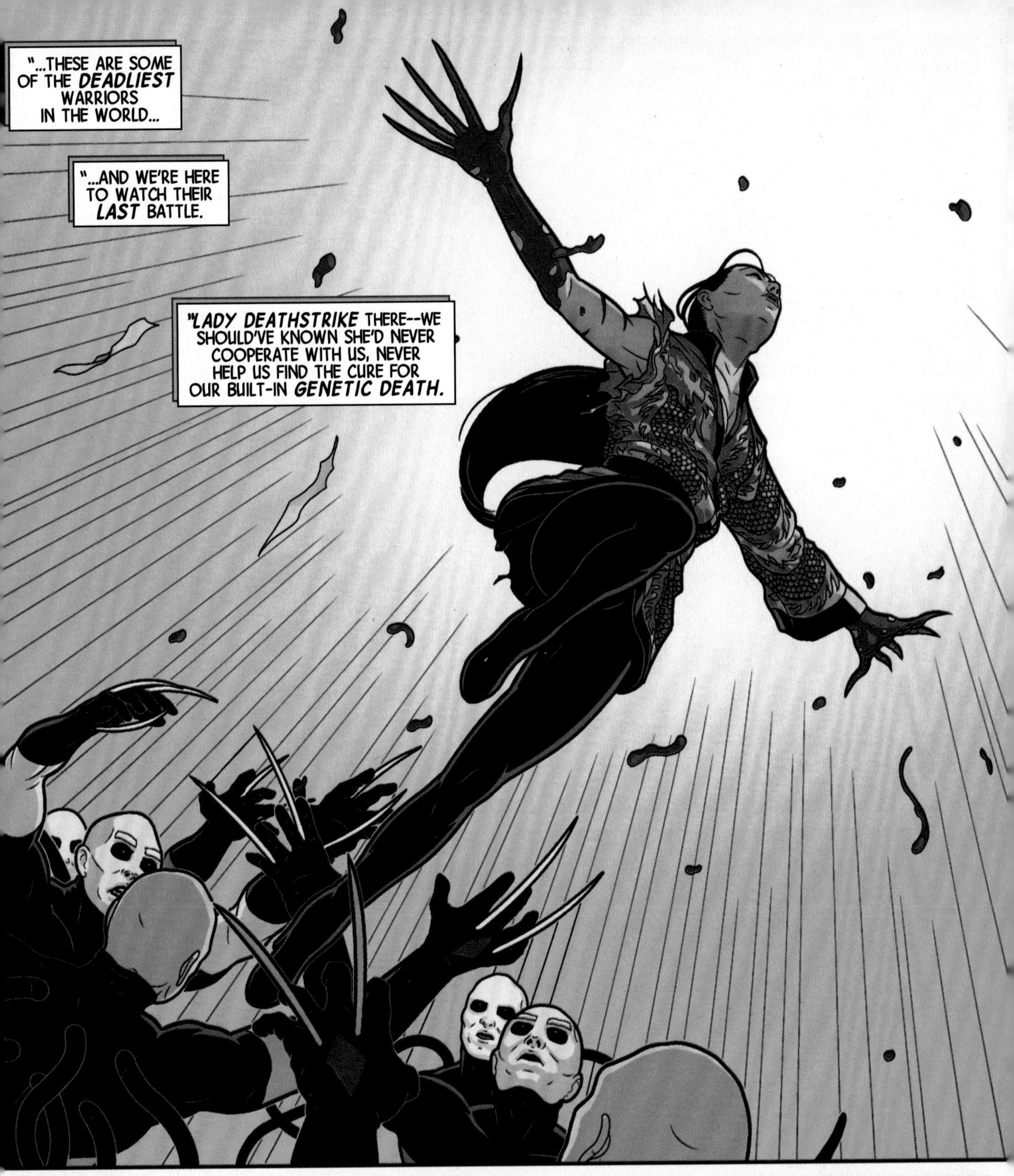
"...THESE ARE SOME OF THE DEADLIEST WARRIORS IN THE WORLD...
"...AND WE'RE HERE TO WATCH THEIR LAST BATTLE.
"LADY DEATHSTRIKE THERE--WE SHOULD'VE KNOWN SHE'D NEVER COOPERATE WITH US, NEVER HELP US FIND THE CURE FOR OUR BUILT-IN GENETIC DEATH.

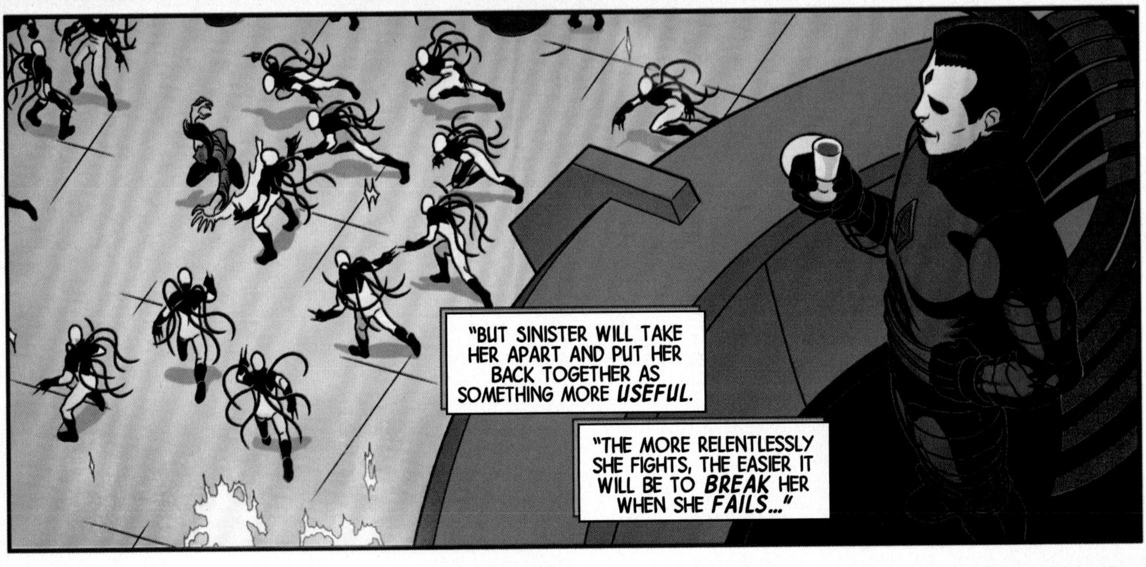
"BUT SINISTER WILL TAKE HER APART AND PUT HER BACK TOGETHER AS SOMETHING MORE USEFUL.
"THE MORE RELENTLESSLY SHE FIGHTS, THE EASIER IT WILL BE TO BREAK HER WHEN SHE FAILS..."

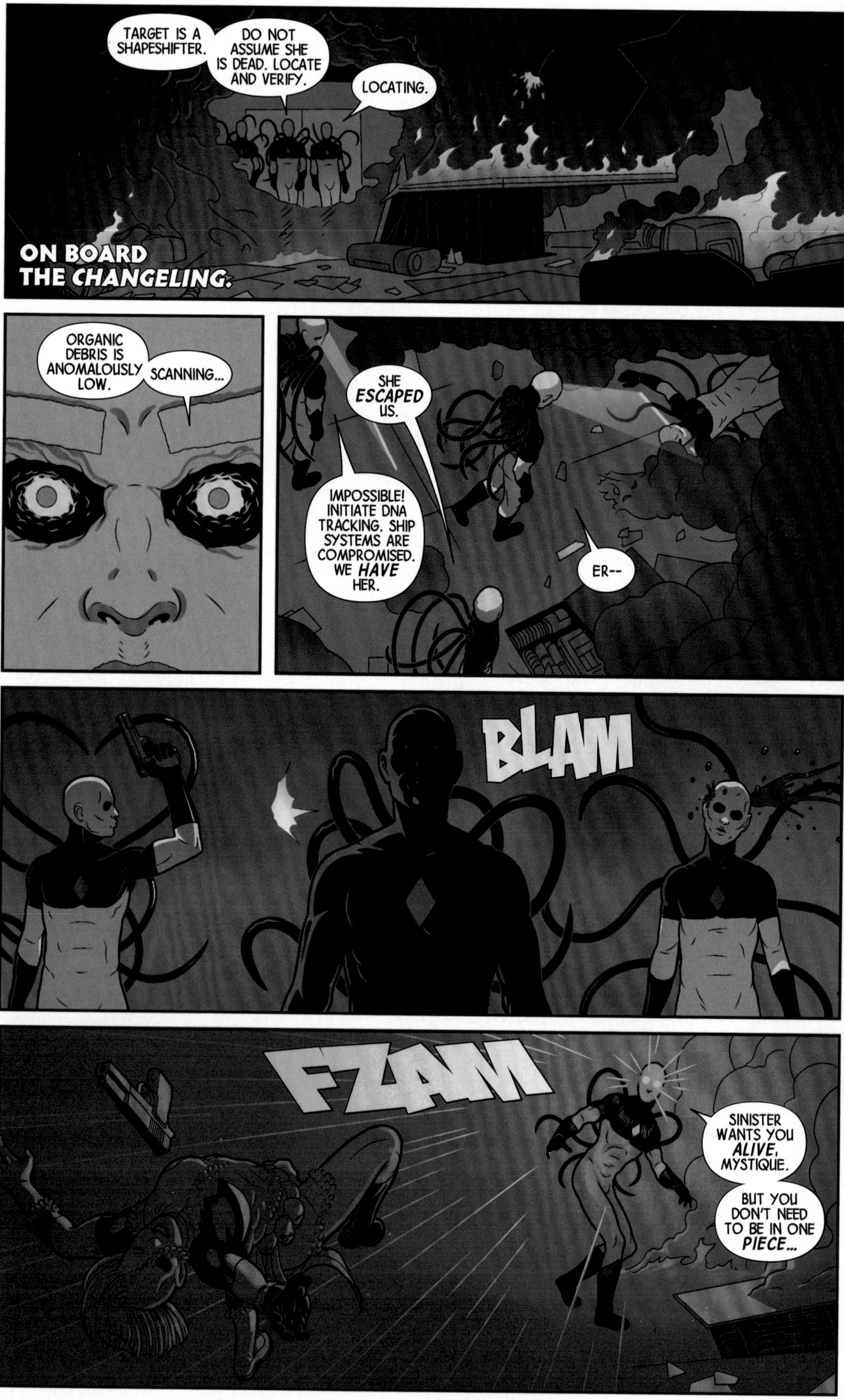
TARGET IS A SHAPESHIFTER.
DO NOT ASSUME SHE IS DEAD. LOCATE AND VERIFY.
LOCATING.
ON BOARD THE CHANGELING.
ORGANIC DEBRIS IS ANOMALOUSLY LOW.
SCANNING...
SHE ESCAPED US.
IMPOSSIBLE! INITIATE DNA TRACKING. SHIP SYSTEMS ARE COMPROMISED. WE HAVE HER.
ER--
BLAM
FZAM
SINISTER WANTS YOU ALIVE, MYSTIQUE.
BUT YOU DON'T NEED TO BE IN ONE PIECE...

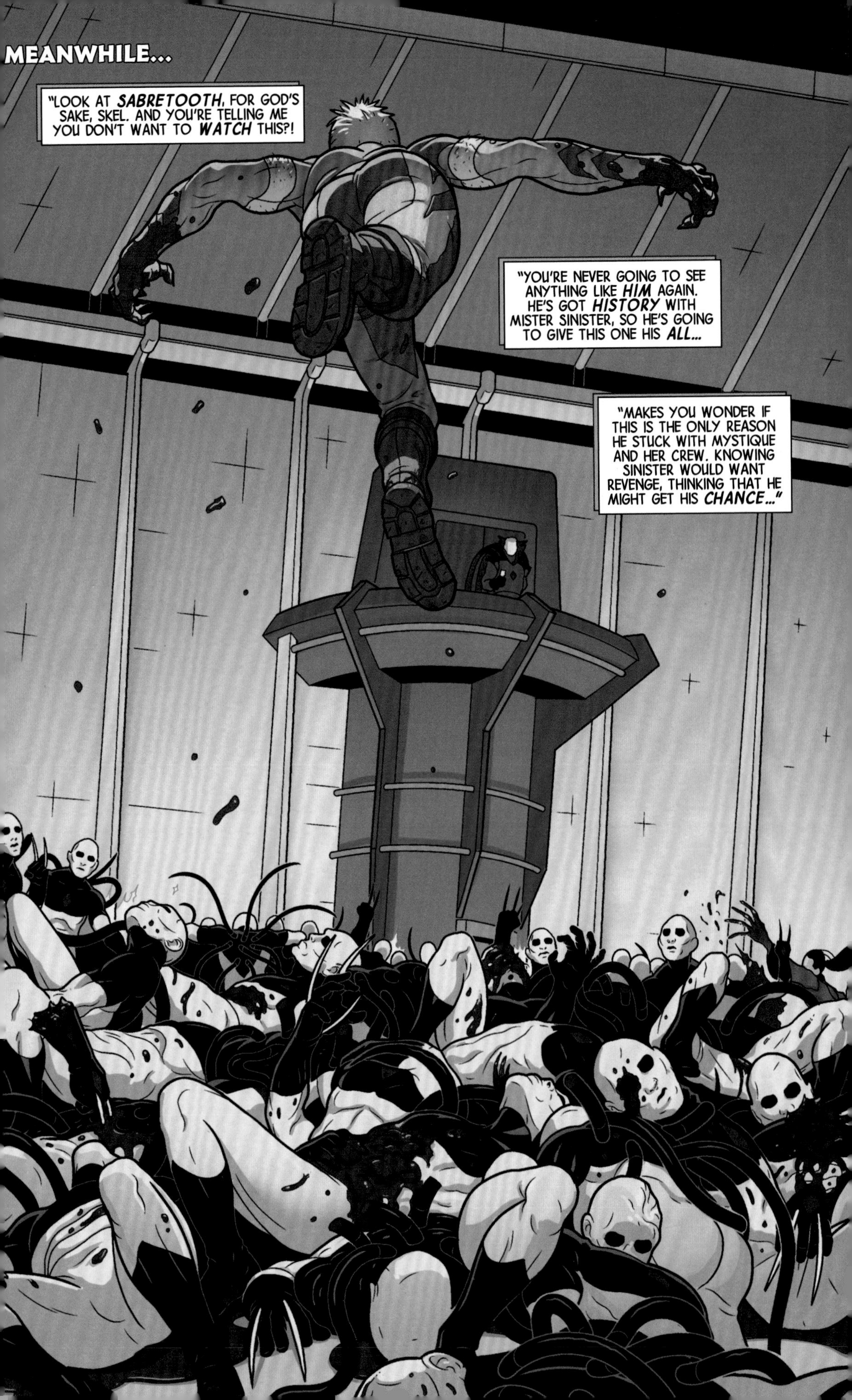
MEANWHILE...
"LOOK AT SABRETOOTH, FOR GOD'S SAKE, SKEL. AND YOU'RE TELLING ME YOU DON'T WANT TO WATCH THIS?!
"YOU'RE NEVER GOING TO SEE ANYTHING LIKE HIM AGAIN. HE'S GOT HISTORY WITH MISTER SINISTER, SO HE'S GOING TO GIVE THIS ONE HIS ALL...
"MAKES YOU WONDER IF THIS IS THE ONLY REASON HE STUCK WITH MYSTIQUE AND HER CREW. KNOWING SINISTER WOULD WANT REVENGE, THINKING THAT HE MIGHT GET HIS CHANCE..."

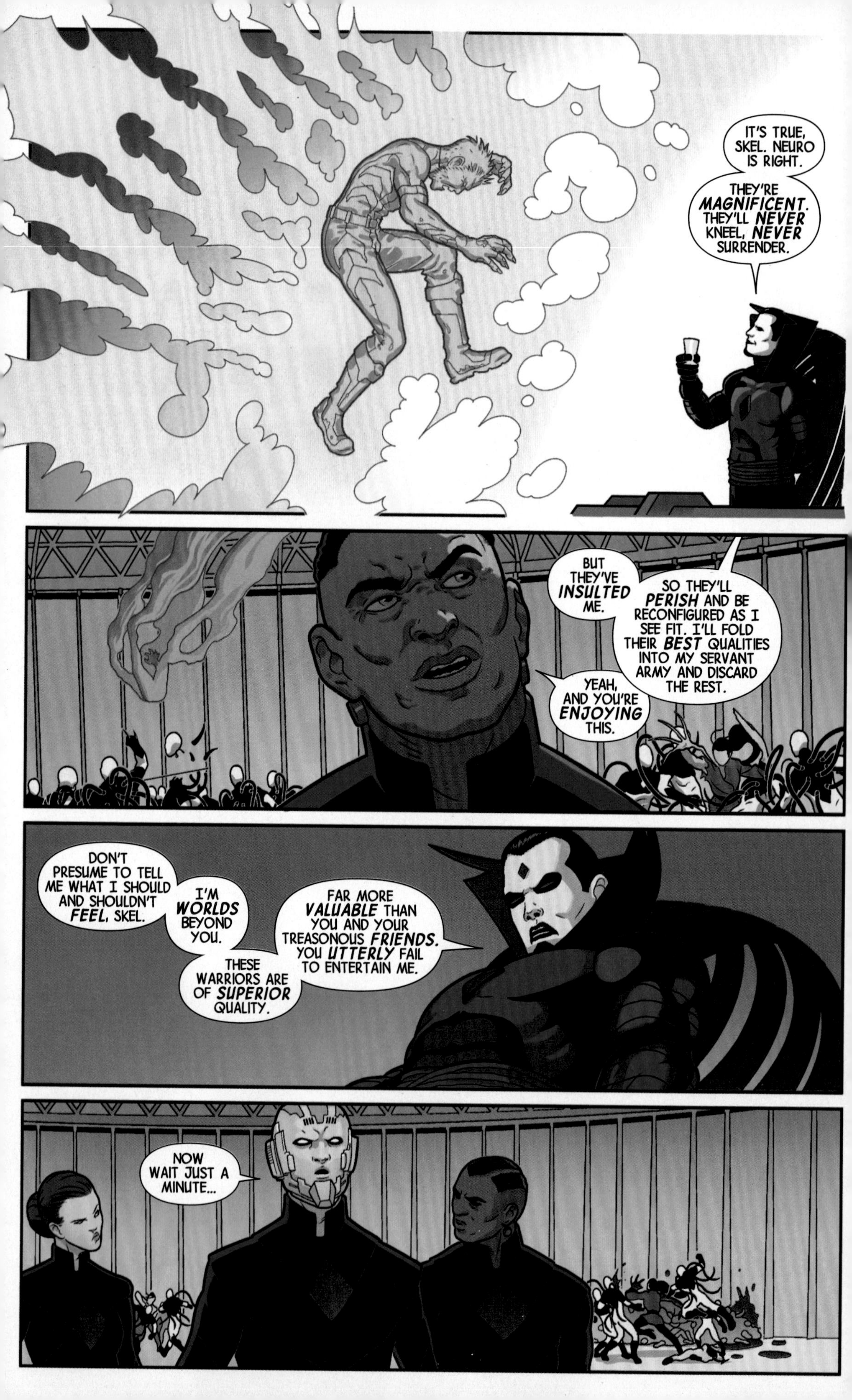
IT'S TRUE, SKEL. NEURO IS RIGHT.
THEY'RE MAGNIFICENT. THEY'LL NEVER KNEEL, NEVER SURRENDER.
BUT THEY'VE INSULTED ME.
SO THEY'LL PERISH AND BE RECONFIGURED AS I SEE FIT. I'LL FOLD THEIR BEST QUALITIES INTO MY SERVANT ARMY AND DISCARD THE REST.
YEAH, AND YOU'RE ENJOYING THIS.
DON'T PRESUME TO TELL ME WHAT I SHOULD AND SHOULDN'T FEEL, SKEL.
I'M WORLDS BEYOND YOU.
THESE WARRIORS ARE OF SUPERIOR QUALITY.
FAR MORE VALUABLE THAN YOU AND YOUR TREASONOUS FRIENDS. YOU UTTERLY FAIL TO ENTERTAIN ME.
NOW WAIT JUST A MINUTE...

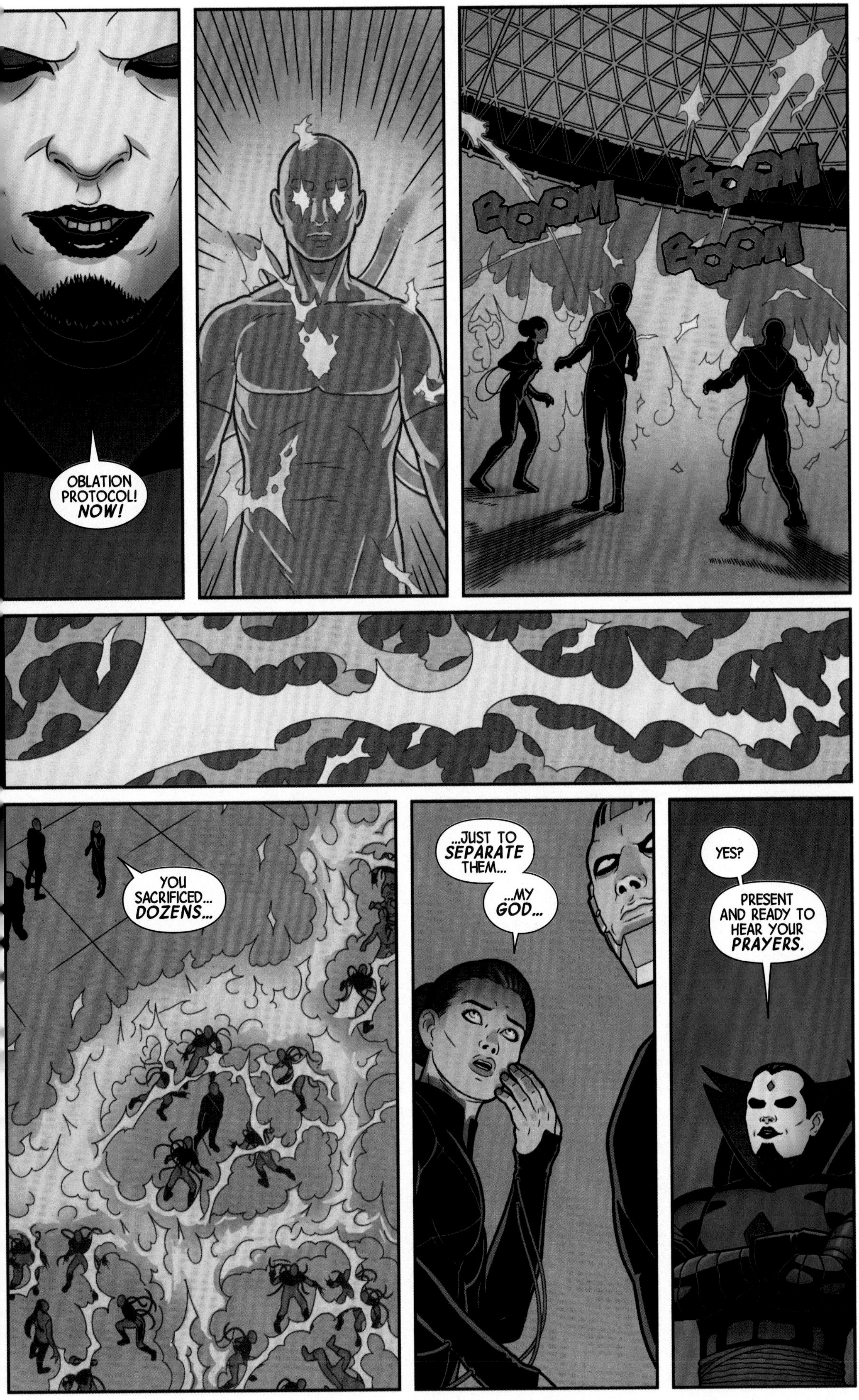
OBLATION PROTOCOL! NOW!
BOOM
BOOM
BOOM
YOU SACRIFICED... DOZENS...
...JUST TO SEPARATE THEM...
...MY GOD...
YES?
PRESENT AND READY TO HEAR YOUR PRAYERS.

OH, POOR BABY.

YOU LOOK CONFUSED.

THERE IS NO ESCAPE, MYSTIQUE.

FOR YOU.

YOU BELIEVE SINISTER SERIOUSLY THOUGHT THREE CLONES COULD HANDLE ME?

HE SENT YOU TO ME. AS A GIFT.

WHAT? NO, I...

...YOU ARE ATTEMPTING TO CONFUSE ME.

BUT I AM ONE OF MISTER SINISTER'S PERFECT CREATIONS. I CANNOT BE TRICKED OR INTIMIDATED.

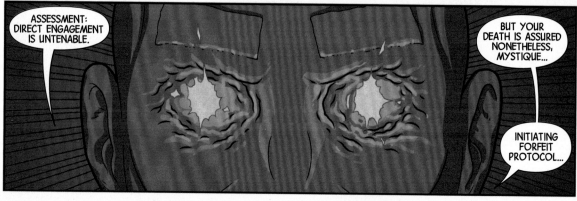

ASSESSMENT: DIRECT ENGAGEMENT IS UNTENABLE.

BUT YOUR DEATH IS ASSURED NONETHELESS, MYSTIQUE...

INITIATING FORFEIT PROTOCOL...

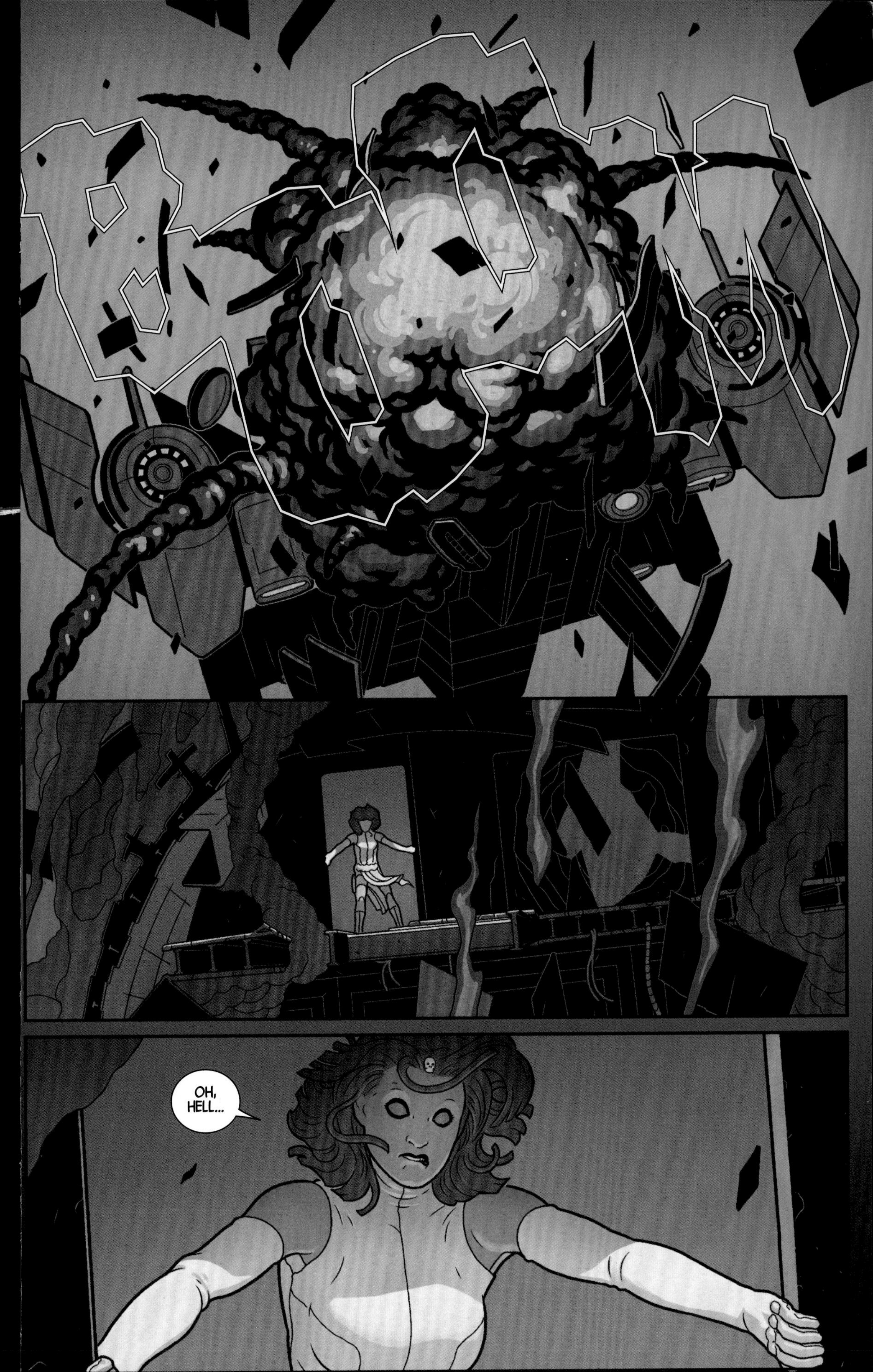
OH, HELL...

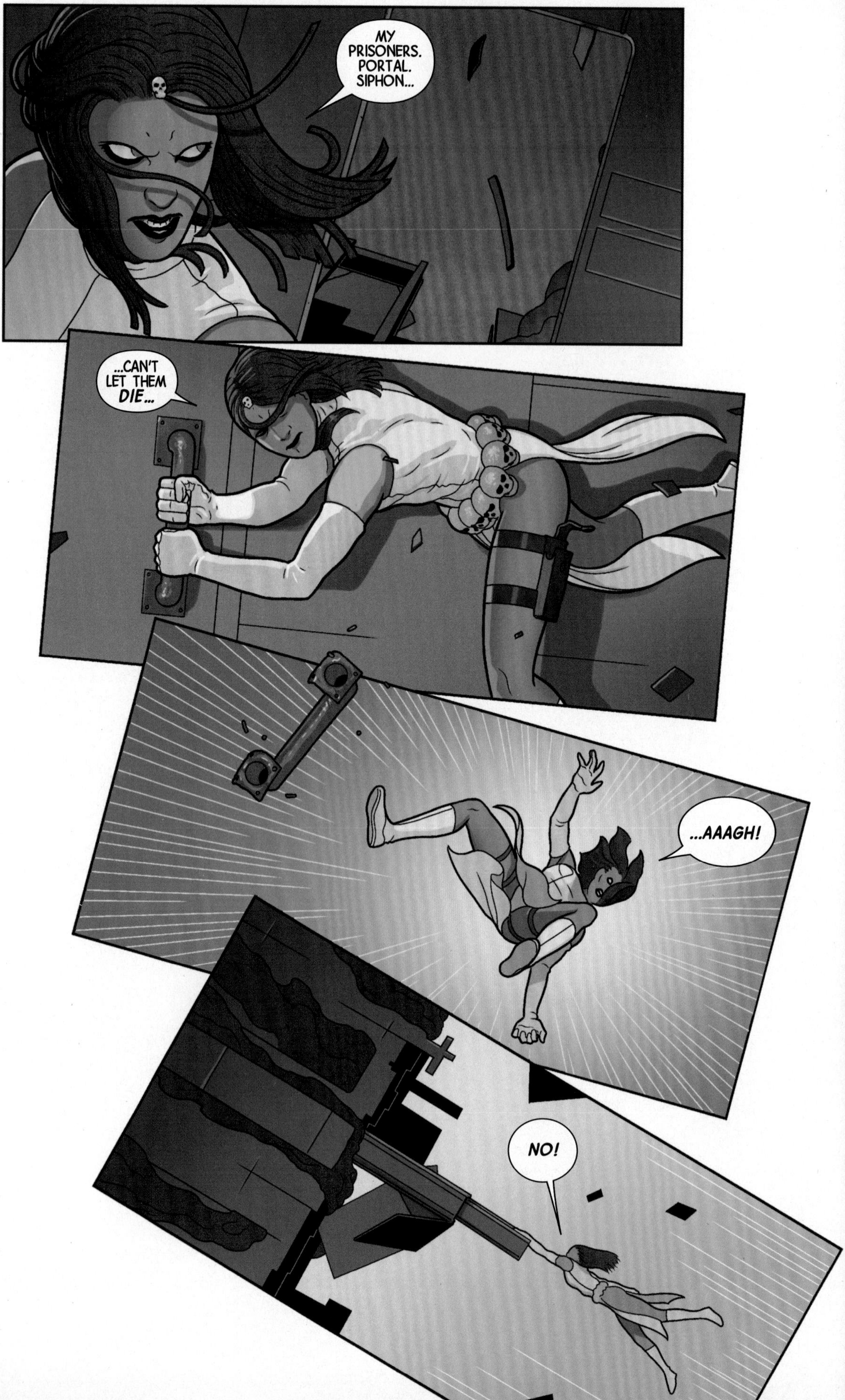
MY PRISONERS. PORTAL. SIPHON...
...CAN'T LET THEM *DIE*...
...AAAGH!
NO!

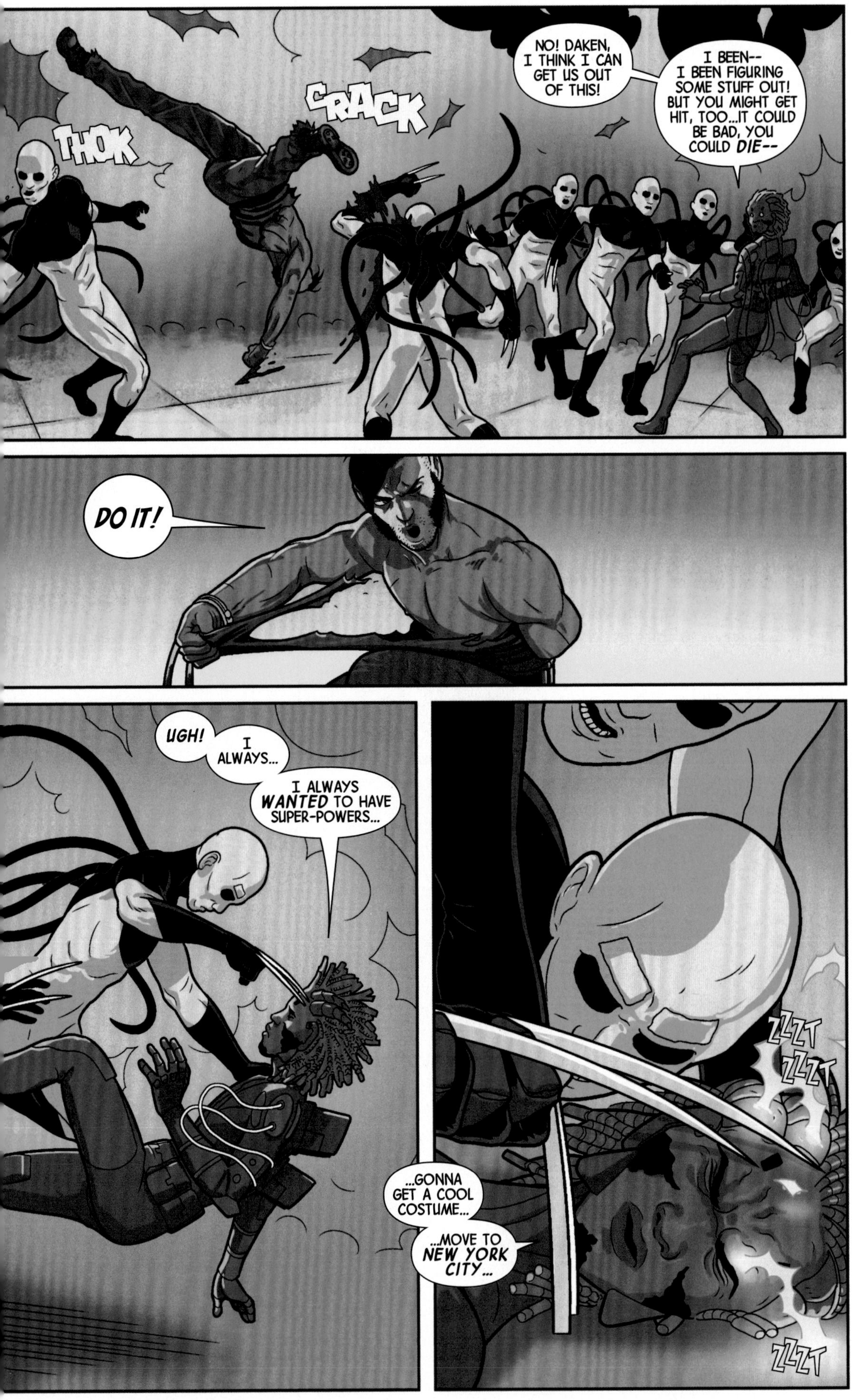
THOK
CRACK
NO! DAKEN, I THINK I CAN GET US OUT OF THIS!
I BEEN-- I BEEN FIGURING SOME STUFF OUT! BUT YOU MIGHT GET HIT, TOO...IT COULD BE BAD, YOU COULD DIE--
DO IT!
UGH!
I ALWAYS...
I ALWAYS WANTED TO HAVE SUPER-POWERS...
...GONNA GET A COOL COSTUME...
...MOVE TO NEW YORK CITY...
ZZZT
ZZZT
ZZZT

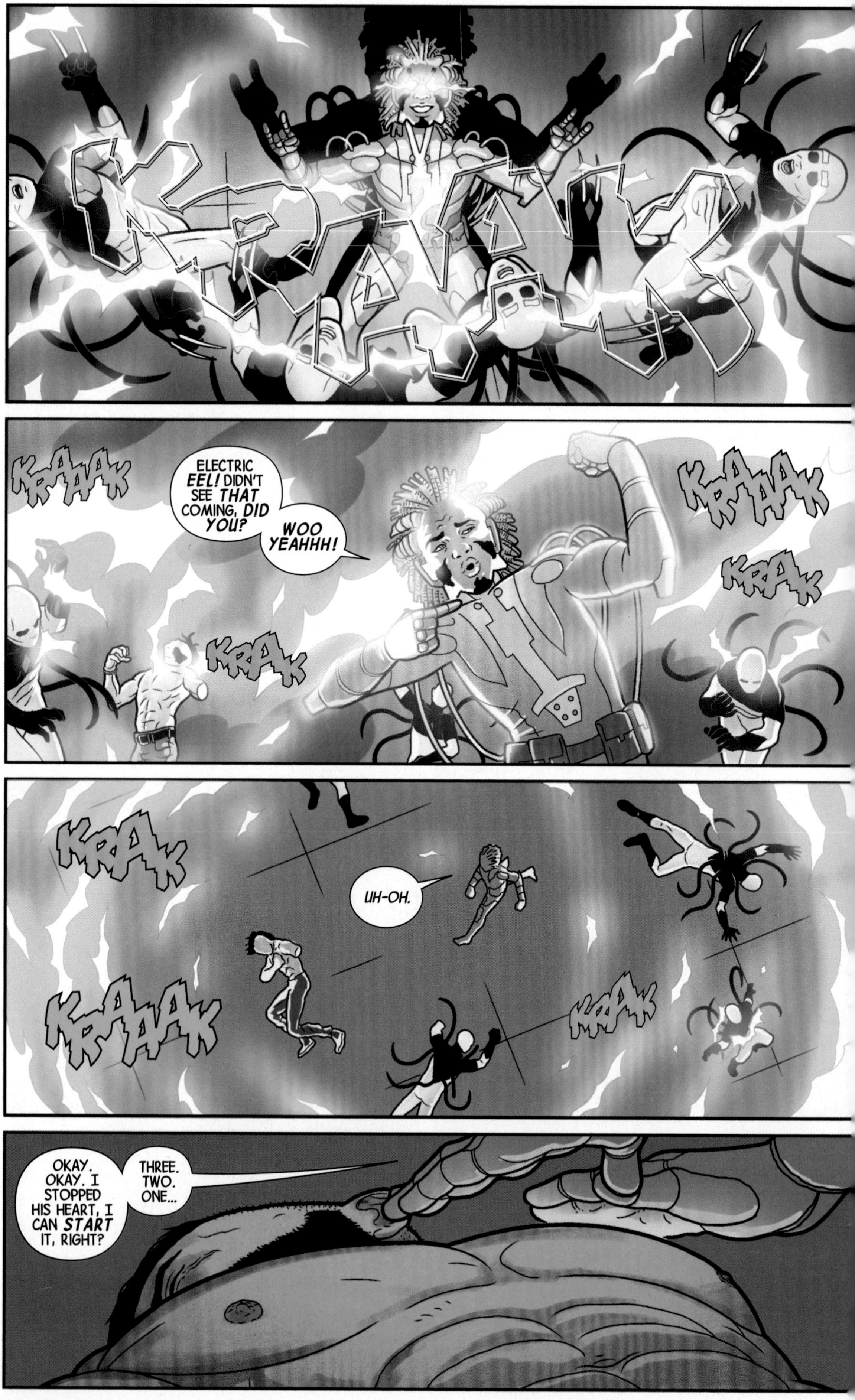
ELECTRIC EEL! DIDN'T SEE THAT COMING, DID YOU?
WOO YEAHHH!
UH-OH.
OKAY. OKAY. I STOPPED HIS HEART, I CAN START IT, RIGHT?
THREE. TWO. ONE...

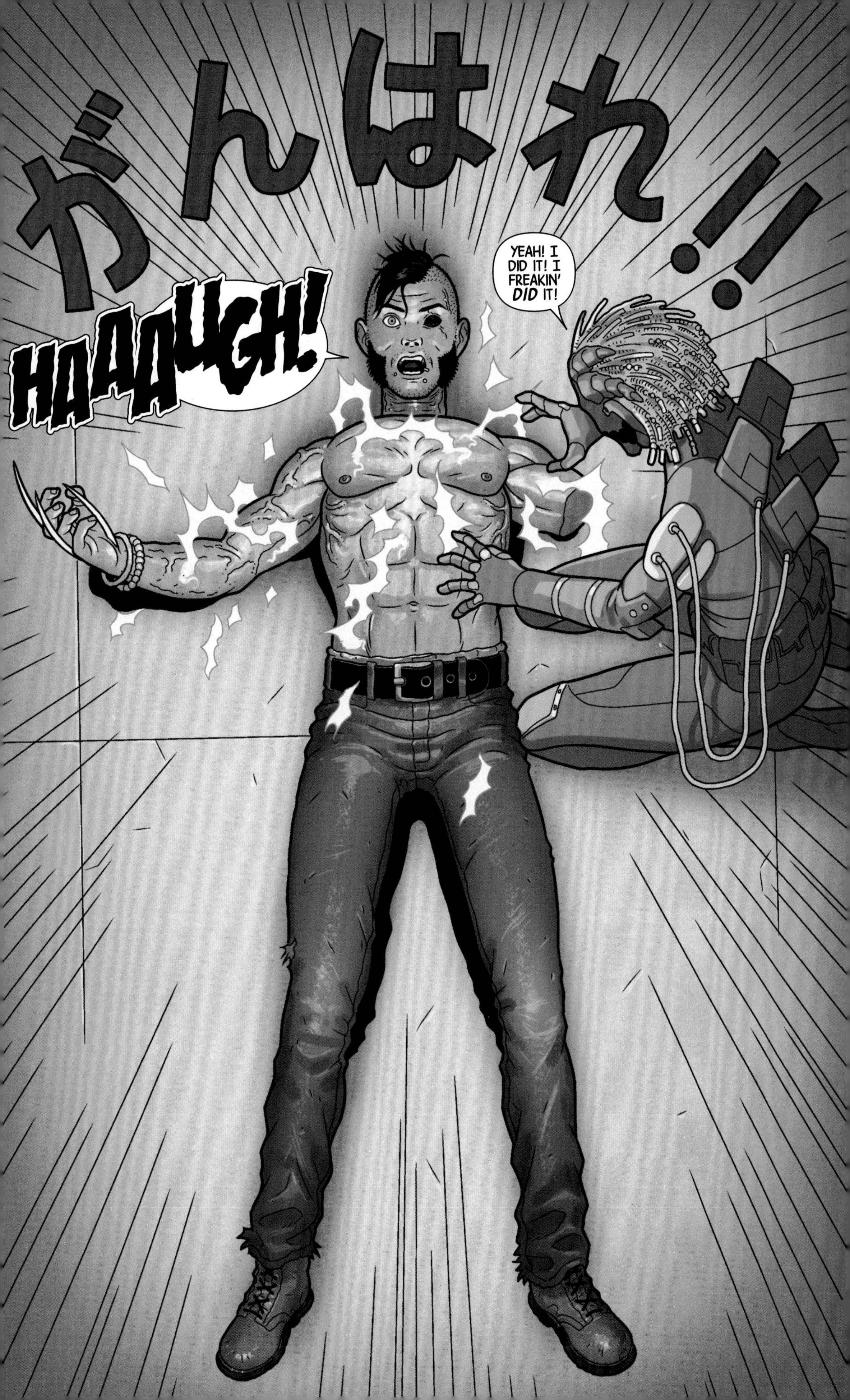
がんばれ!!!
HAAAUGH!
YEAH! I DID IT! I FREAKIN' DID IT!

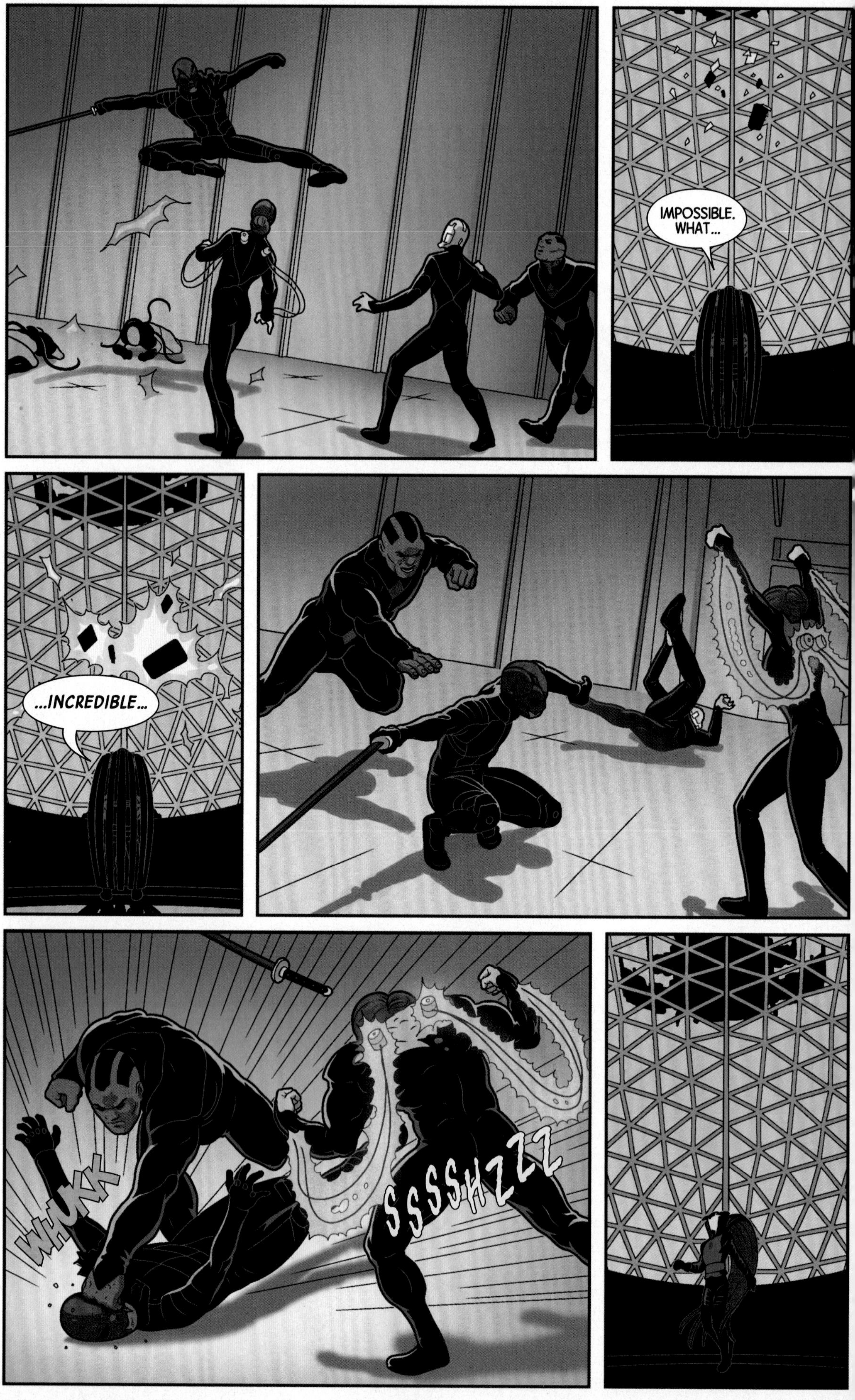
IMPOSSIBLE. WHAT...
...INCREDIBLE...
WHUKK
SSSSHZZZ

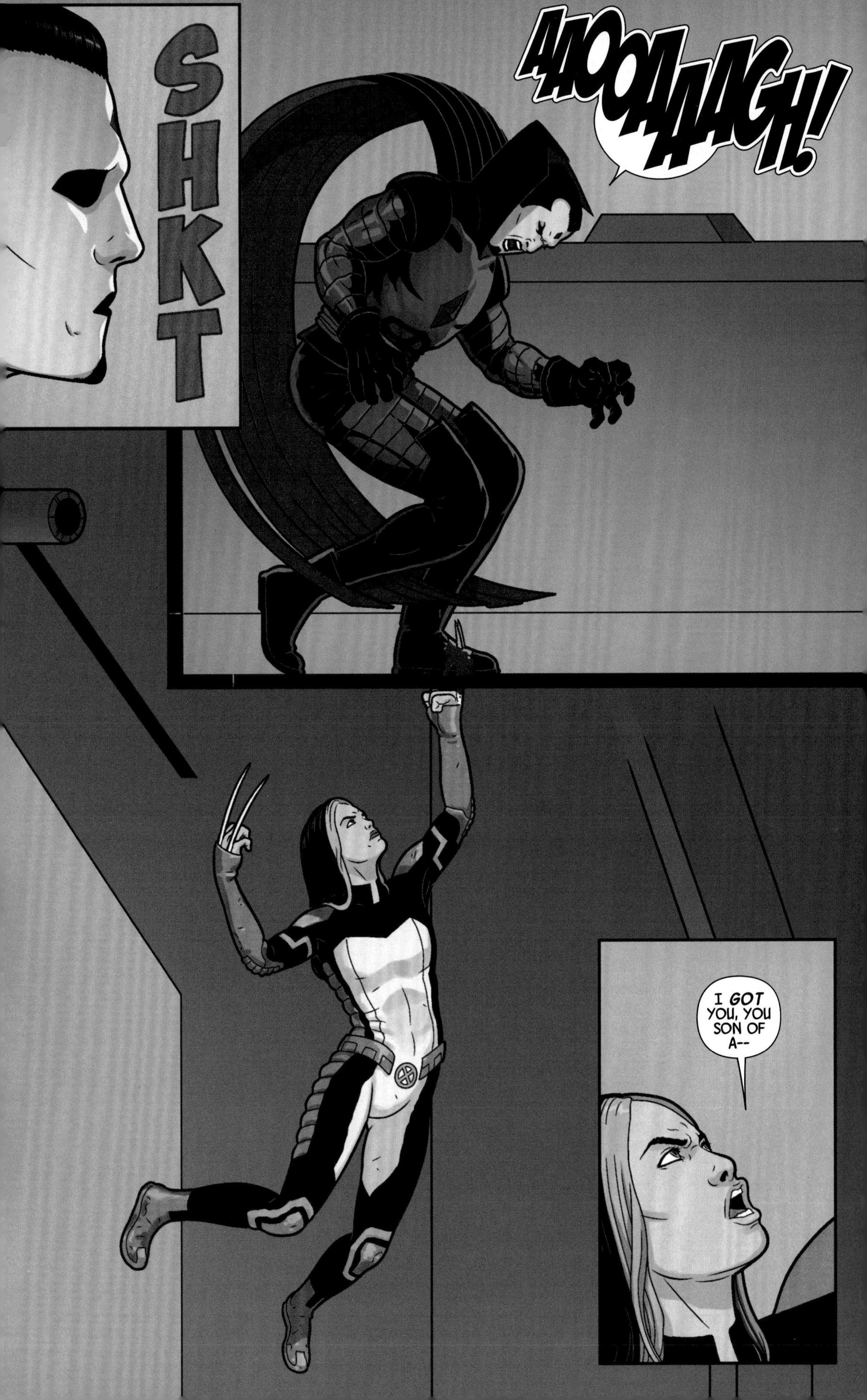
SHKT
AAOOAAAAGH!
I GOT YOU, YOU SON OF A--

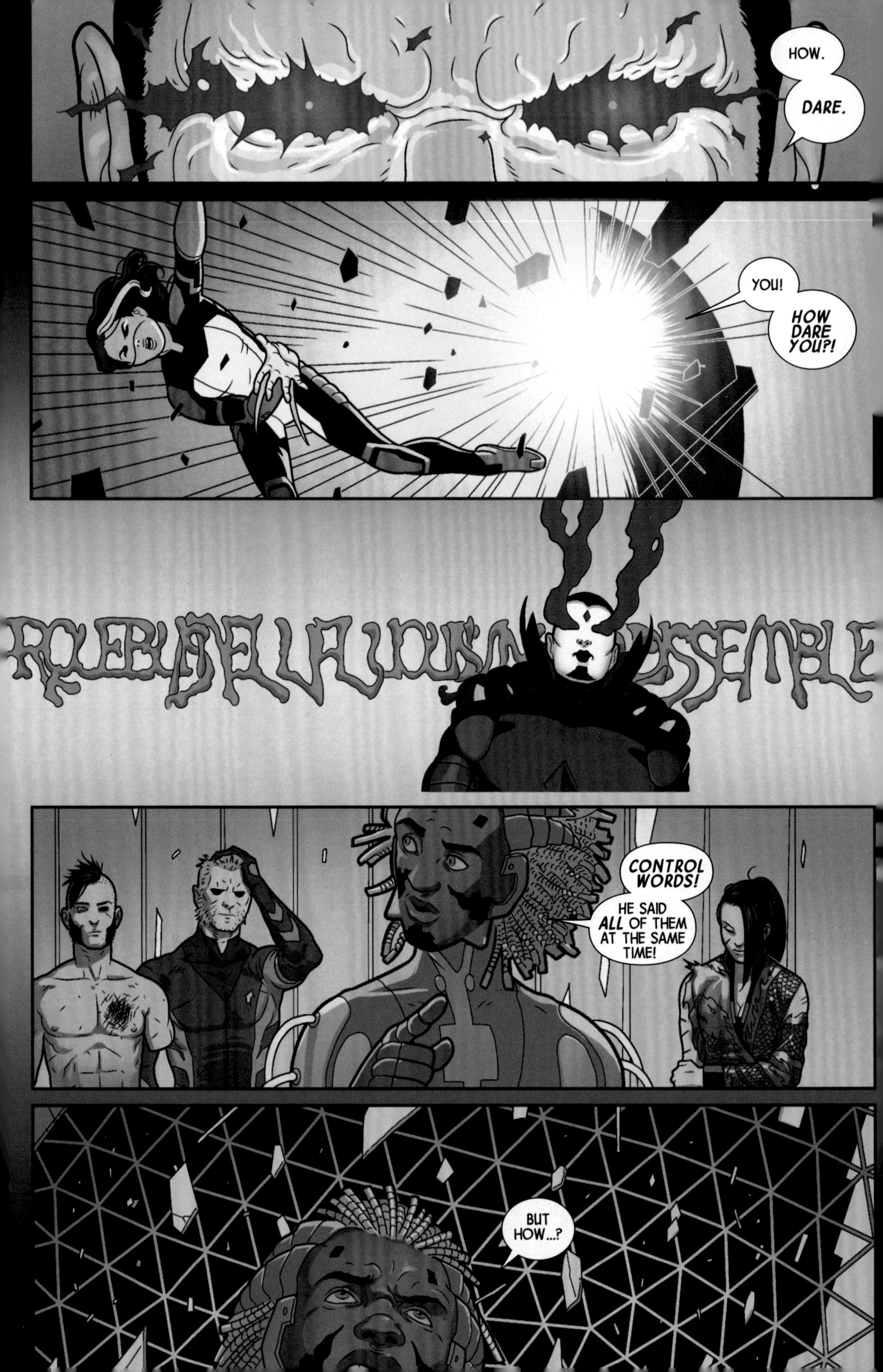
HOW.
DARE.
YOU!
HOW DARE YOU?!
CONTROL WORDS!
HE SAID ALL OF THEM AT THE SAME TIME!
BUT HOW...?

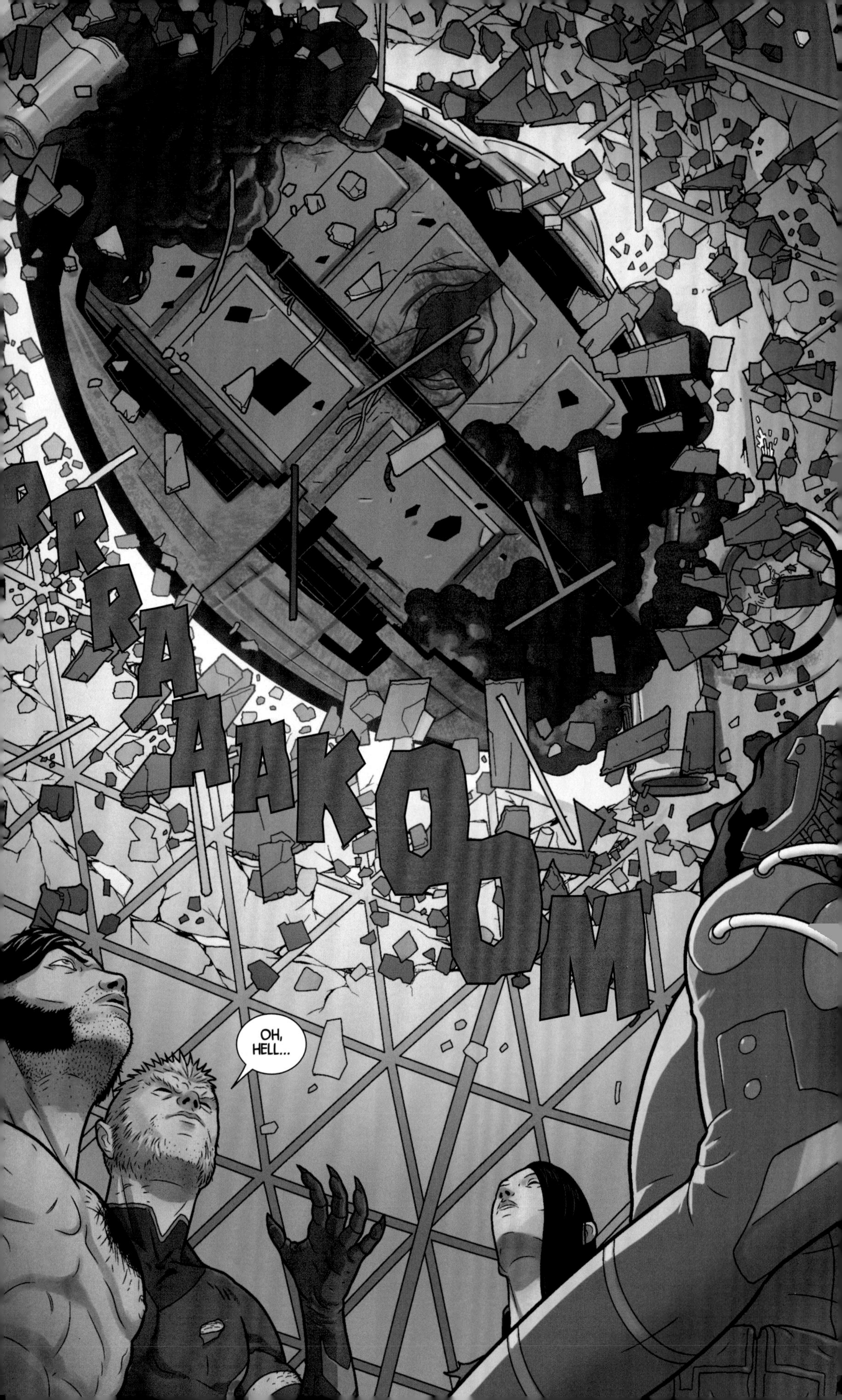
RRRAAAKOOOM
OH, HELL...

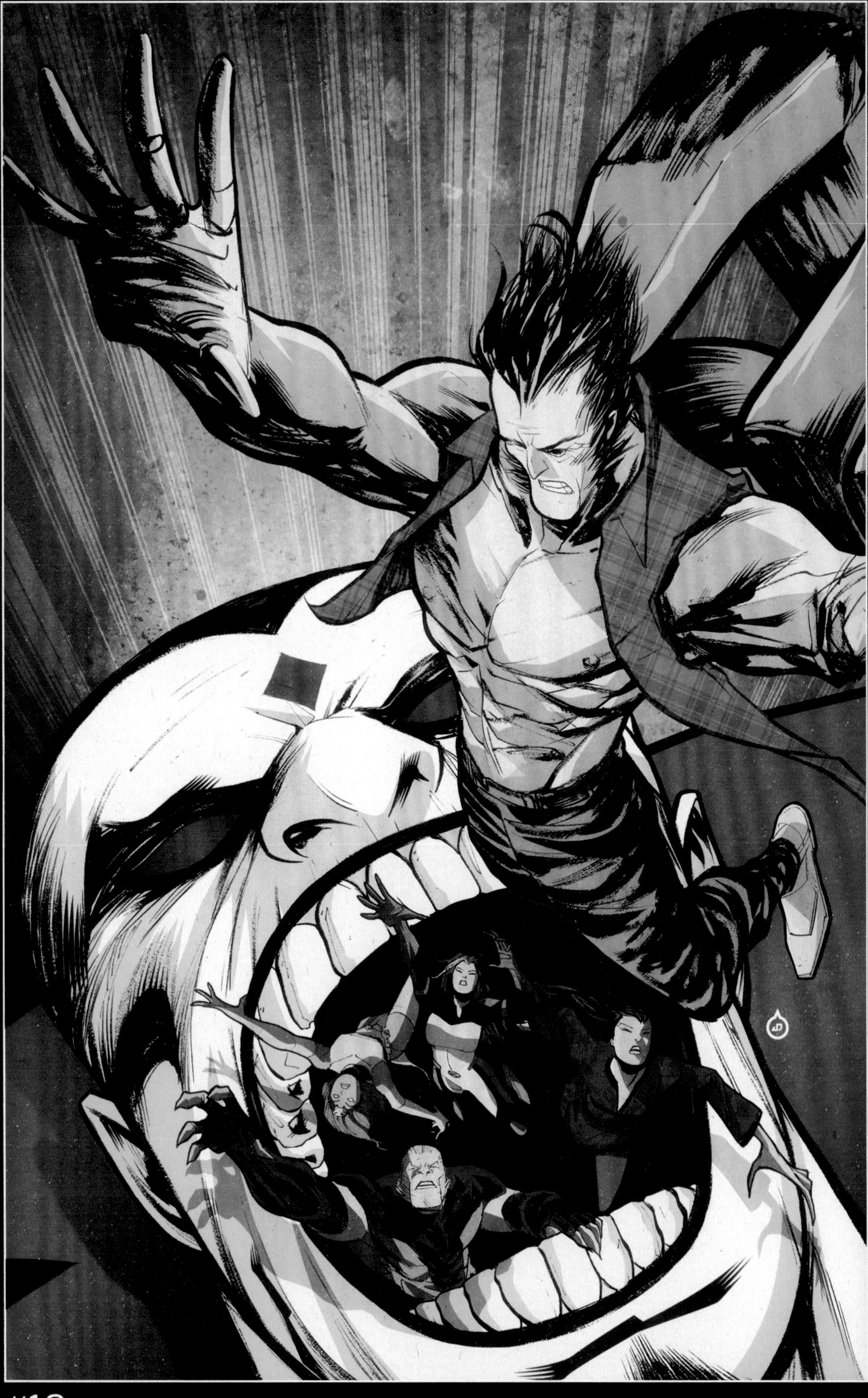

#18

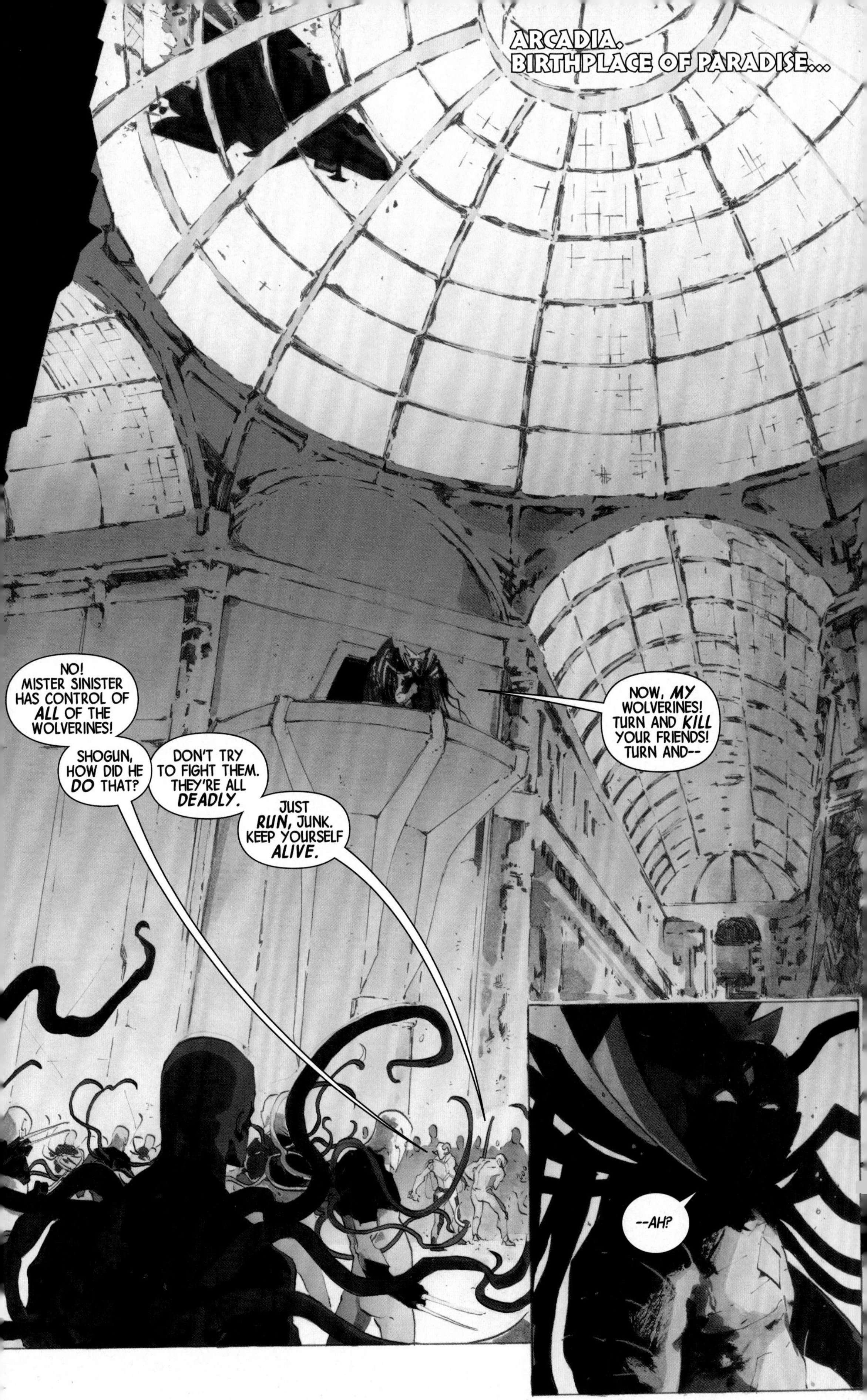
ARCADIA. BIRTHPLACE OF PARADISE...
NOW, MY WOLVERINES! TURN AND KILL YOUR FRIENDS! TURN AND--
NO! MISTER SINISTER HAS CONTROL OF ALL OF THE WOLVERINES!
SHOGUN, HOW DID HE DO THAT?
DON'T TRY TO FIGHT THEM. THEY'RE ALL DEADLY.
JUST RUN, JUNK. KEEP YOURSELF ALIVE.
--AH?

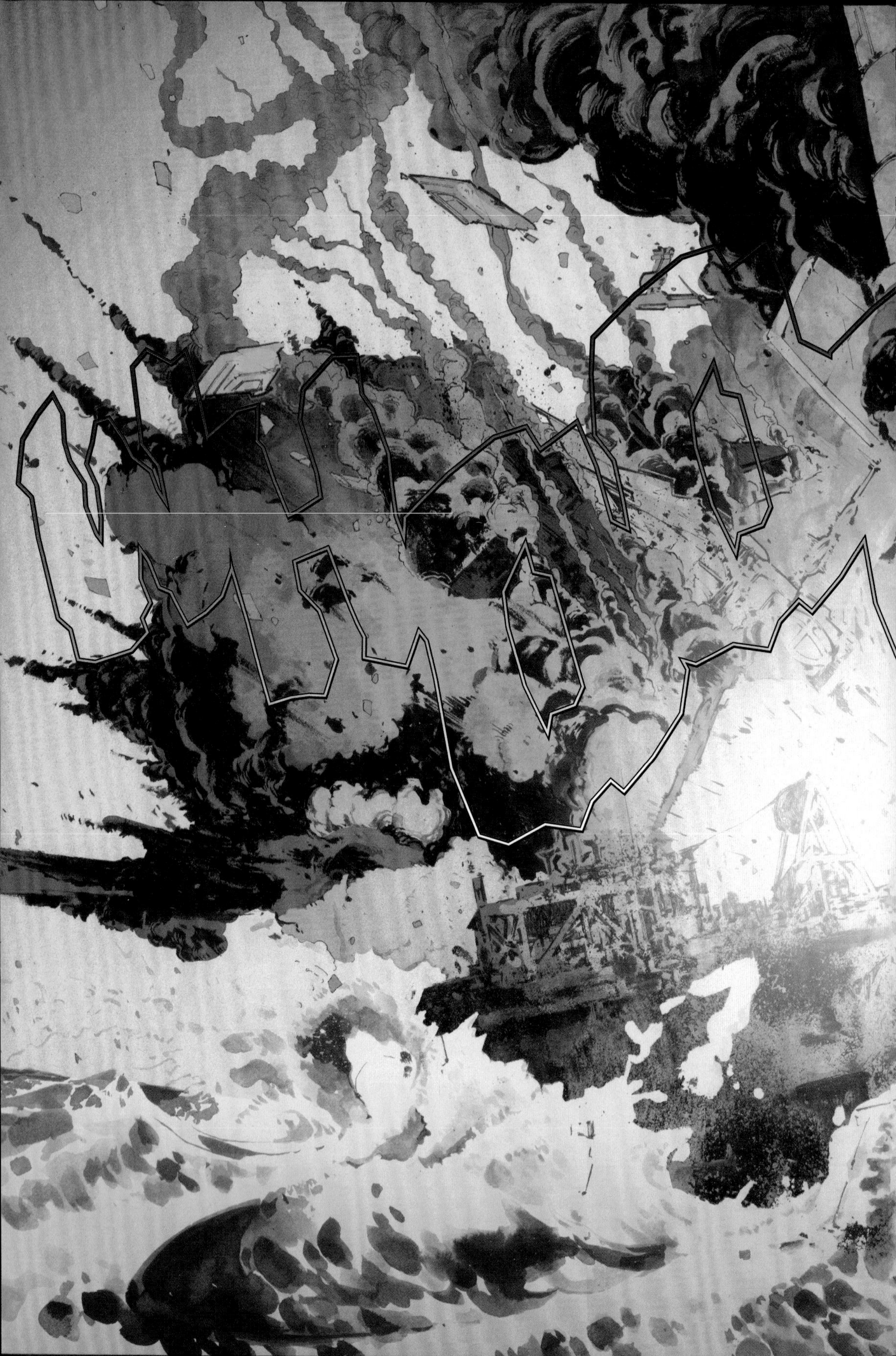

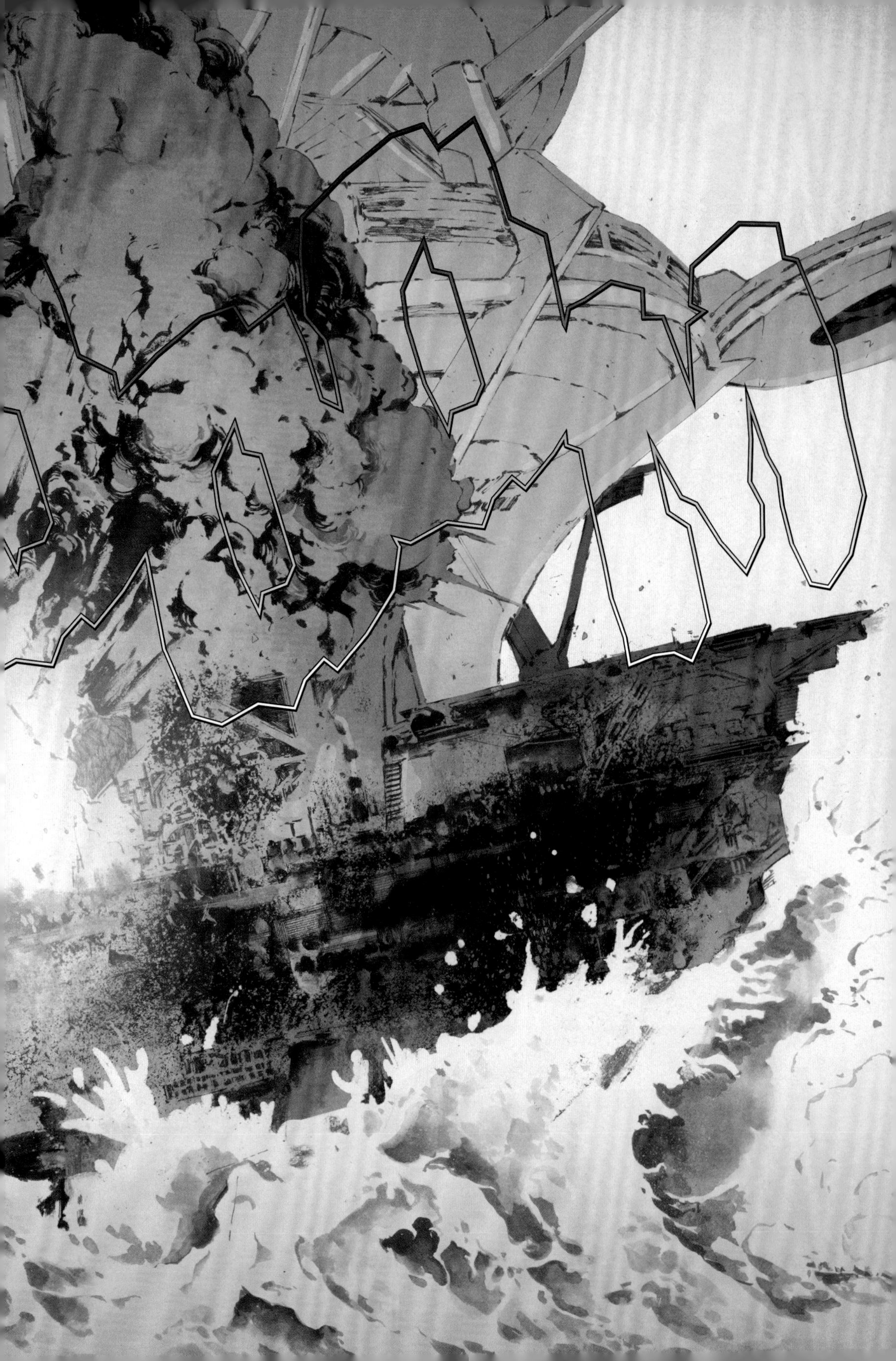

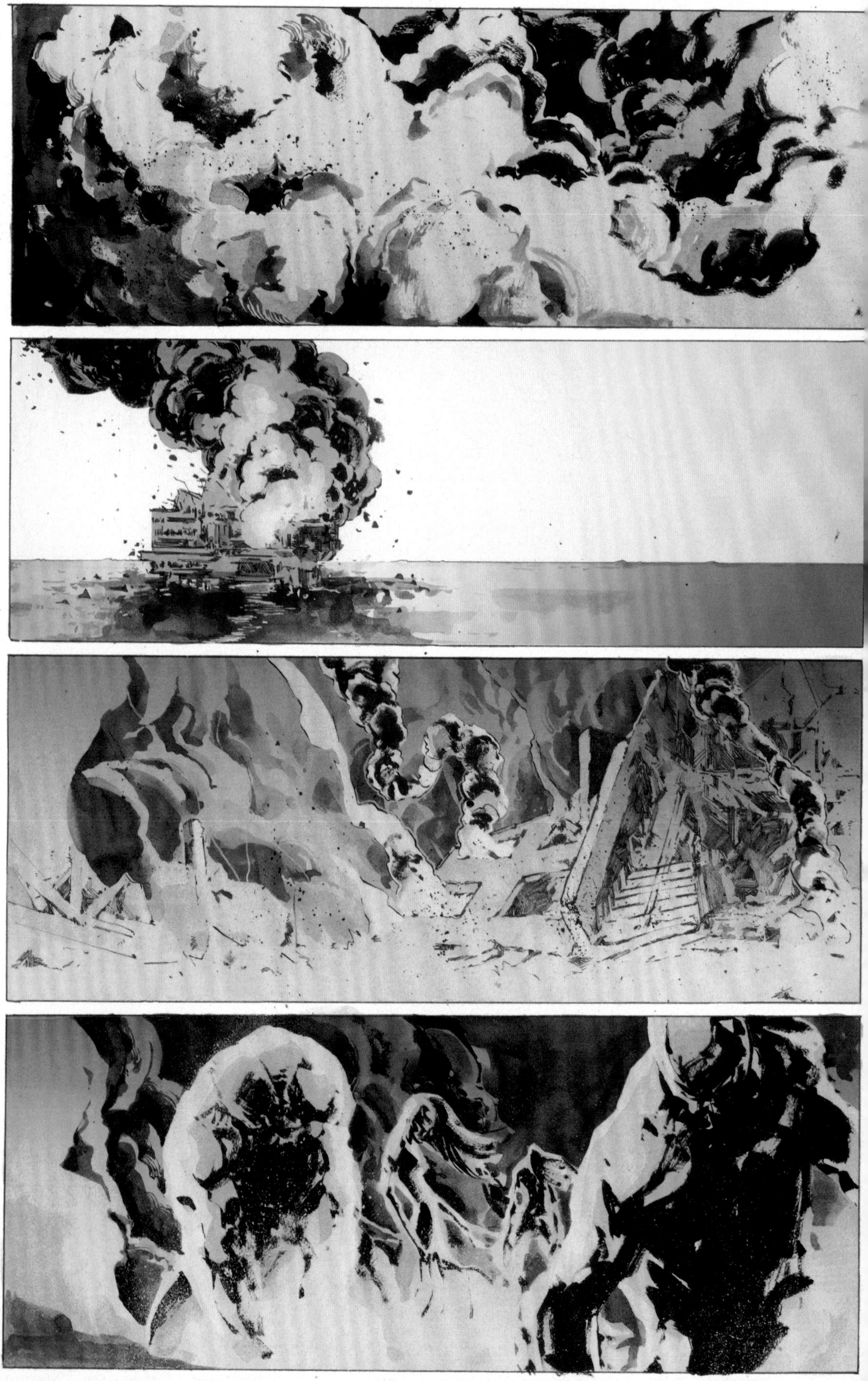

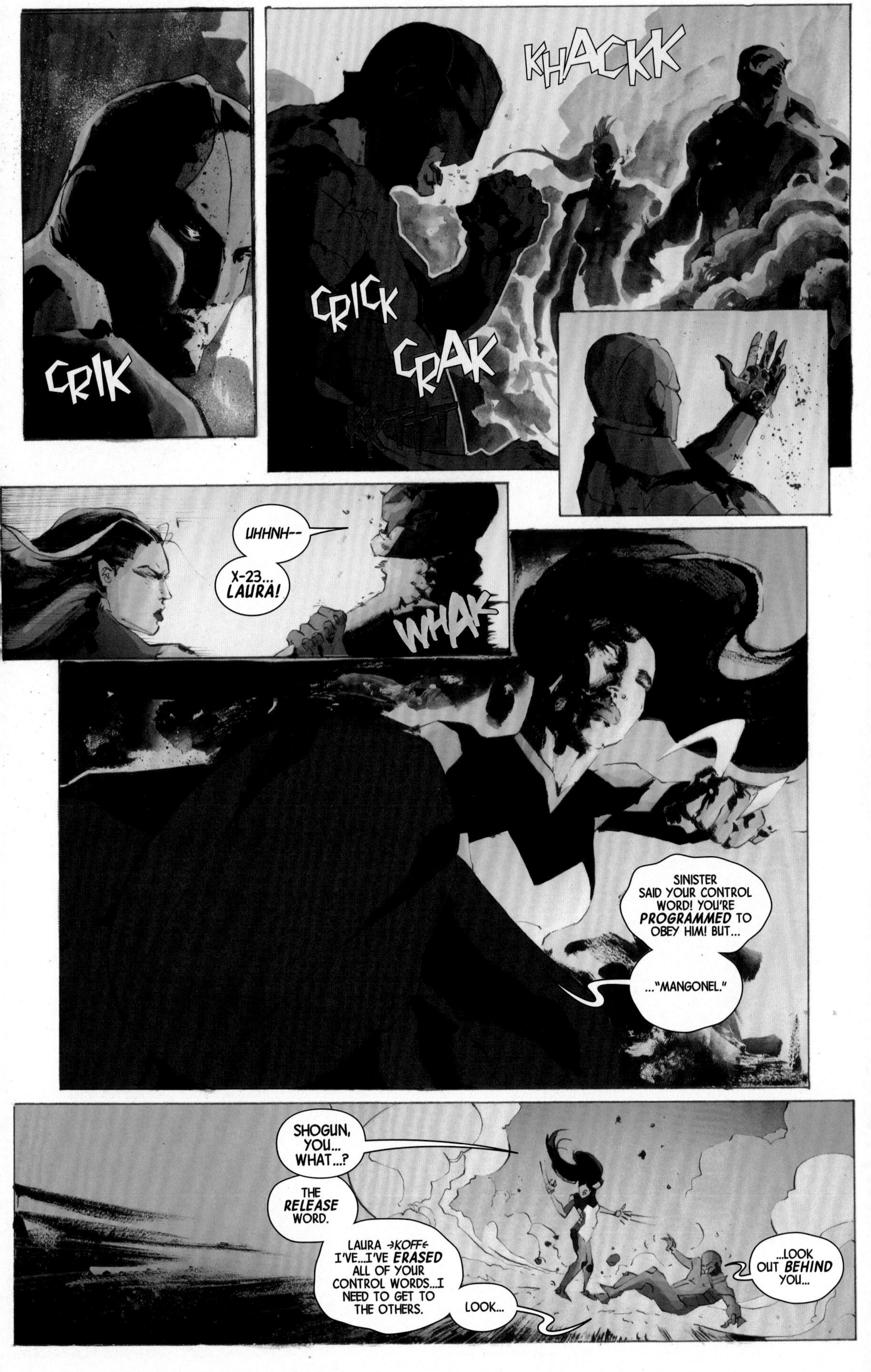
CRIK
KHACKK
CRICK
CRAK
UHHNH--
X-23... LAURA!
WHAK
SINISTER SAID YOUR CONTROL WORD! YOU'RE PROGRAMMED TO OBEY HIM! BUT...
..."MANGONEL."
SHOGUN, YOU... WHAT...?
THE RELEASE WORD.
LAURA →KOFF← I'VE...I'VE ERASED ALL OF YOUR CONTROL WORDS...I NEED TO GET TO THE OTHERS.
LOOK...
...LOOK OUT BEHIND YOU...

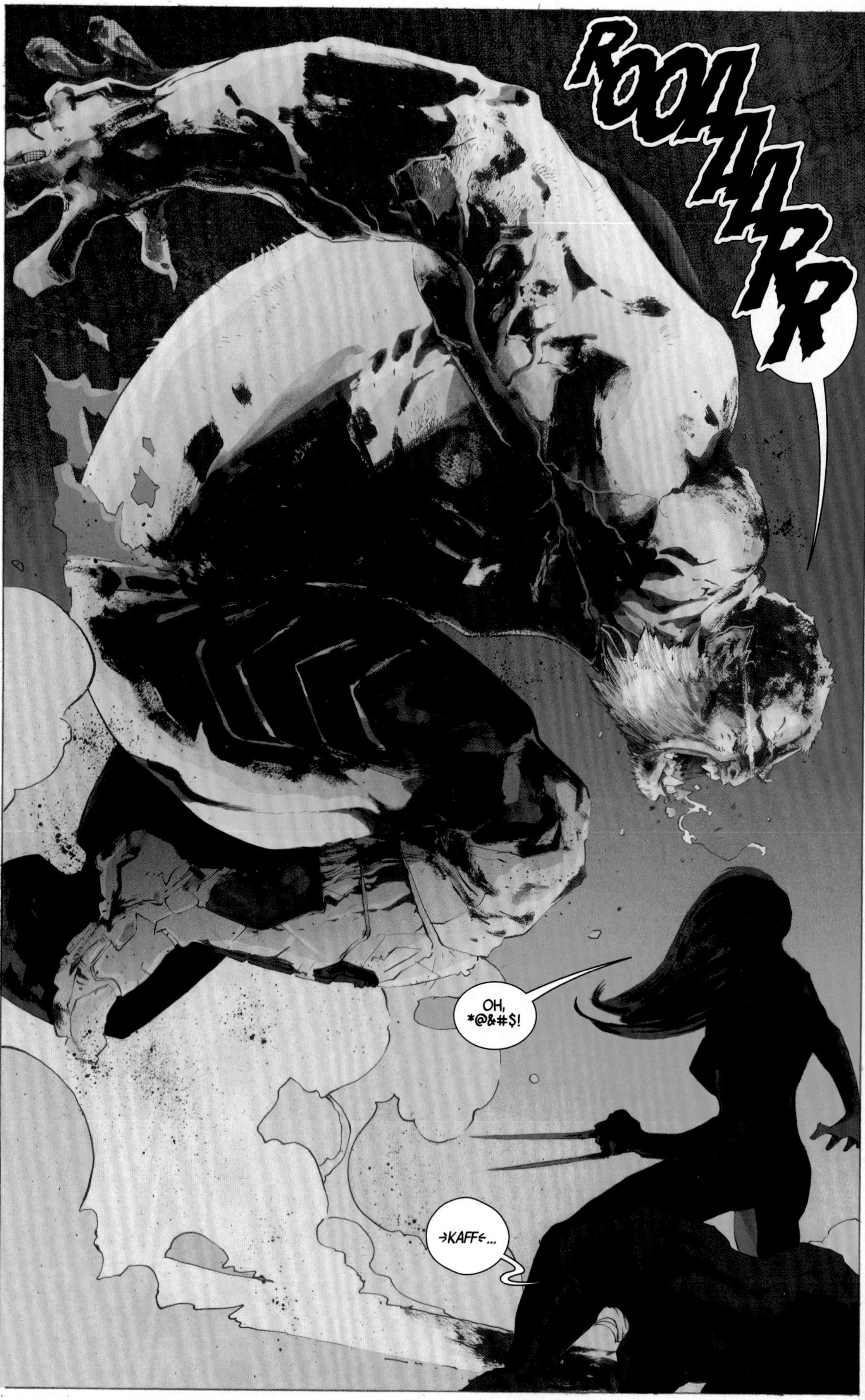
ROOOAAARR
OH, *@&#$!
→KAFF←...

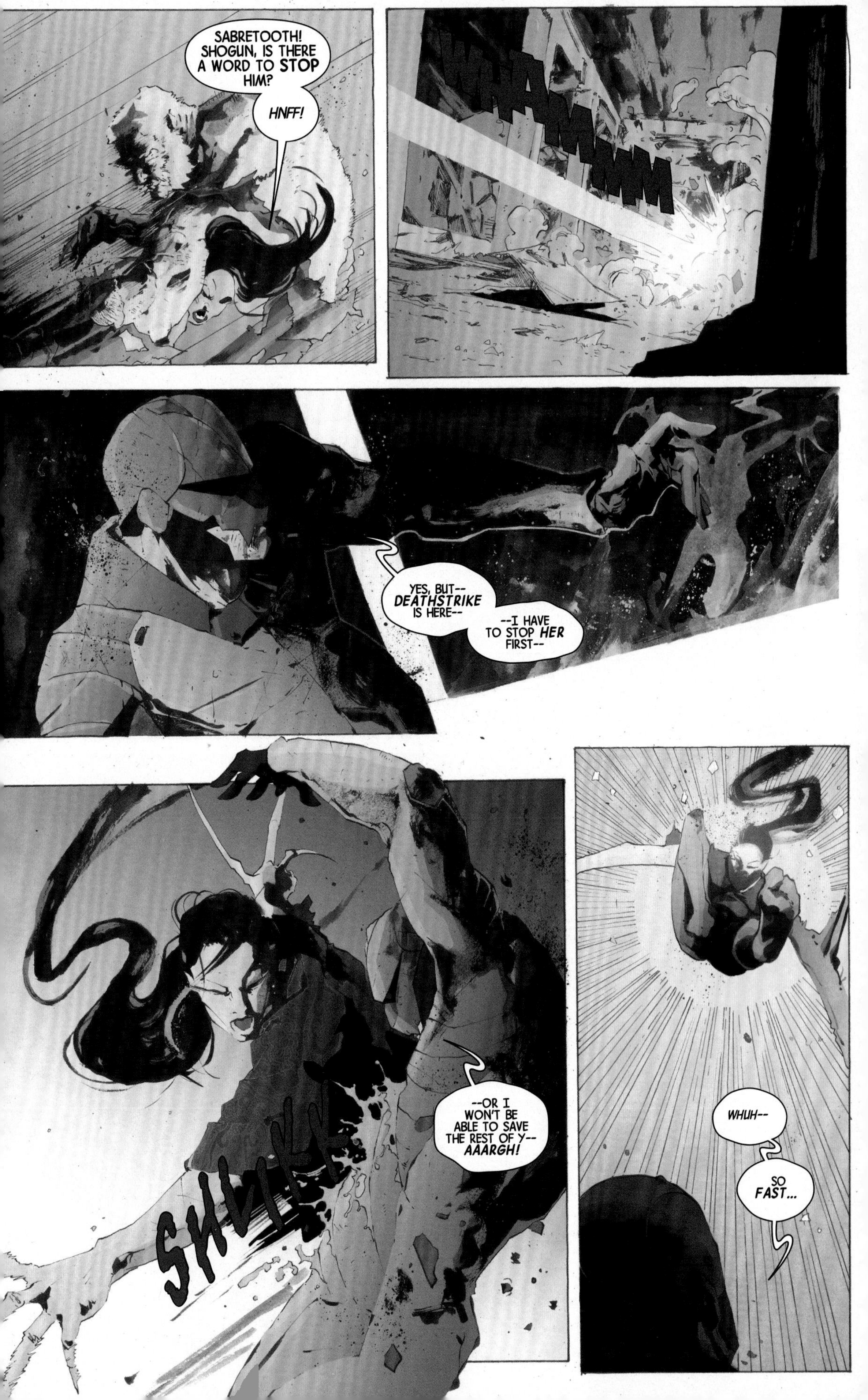
SABRETOOTH! SHOGUN, IS THERE A WORD TO STOP HIM?
HNFF!
WHAMMMM
YES, BUT-- DEATHSTRIKE IS HERE--
--I HAVE TO STOP HER FIRST--
--OR I WON'T BE ABLE TO SAVE THE REST OF Y-- AAARGH!
SHUKK
WHUH--
SO FAST...

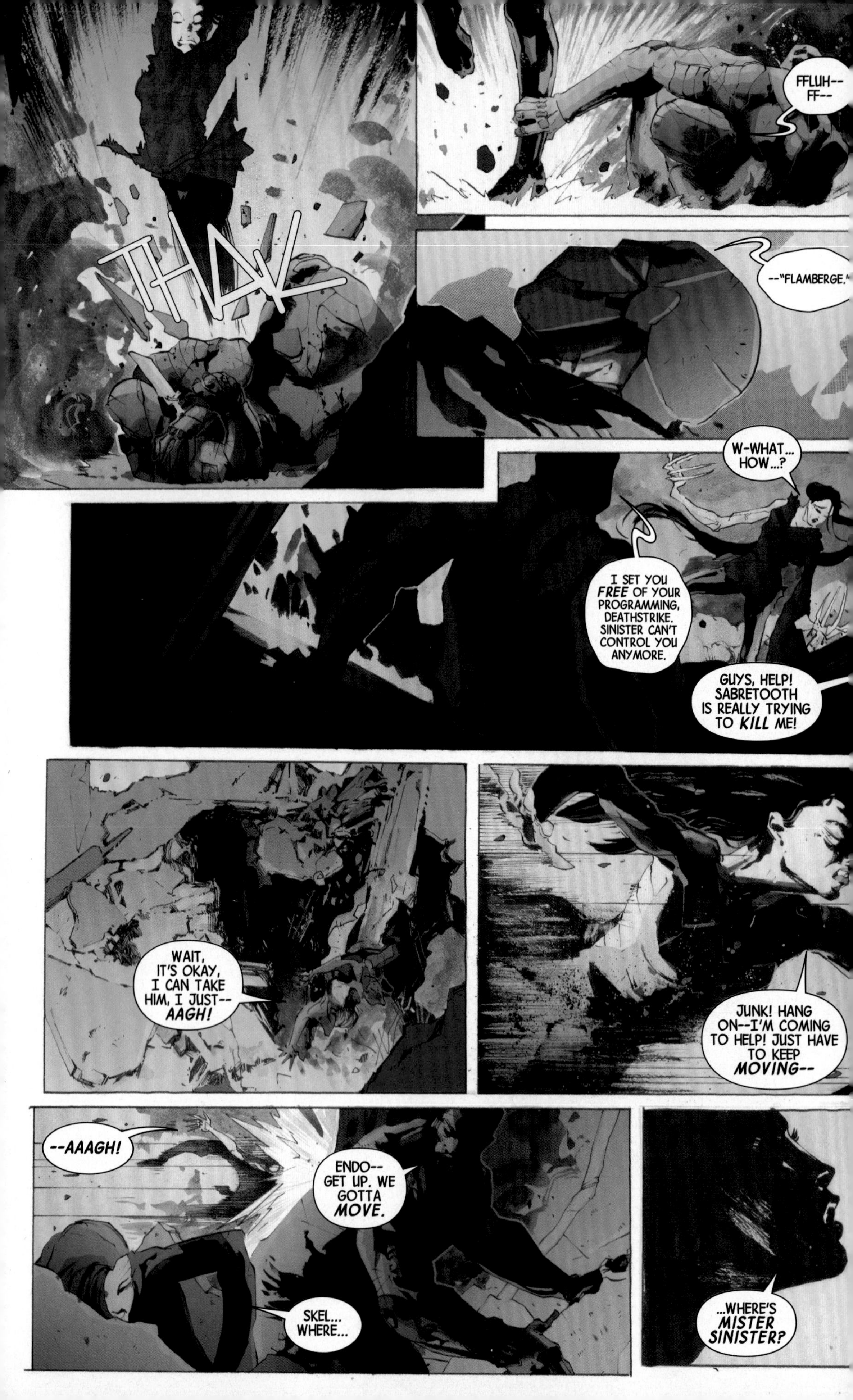
THAK
FFLUH--FF--
--"FLAMBERGE."
W-WHAT... HOW...?
I SET YOU FREE OF YOUR PROGRAMMING, DEATHSTRIKE. SINISTER CAN'T CONTROL YOU ANYMORE.
GUYS, HELP! SABRETOOTH IS REALLY TRYING TO KILL ME!
WAIT, IT'S OKAY, I CAN TAKE HIM, I JUST--AAGH!
JUNK! HANG ON--I'M COMING TO HELP! JUST HAVE TO KEEP MOVING--
--AAAGH!
ENDO--GET UP. WE GOTTA MOVE.
SKEL... WHERE...
...WHERE'S MISTER SINISTER?

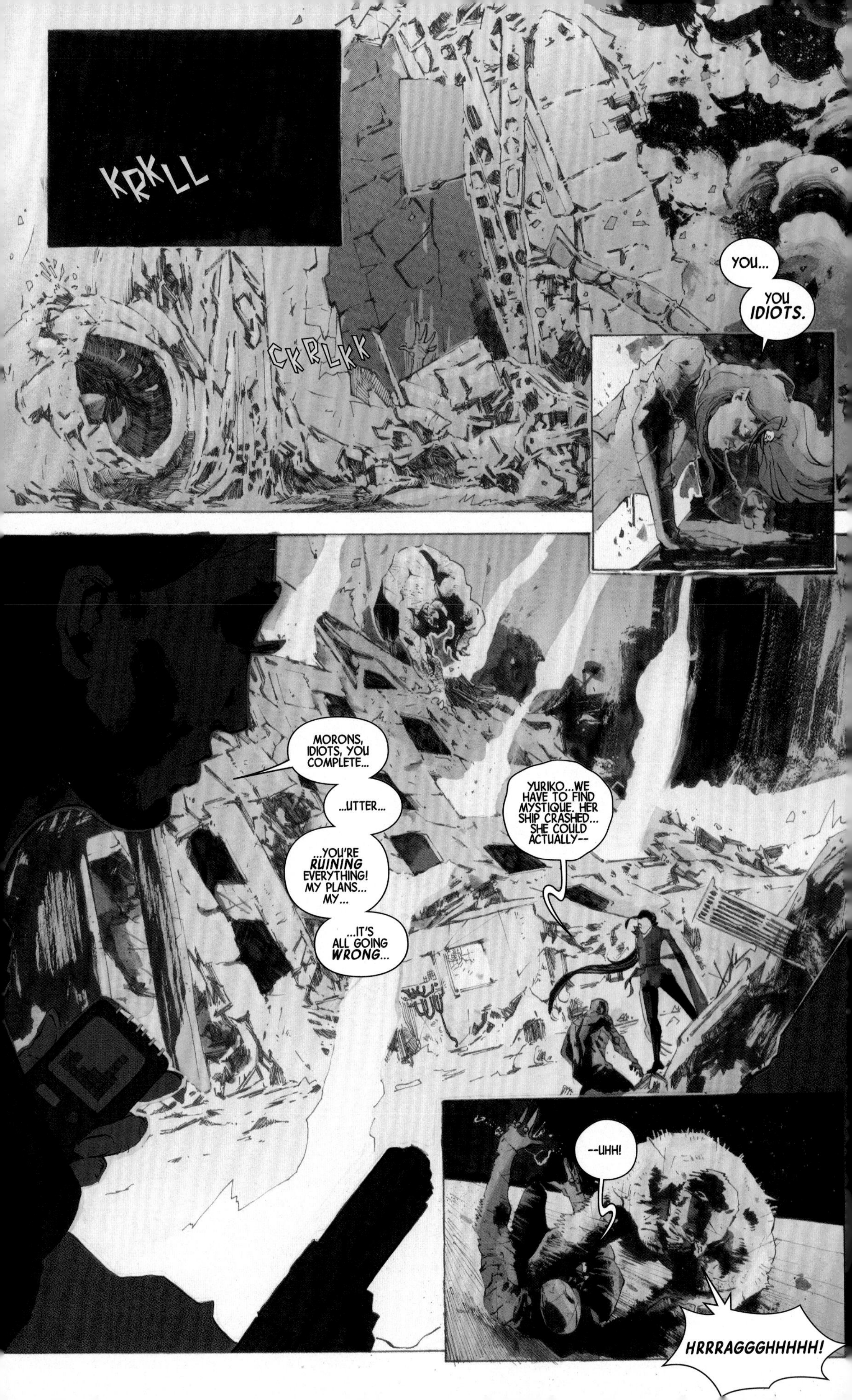
KRKLL
CKRLKK
YOU...
YOU IDIOTS.
MORONS, IDIOTS, YOU COMPLETE...
...UTTER...
...YOU'RE RUINING EVERYTHING! MY PLANS... MY...
...IT'S ALL GOING WRONG...
YURIKO...WE HAVE TO FIND MYSTIQUE. HER SHIP CRASHED... SHE COULD ACTUALLY--
--UHH!
HRRRAGGGHHHHH!

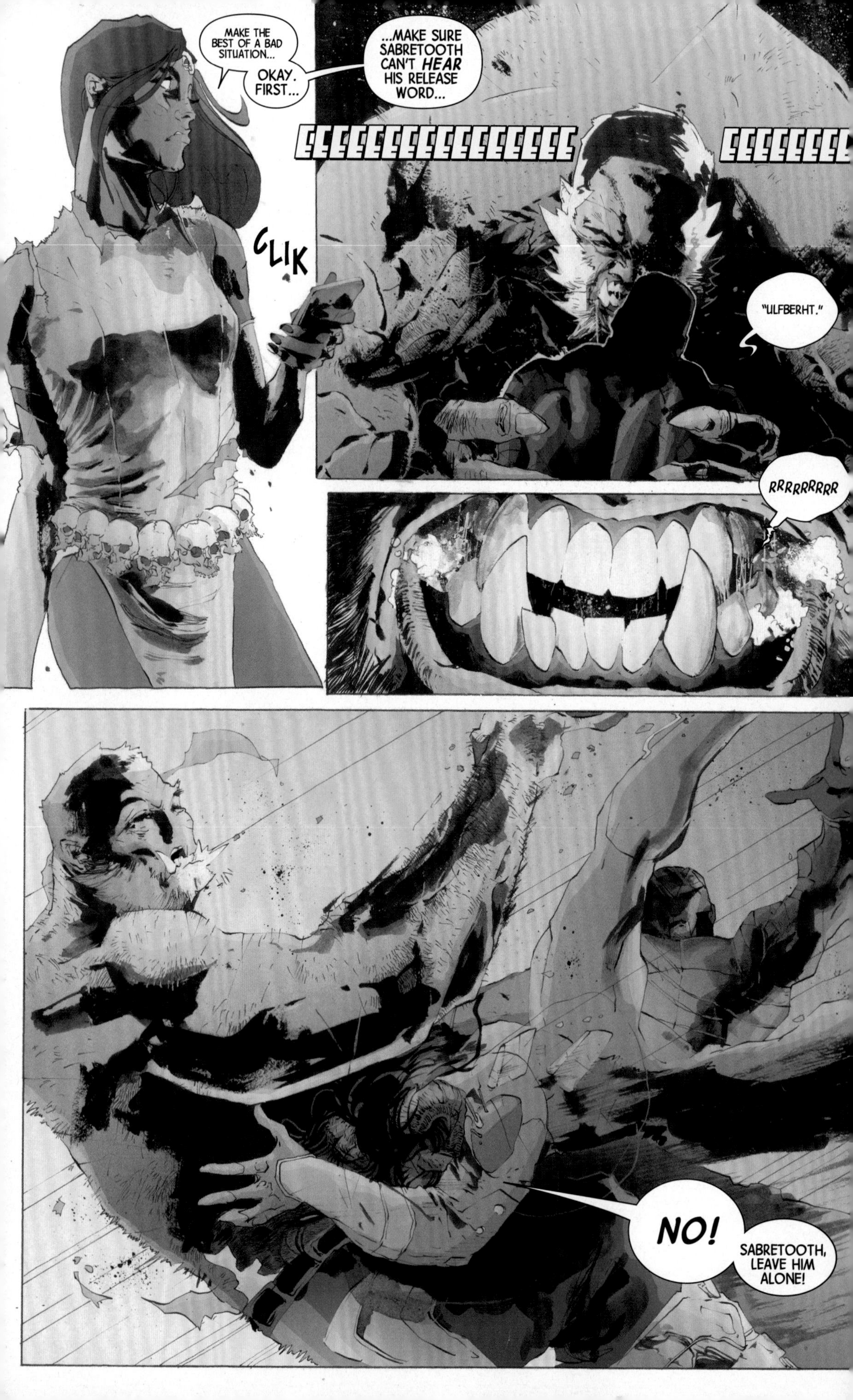
MAKE THE BEST OF A BAD SITUATION...
OKAY. FIRST...
...MAKE SURE SABRETOOTH CAN'T HEAR HIS RELEASE WORD...
EEEEEEEEEEEEEEEE
EEEEEEEE
CLIK
"ULFBERHT."
RRRRRRRRR
NO!
SABRETOOTH, LEAVE HIM ALONE!

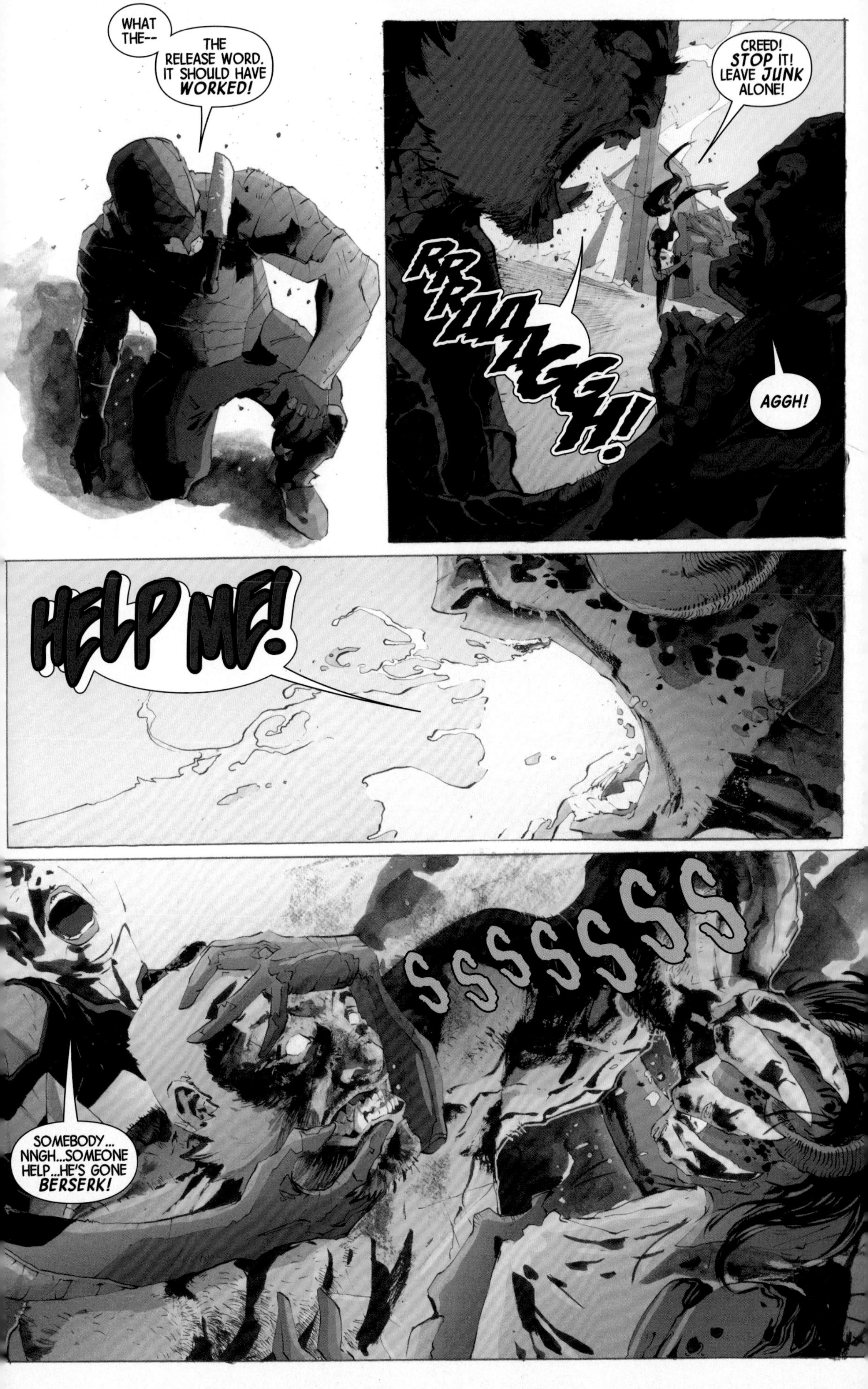
WHAT THE--
THE RELEASE WORD. IT SHOULD HAVE WORKED!
CREED! STOP IT! LEAVE JUNK ALONE!
RRRAAAGGH!
AGGH!
HELP ME!
SSSSSSSS
SOMEBODY... NNGH...SOMEONE HELP...HE'S GONE BERSERK!

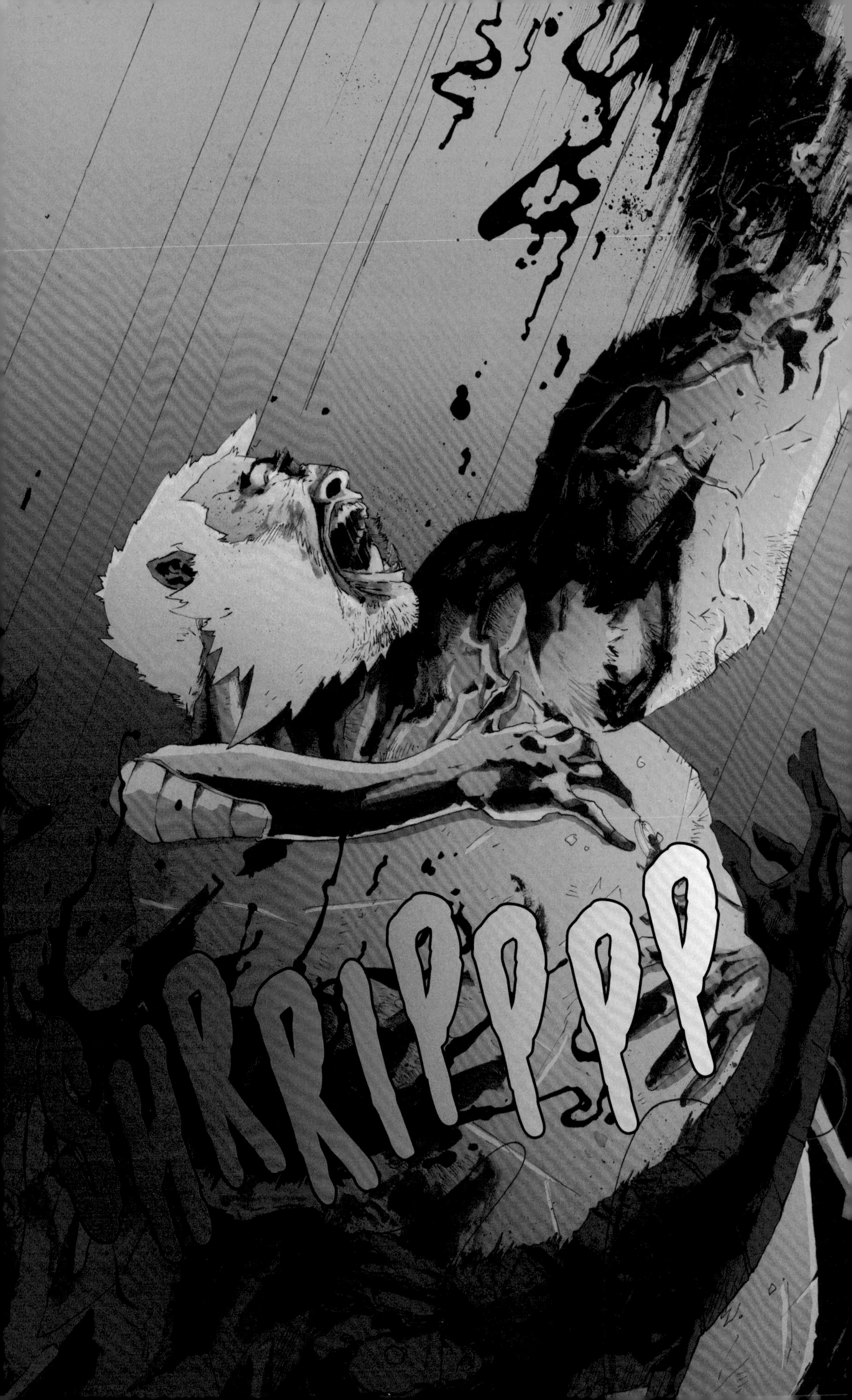
RRIPPPP

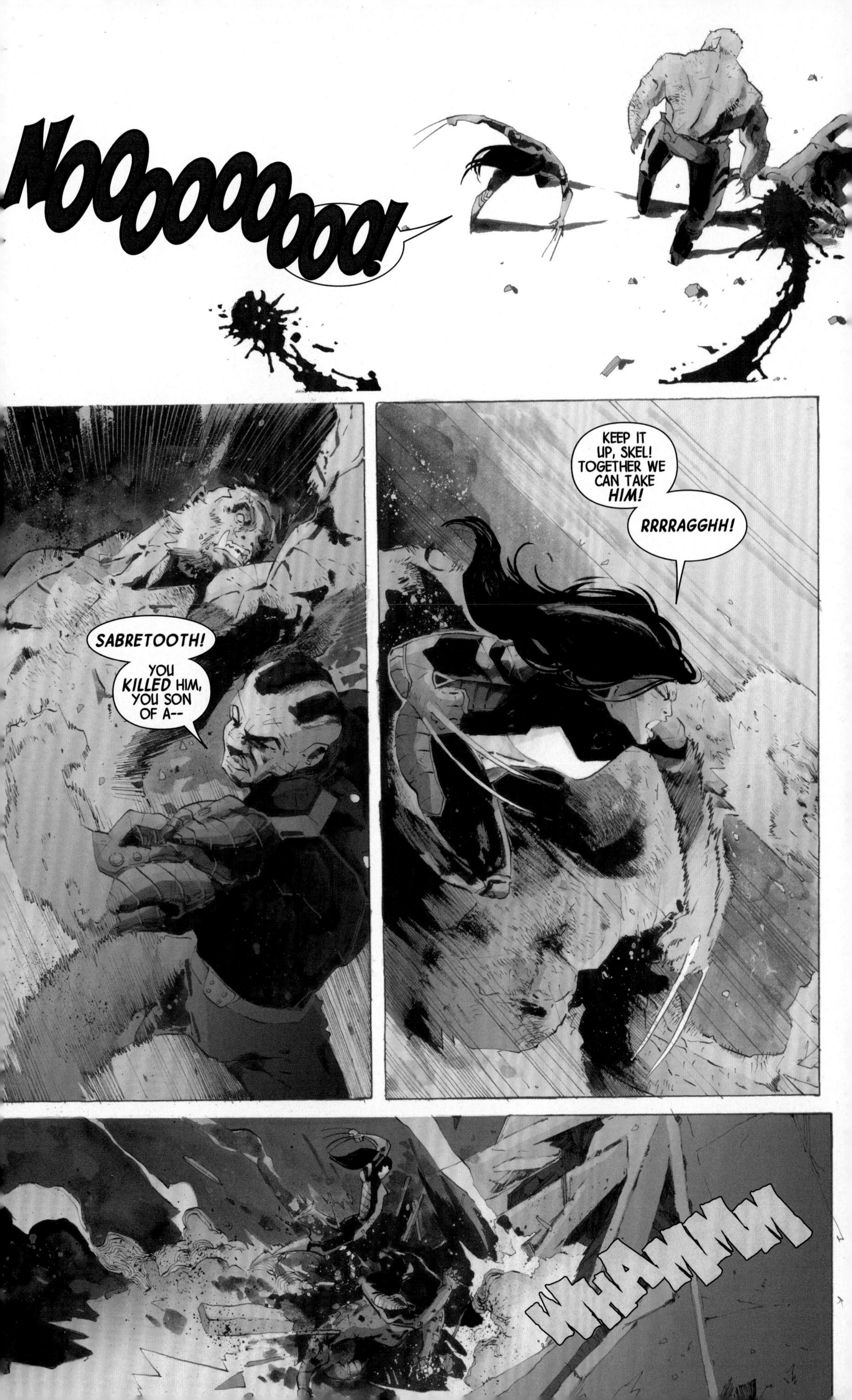
NOOOOOOOOOO!
SABRETOOTH!
YOU KILLED HIM, YOU SON OF A--
KEEP IT UP, SKEL! TOGETHER WE CAN TAKE HIM!
RRRRAGGHH!
WHAMMM

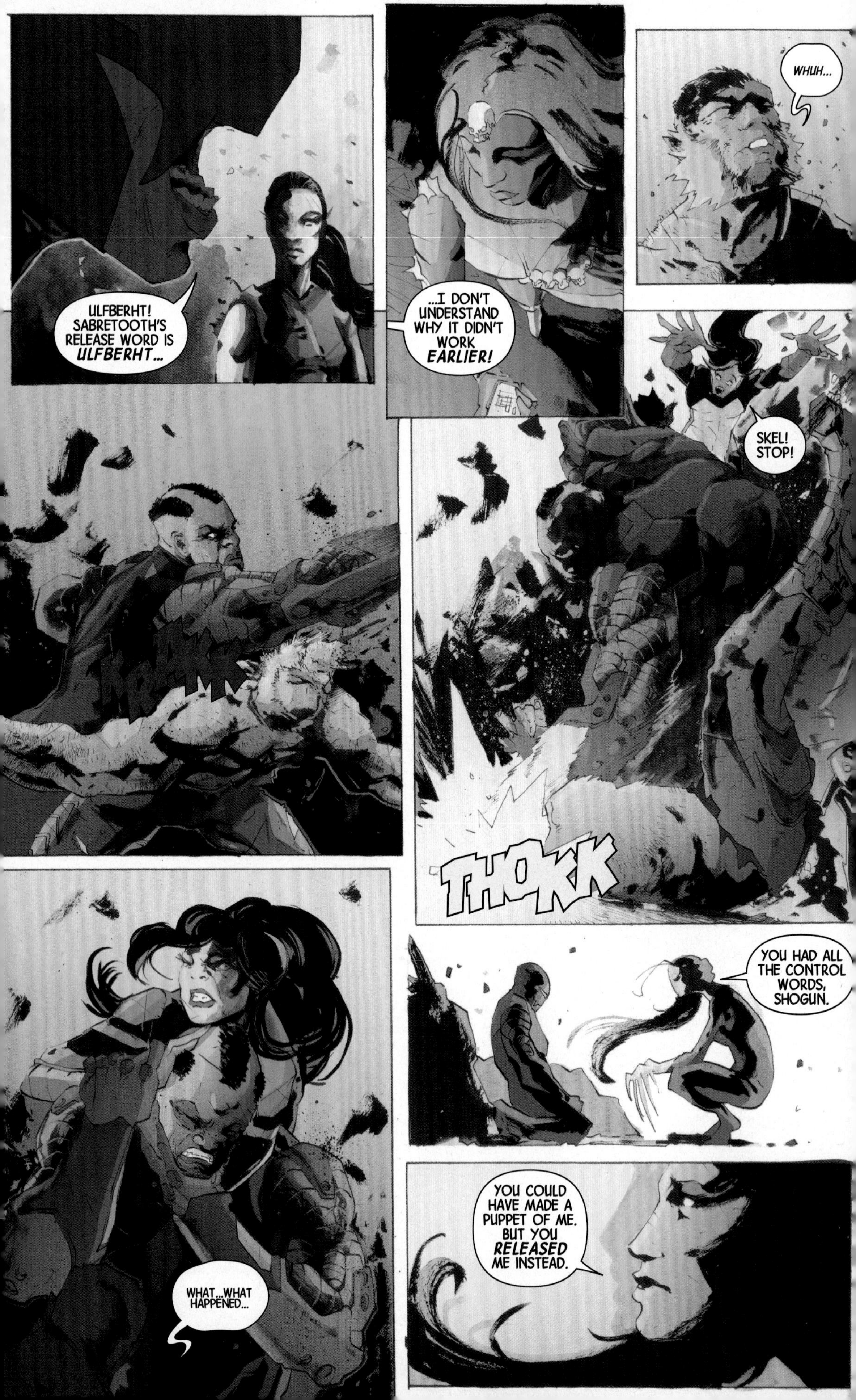
ULFBERHT! SABRETOOTH'S RELEASE WORD IS ULFBERHT...
...I DON'T UNDERSTAND WHY IT DIDN'T WORK EARLIER!
WHUH...
SKEL! STOP!
THOKK
WHAT...WHAT HAPPENED...
YOU HAD ALL THE CONTROL WORDS, SHOGUN.
YOU COULD HAVE MADE A PUPPET OF ME. BUT YOU RELEASED ME INSTEAD.

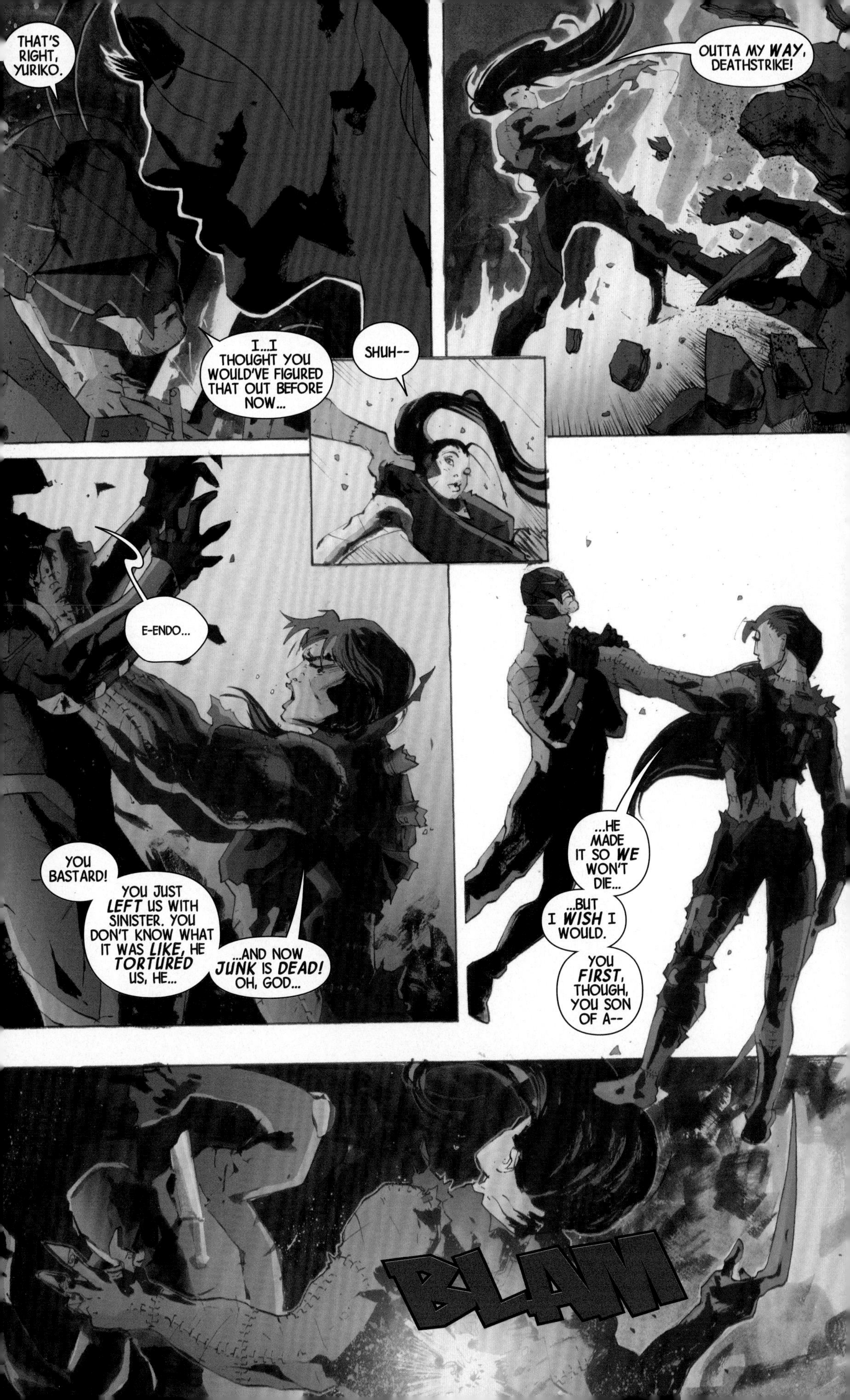
THAT'S RIGHT, YURIKO.
OUTTA MY WAY, DEATHSTRIKE!
I...I THOUGHT YOU WOULD'VE FIGURED THAT OUT BEFORE NOW...
SHUH--
E-ENDO...
YOU BASTARD!
YOU JUST LEFT US WITH SINISTER. YOU DON'T KNOW WHAT IT WAS LIKE, HE TORTURED US, HE...
...AND NOW JUNK IS DEAD! OH, GOD...
...HE MADE IT SO WE WON'T DIE...
...BUT I WISH I WOULD.
YOU FIRST, THOUGH, YOU SON OF A--
BLAM

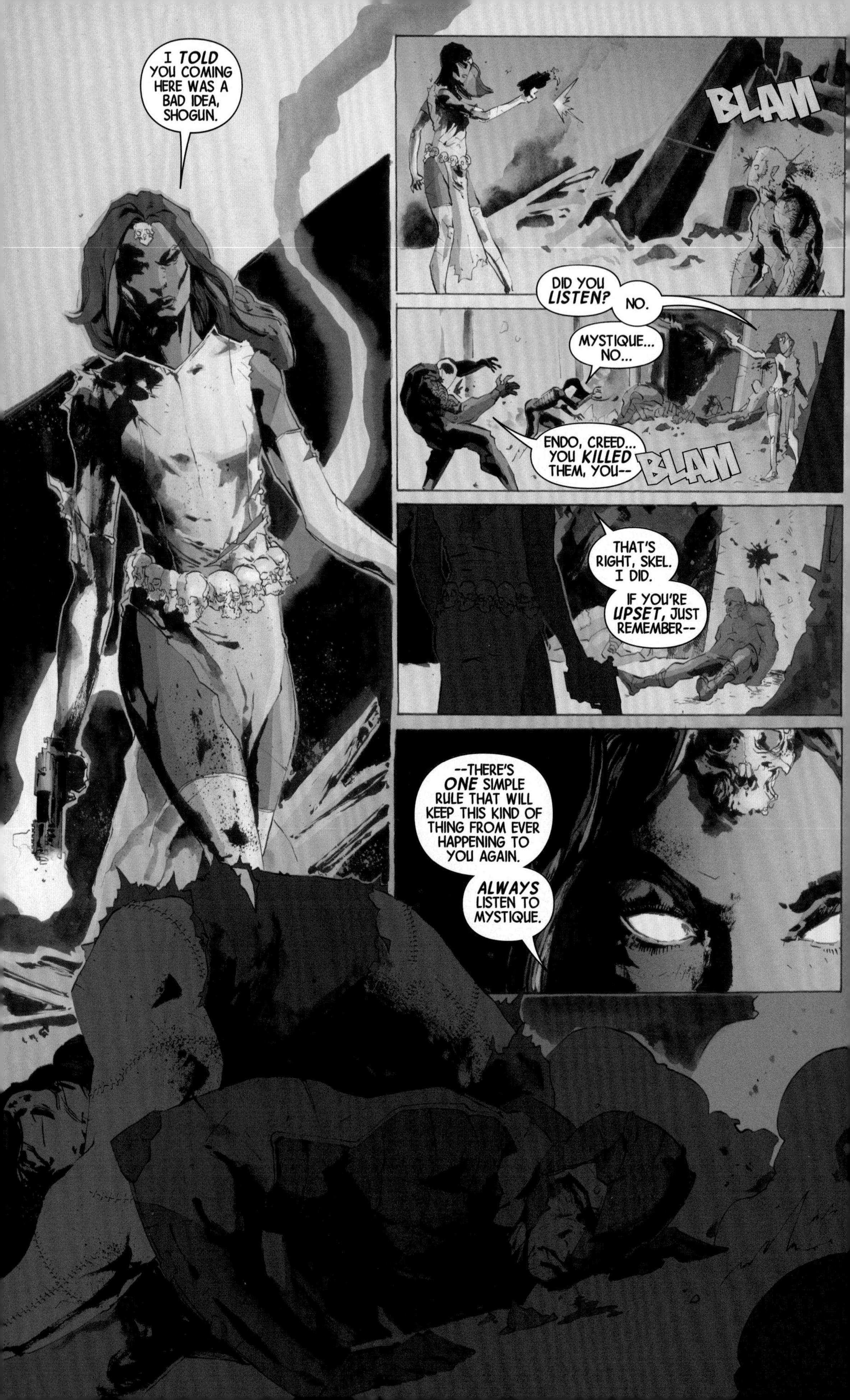
I TOLD YOU COMING HERE WAS A BAD IDEA, SHOGUN.
BLAM
DID YOU LISTEN?
NO.
MYSTIQUE... NO...
ENDO, CREED... YOU KILLED THEM, YOU--
BLAM
THAT'S RIGHT, SKEL. I DID.
IF YOU'RE UPSET, JUST REMEMBER--
--THERE'S ONE SIMPLE RULE THAT WILL KEEP THIS KIND OF THING FROM EVER HAPPENING TO YOU AGAIN.
ALWAYS LISTEN TO MYSTIQUE.

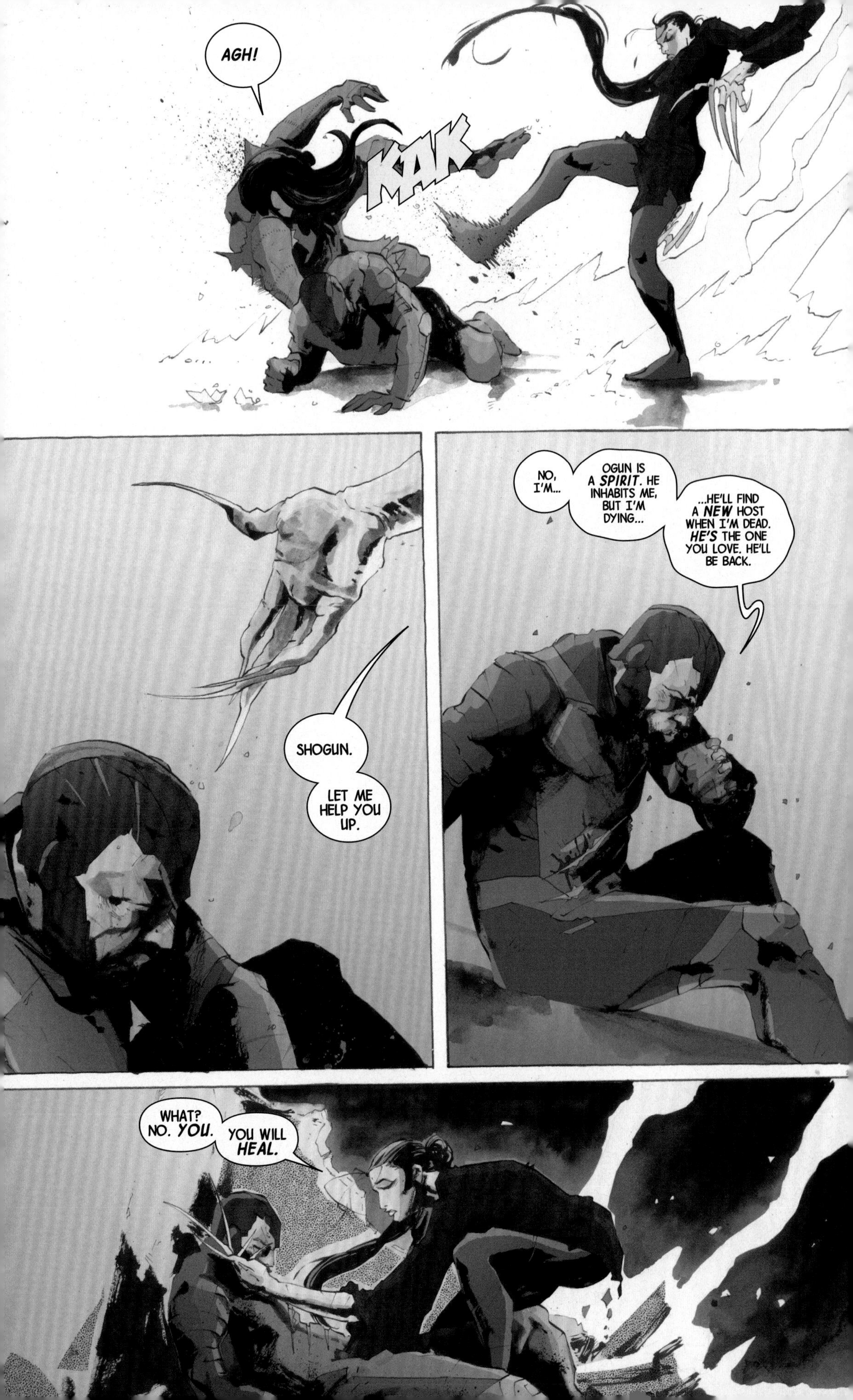
AGH!
KAK
SHOGUN.
LET ME HELP YOU UP.
NO, I'M...
OGUN IS A SPIRIT. HE INHABITS ME, BUT I'M DYING...
...HE'LL FIND A NEW HOST WHEN I'M DEAD. HE'S THE ONE YOU LOVE. HE'LL BE BACK.
WHAT? NO. YOU.
YOU WILL HEAL.

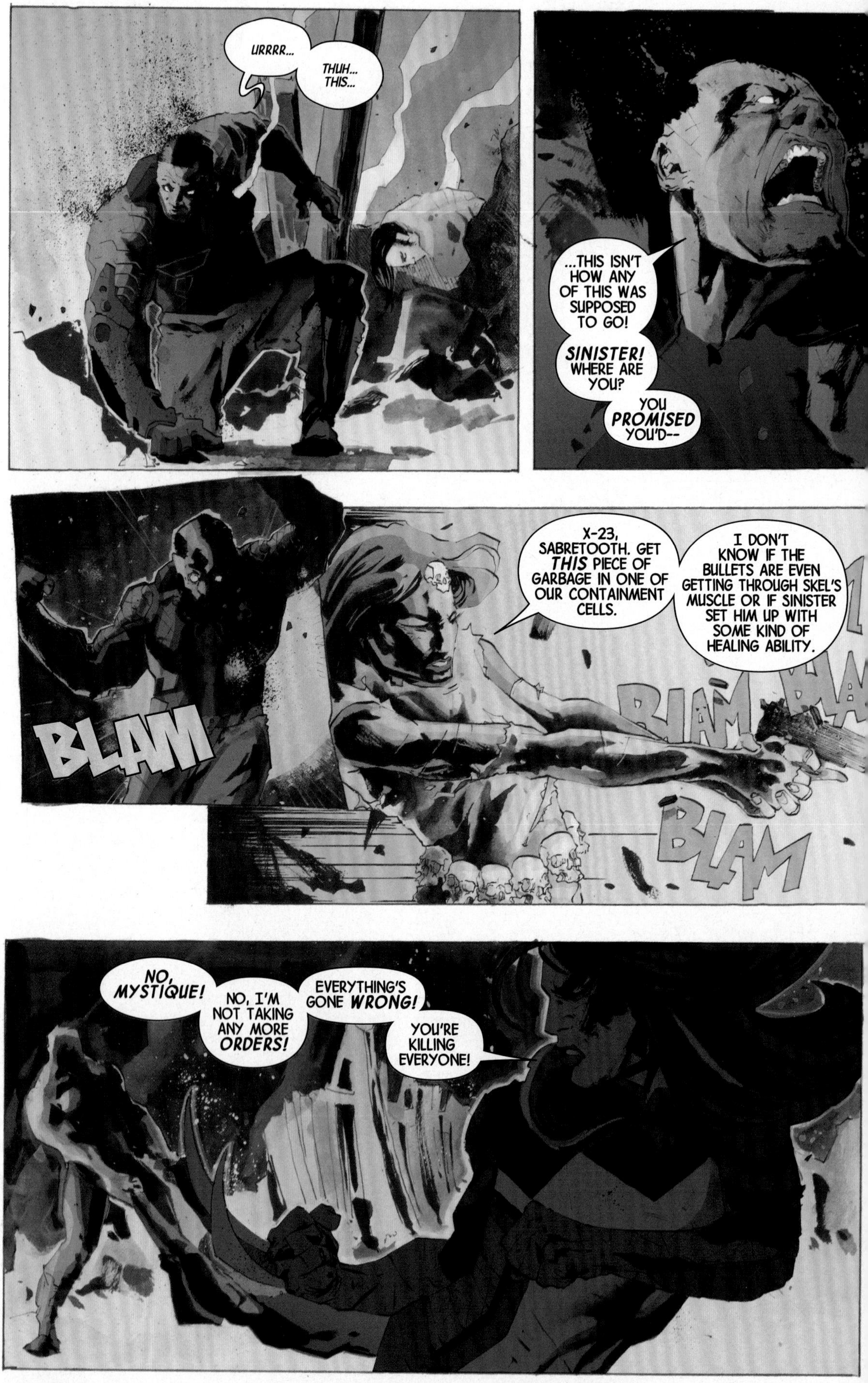
URRRR...
THUH... THIS...
...THIS ISN'T HOW ANY OF THIS WAS SUPPOSED TO GO!
SINISTER! WHERE ARE YOU?
YOU PROMISED YOU'D--
X-23, SABRETOOTH. GET THIS PIECE OF GARBAGE IN ONE OF OUR CONTAINMENT CELLS.
I DON'T KNOW IF THE BULLETS ARE EVEN GETTING THROUGH SKEL'S MUSCLE OR IF SINISTER SET HIM UP WITH SOME KIND OF HEALING ABILITY.
BLAM
BLAM
BLAM
NO, MYSTIQUE!
NO, I'M NOT TAKING ANY MORE ORDERS!
EVERYTHING'S GONE WRONG!
YOU'RE KILLING EVERYONE!

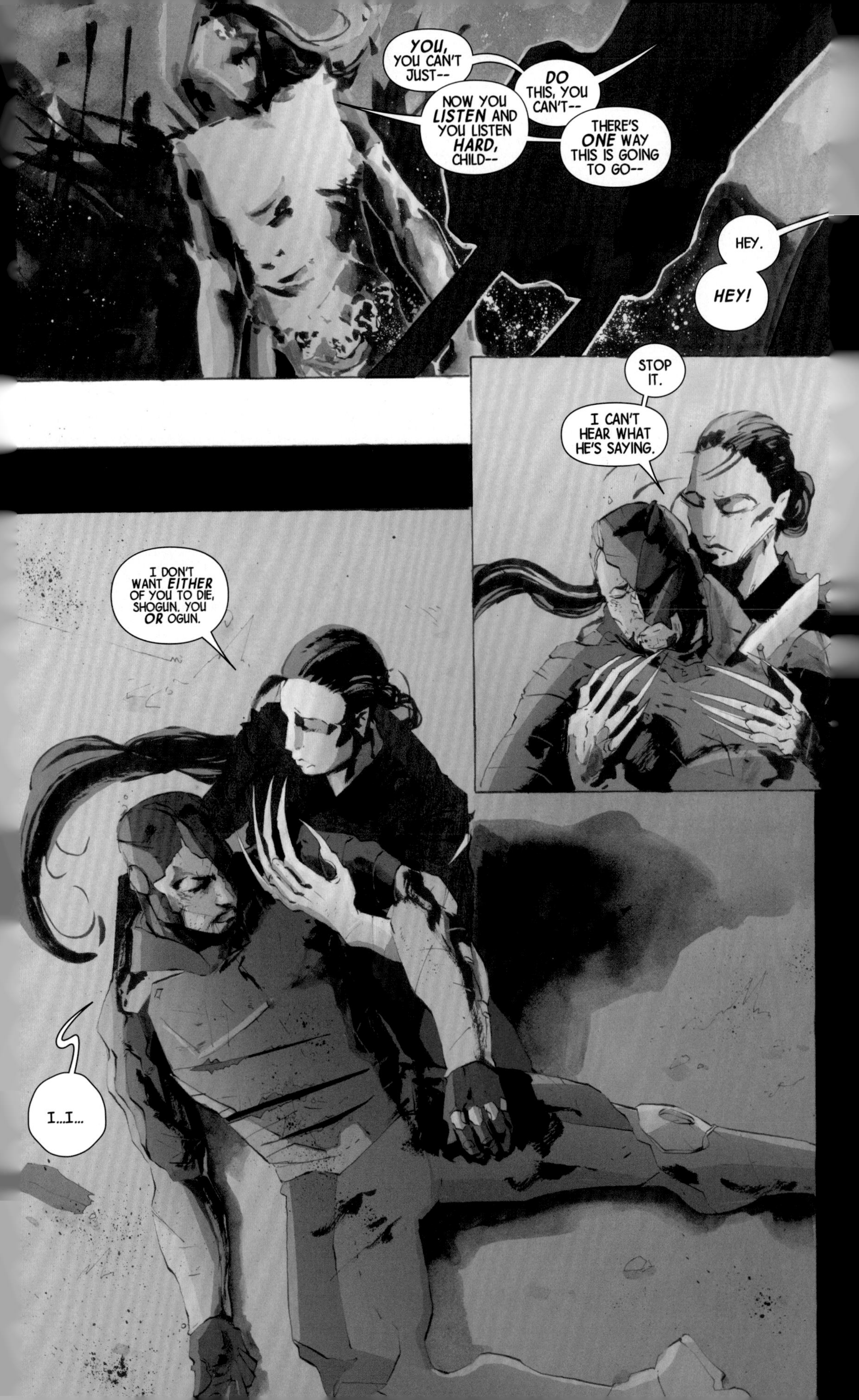
YOU, YOU CAN'T JUST--
DO THIS, YOU CAN'T--
NOW YOU LISTEN AND YOU LISTEN HARD, CHILD--
THERE'S ONE WAY THIS IS GOING TO GO--
HEY.
HEY!
STOP IT.
I CAN'T HEAR WHAT HE'S SAYING.
I DON'T WANT EITHER OF YOU TO DIE, SHOGUN. YOU OR OGUN.
I...I...

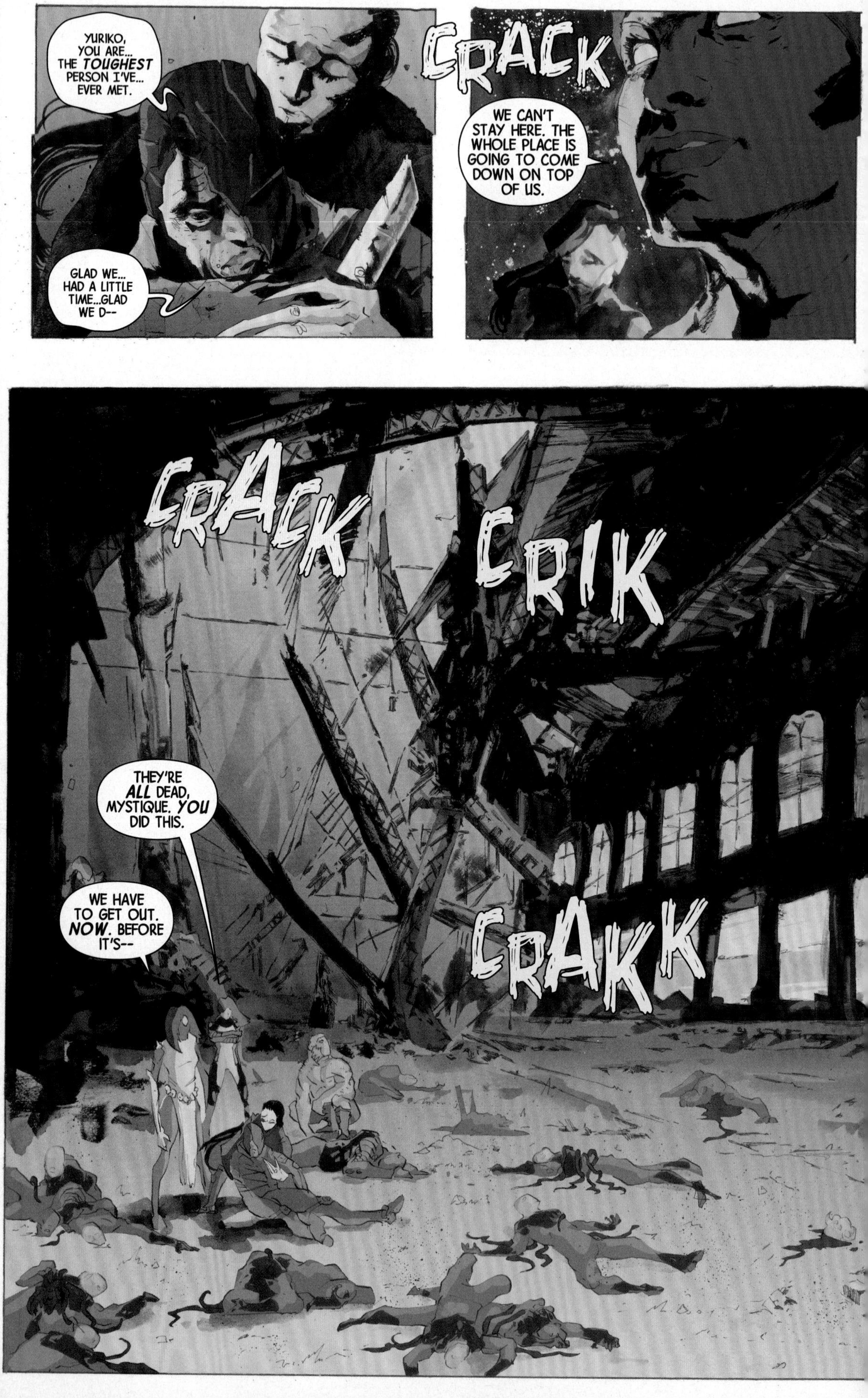
YURIKO, YOU ARE... THE TOUGHEST PERSON I'VE... EVER MET.
GLAD WE... HAD A LITTLE TIME...GLAD WE D--
CRACK
WE CAN'T STAY HERE. THE WHOLE PLACE IS GOING TO COME DOWN ON TOP OF US.
CRACK
CRIK
THEY'RE ALL DEAD, MYSTIQUE. YOU DID THIS.
WE HAVE TO GET OUT. NOW. BEFORE IT'S--
CRAKK

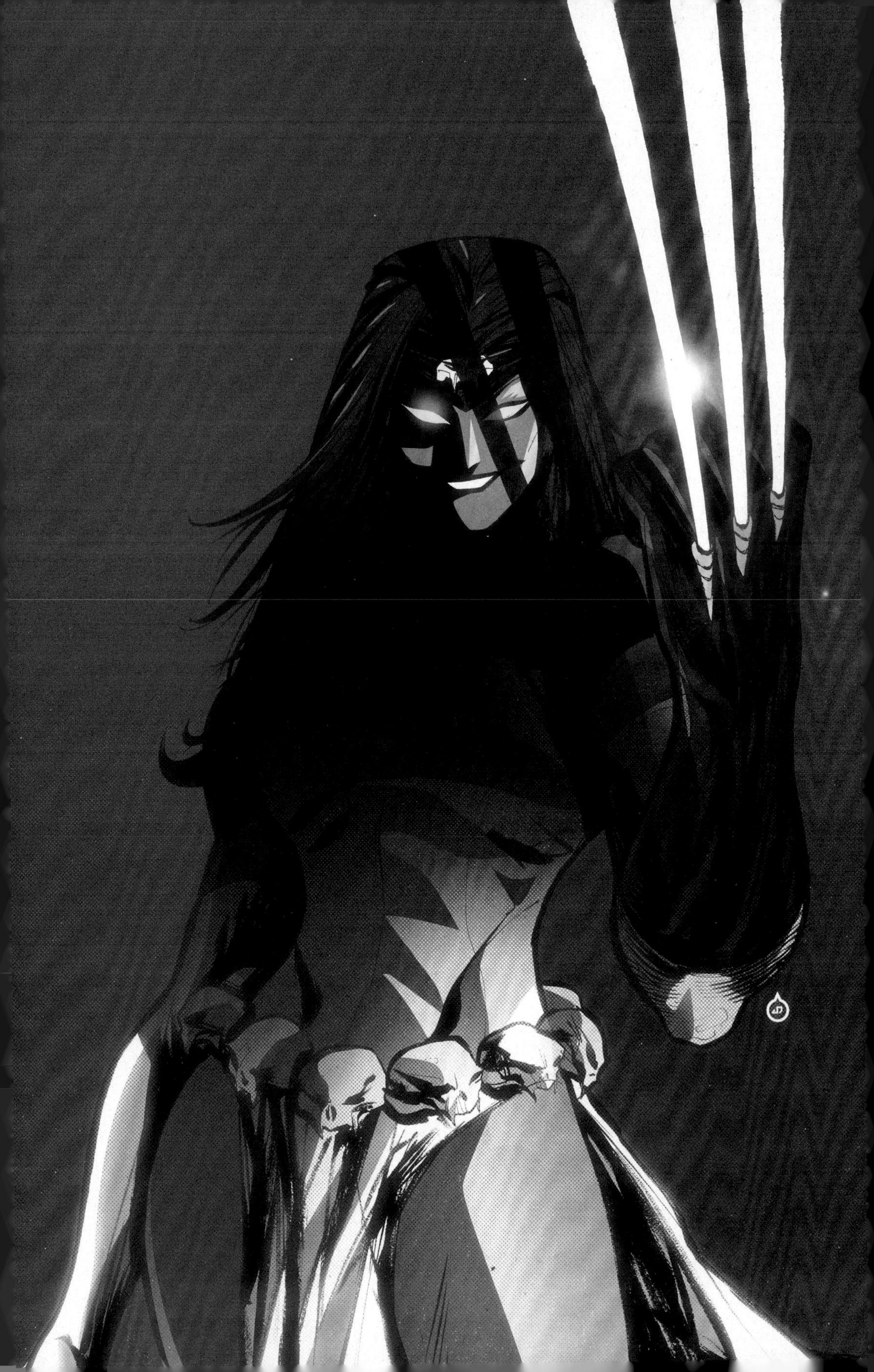

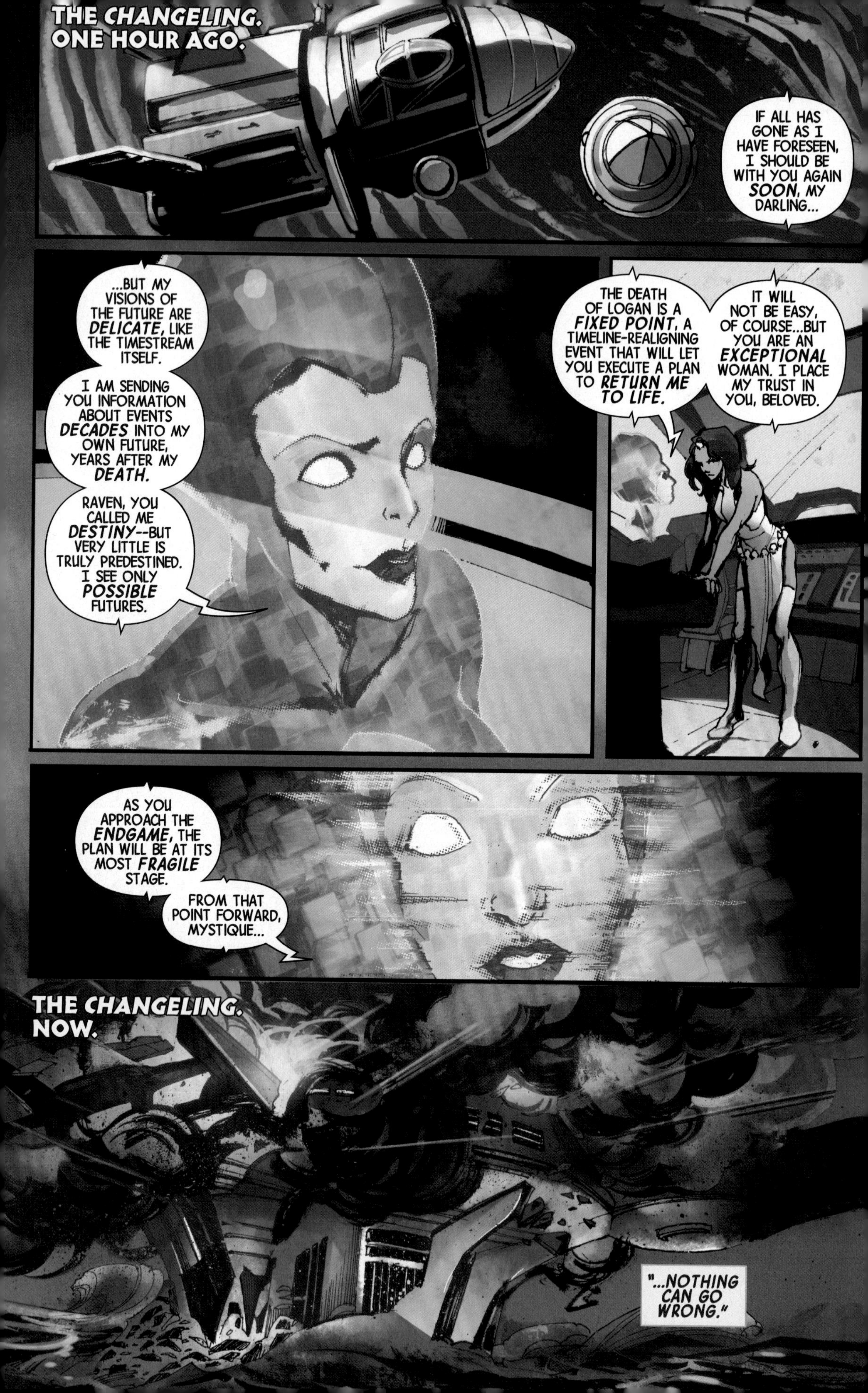
THE CHANGELING. ONE HOUR AGO.
IF ALL HAS GONE AS I HAVE FORESEEN, I SHOULD BE WITH YOU AGAIN SOON, MY DARLING...
...BUT MY VISIONS OF THE FUTURE ARE DELICATE, LIKE THE TIMESTREAM ITSELF.
I AM SENDING YOU INFORMATION ABOUT EVENTS DECADES INTO MY OWN FUTURE, YEARS AFTER MY DEATH.
RAVEN, YOU CALLED ME DESTINY--BUT VERY LITTLE IS TRULY PREDESTINED. I SEE ONLY POSSIBLE FUTURES.
THE DEATH OF LOGAN IS A FIXED POINT, A TIMELINE-REALIGNING EVENT THAT WILL LET YOU EXECUTE A PLAN TO RETURN ME TO LIFE.
IT WILL NOT BE EASY, OF COURSE...BUT YOU ARE AN EXCEPTIONAL WOMAN. I PLACE MY TRUST IN YOU, BELOVED.
AS YOU APPROACH THE ENDGAME, THE PLAN WILL BE AT ITS MOST FRAGILE STAGE.
FROM THAT POINT FORWARD, MYSTIQUE...
THE CHANGELING. NOW.
"...NOTHING CAN GO WRONG."

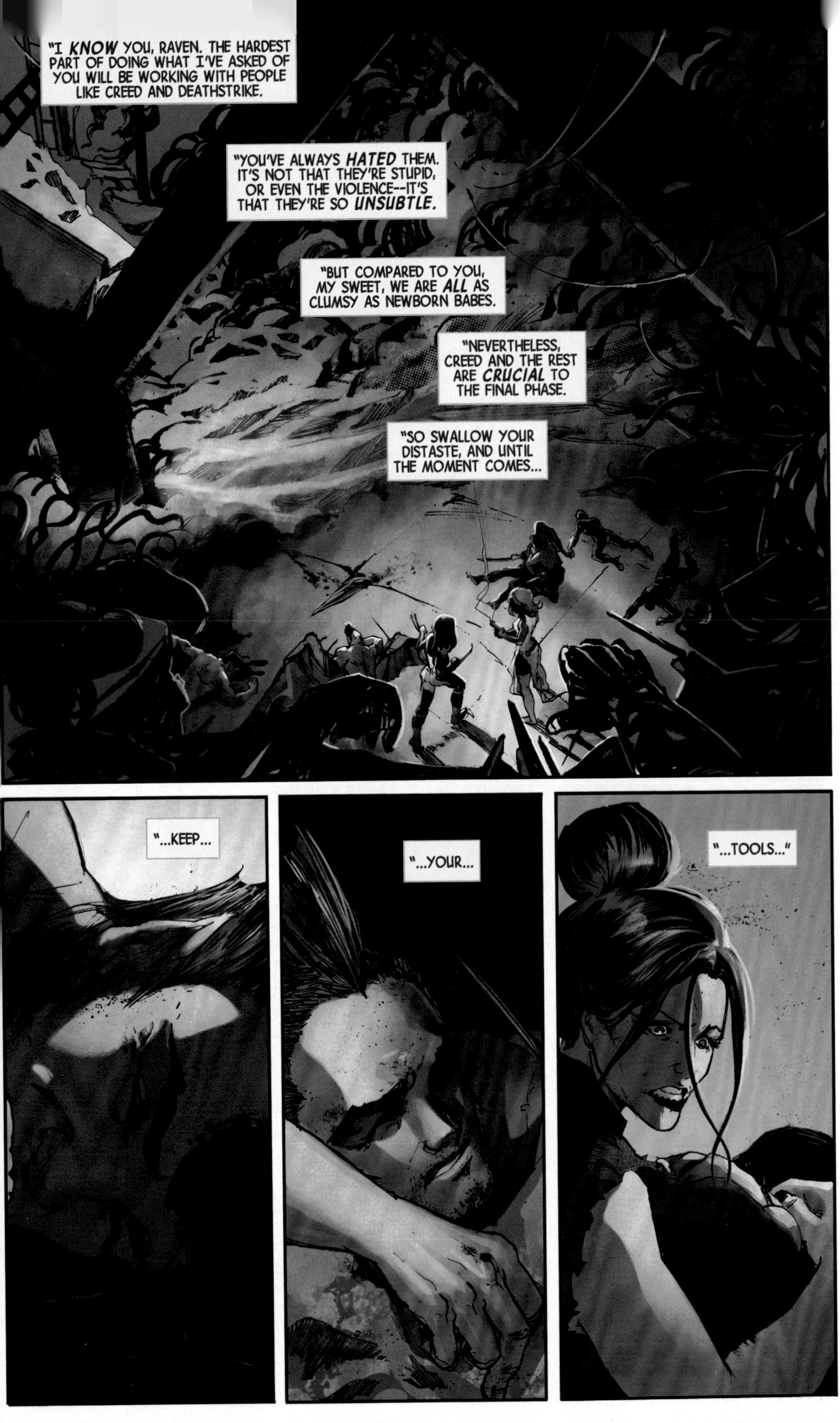
"I KNOW YOU, RAVEN. THE HARDEST PART OF DOING WHAT I'VE ASKED OF YOU WILL BE WORKING WITH PEOPLE LIKE CREED AND DEATHSTRIKE.
"YOU'VE ALWAYS HATED THEM. IT'S NOT THAT THEY'RE STUPID, OR EVEN THE VIOLENCE--IT'S THAT THEY'RE SO UNSUBTLE.
"BUT COMPARED TO YOU, MY SWEET, WE ARE ALL AS CLUMSY AS NEWBORN BABES.
"NEVERTHELESS, CREED AND THE REST ARE CRUCIAL TO THE FINAL PHASE.
"SO SWALLOW YOUR DISTASTE, AND UNTIL THE MOMENT COMES...
"...KEEP...
"...YOUR...
"...TOOLS..."

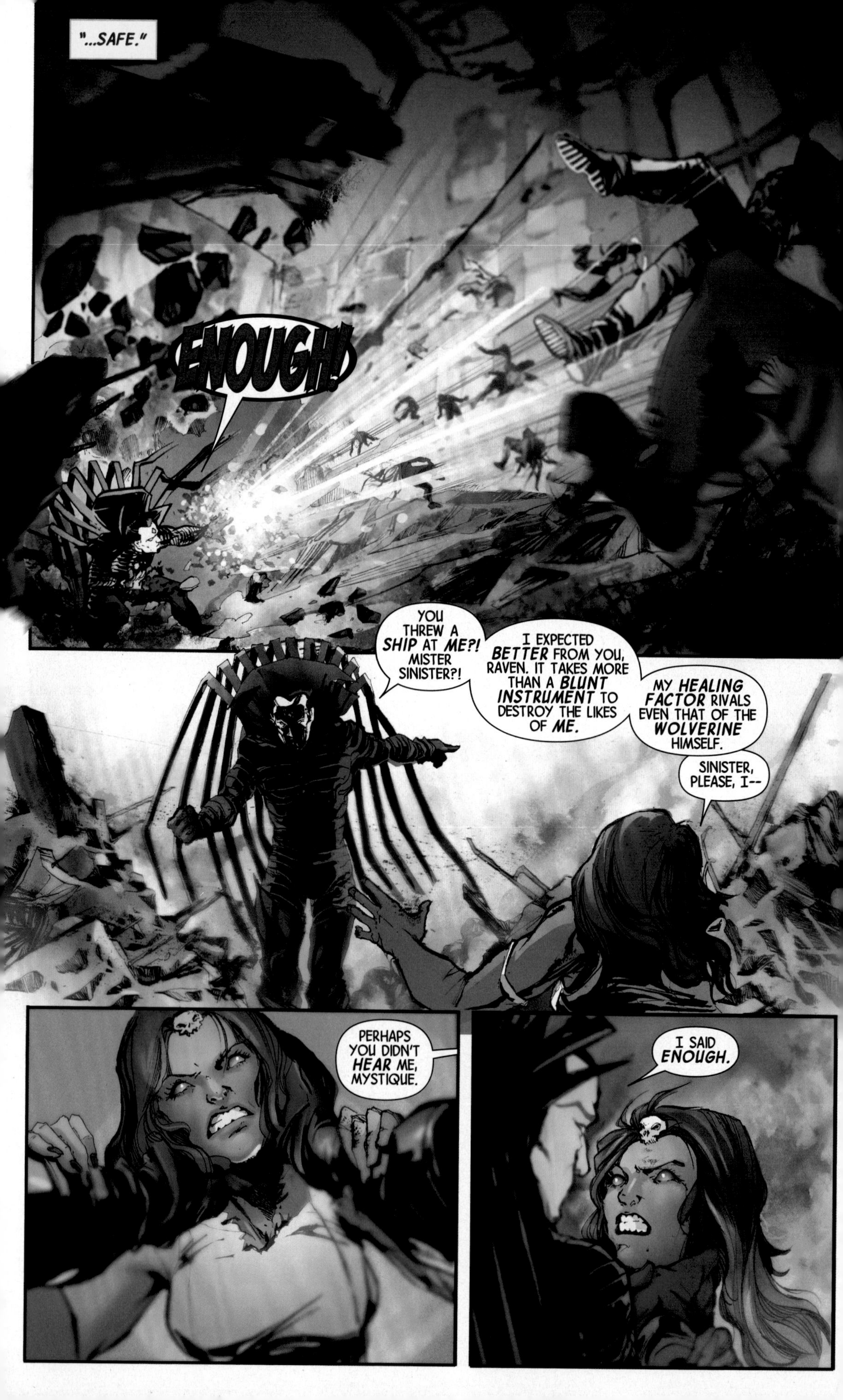

"...SAFE."
ENOUGH!
YOU THREW A SHIP AT ME?! MISTER SINISTER?!
I EXPECTED BETTER FROM YOU, RAVEN. IT TAKES MORE THAN A BLUNT INSTRUMENT TO DESTROY THE LIKES OF ME.
MY HEALING FACTOR RIVALS EVEN THAT OF THE WOLVERINE HIMSELF.
SINISTER, PLEASE, I--
PERHAPS YOU DIDN'T HEAR ME, MYSTIQUE.
I SAID ENOUGH.

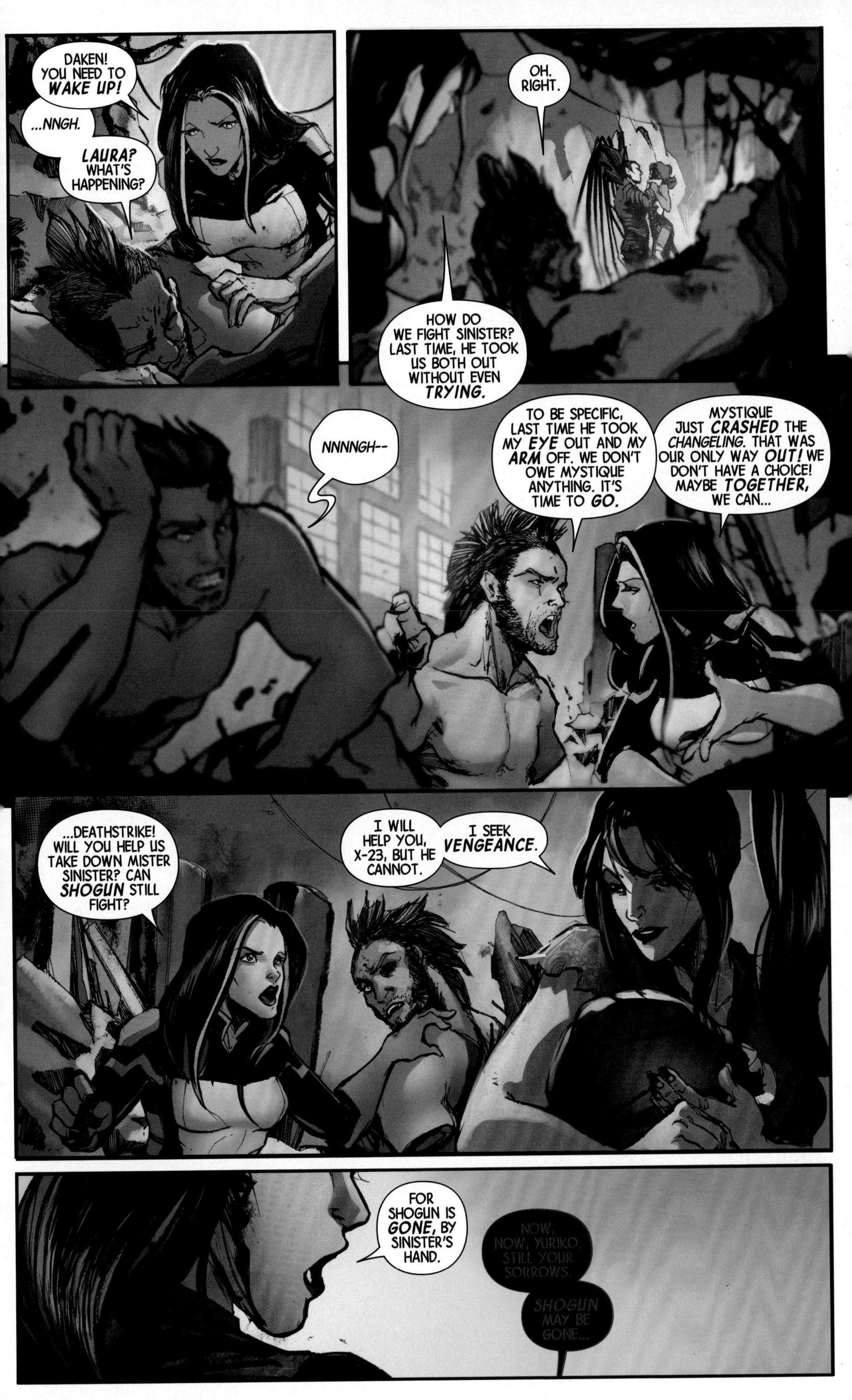
DAKEN! YOU NEED TO WAKE UP!
...NNGH.
LAURA? WHAT'S HAPPENING?
OH. RIGHT.
HOW DO WE FIGHT SINISTER? LAST TIME, HE TOOK US BOTH OUT WITHOUT EVEN TRYING.
NNNNGH--
TO BE SPECIFIC, LAST TIME HE TOOK MY EYE OUT AND MY ARM OFF. WE DON'T OWE MYSTIQUE ANYTHING. IT'S TIME TO GO.
MYSTIQUE JUST CRASHED THE CHANGELING. THAT WAS OUR ONLY WAY OUT! WE DON'T HAVE A CHOICE! MAYBE TOGETHER, WE CAN...
...DEATHSTRIKE! WILL YOU HELP US TAKE DOWN MISTER SINISTER? CAN SHOGUN STILL FIGHT?
I WILL HELP YOU, X-23, BUT HE CANNOT.
I SEEK VENGEANCE.
FOR SHOGUN IS GONE, BY SINISTER'S HAND.
NOW, NOW, YURIKO. STILL YOUR SORROWS.
SHOGUN MAY BE GONE...

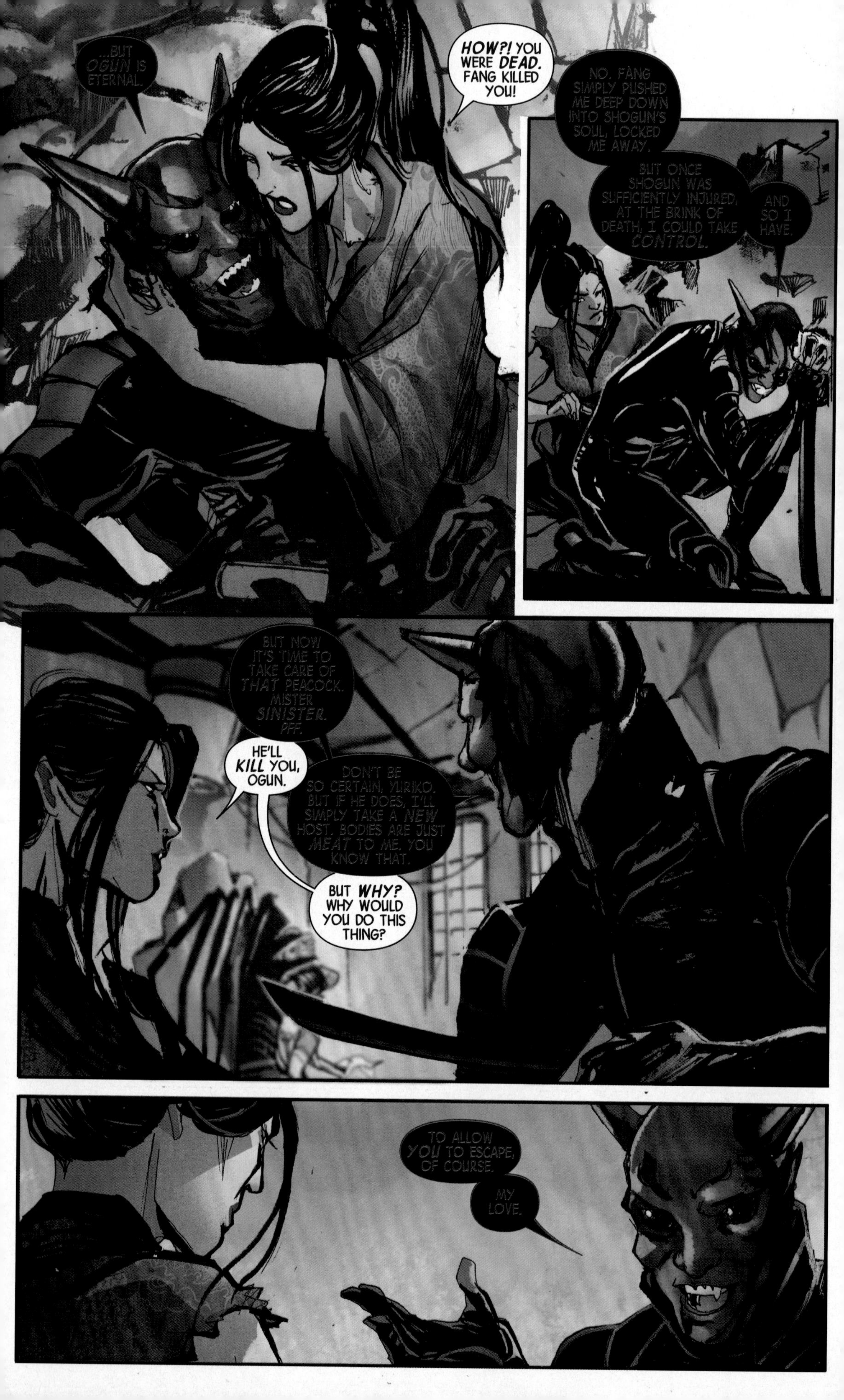
...BUT OGUN IS ETERNAL.
HOW?! YOU WERE DEAD. FANG KILLED YOU!
NO. FANG SIMPLY PUSHED ME DEEP DOWN INTO SHOGUN'S SOUL, LOCKED ME AWAY.
BUT ONCE SHOGUN WAS SUFFICIENTLY INJURED, AT THE BRINK OF DEATH, I COULD TAKE CONTROL.
AND SO I HAVE.
BUT NOW IT'S TIME TO TAKE CARE OF THAT PEACOCK. MISTER SINISTER. PFF.
HE'LL KILL YOU, OGUN.
DON'T BE SO CERTAIN, YURIKO. BUT IF HE DOES, I'LL SIMPLY TAKE A NEW HOST. BODIES ARE JUST MEAT TO ME. YOU KNOW THAT.
BUT WHY? WHY WOULD YOU DO THIS THING?
TO ALLOW YOU TO ESCAPE, OF COURSE.
MY LOVE.

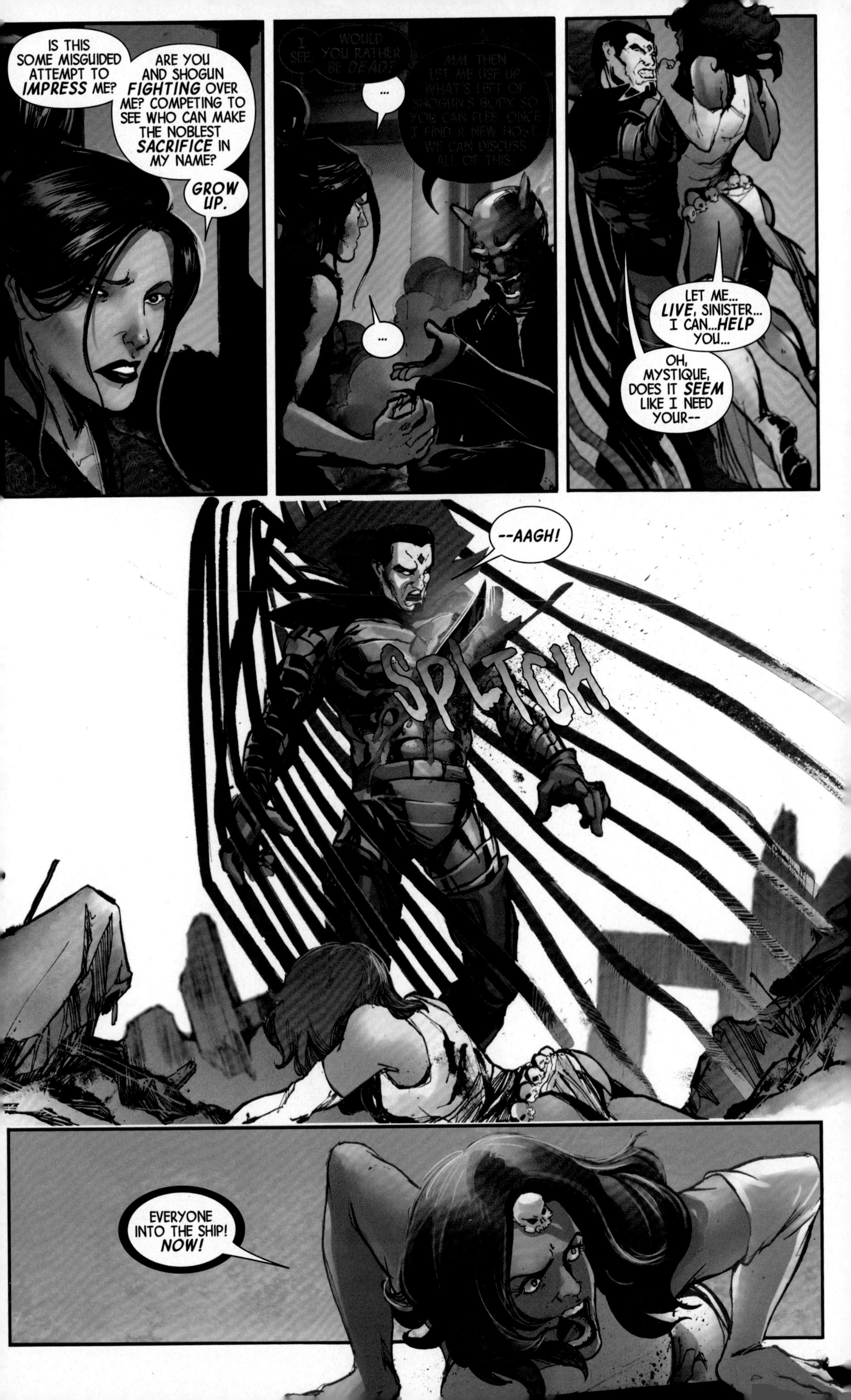
IS THIS SOME MISGUIDED ATTEMPT TO IMPRESS ME?
ARE YOU AND SHOGUN FIGHTING OVER ME? COMPETING TO SEE WHO CAN MAKE THE NOBLEST SACRIFICE IN MY NAME?
GROW UP.
I SEE.
WOULD YOU RATHER BE DEAD?
...
MM. THEN LET ME USE UP WHAT'S LEFT OF SHOGUN'S BODY SO YOU CAN FLEE. ONCE I FIND A NEW HOST, WE CAN DISCUSS ALL OF THIS.
...
LET ME... LIVE, SINISTER... I CAN...HELP YOU...
OH, MYSTIQUE, DOES IT SEEM LIKE I NEED YOUR--
--AAGH!
SPLTCH
EVERYONE INTO THE SHIP! NOW!

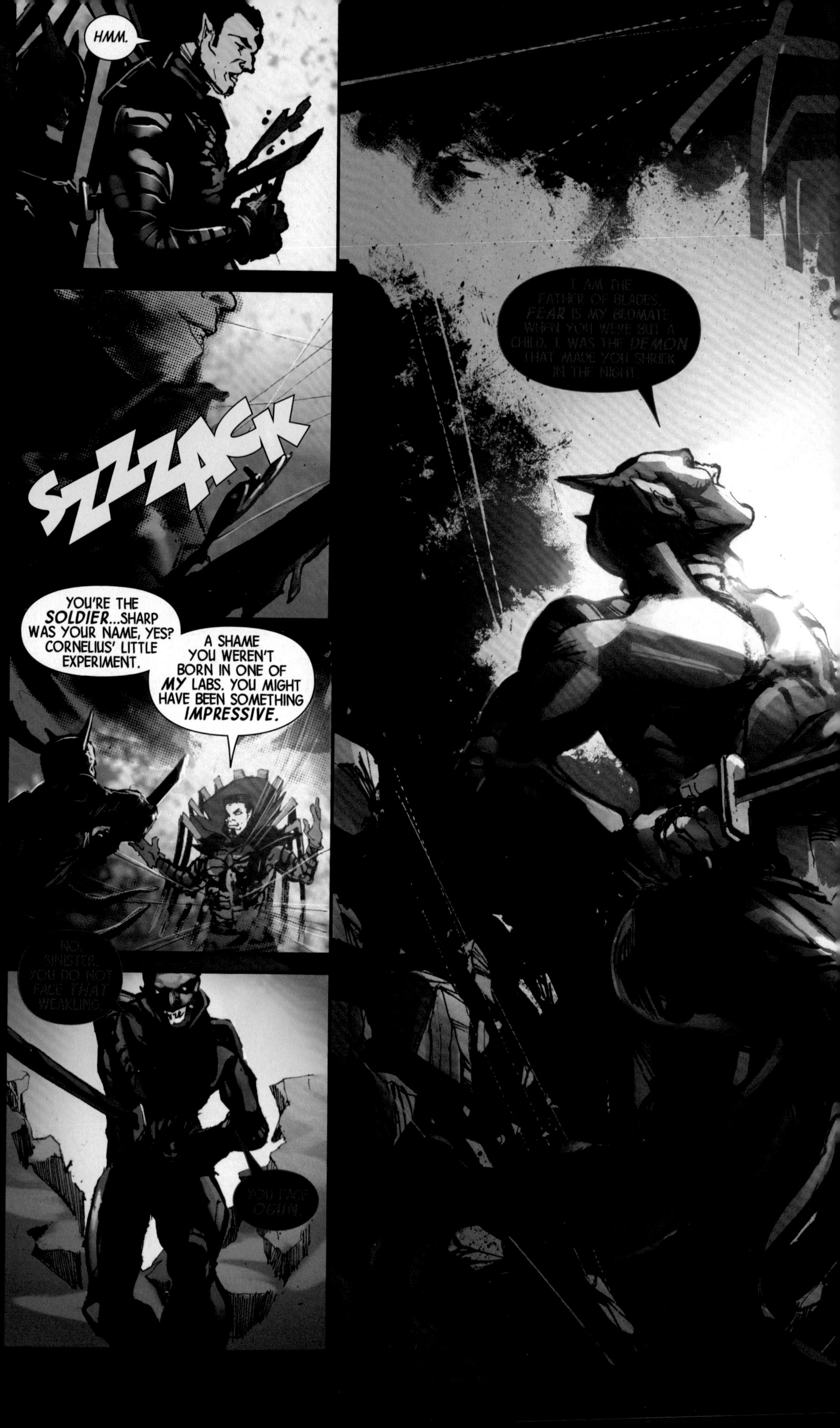
HMM.
SZZZACK
YOU'RE THE SOLDIER...SHARP WAS YOUR NAME, YES? CORNELIUS' LITTLE EXPERIMENT.
A SHAME YOU WEREN'T BORN IN ONE OF MY LABS. YOU MIGHT HAVE BEEN SOMETHING IMPRESSIVE.
NO, SINISTER. YOU DO NOT FACE THAT WEAKLING.
YOU FACE ODIN.
I AM THE FATHER OF BLADES. FEAR IS MY BEDMATE. WHEN YOU WERE BUT A CHILD, I WAS THE DEMON THAT MADE YOU SHRIEK IN THE NIGHT.

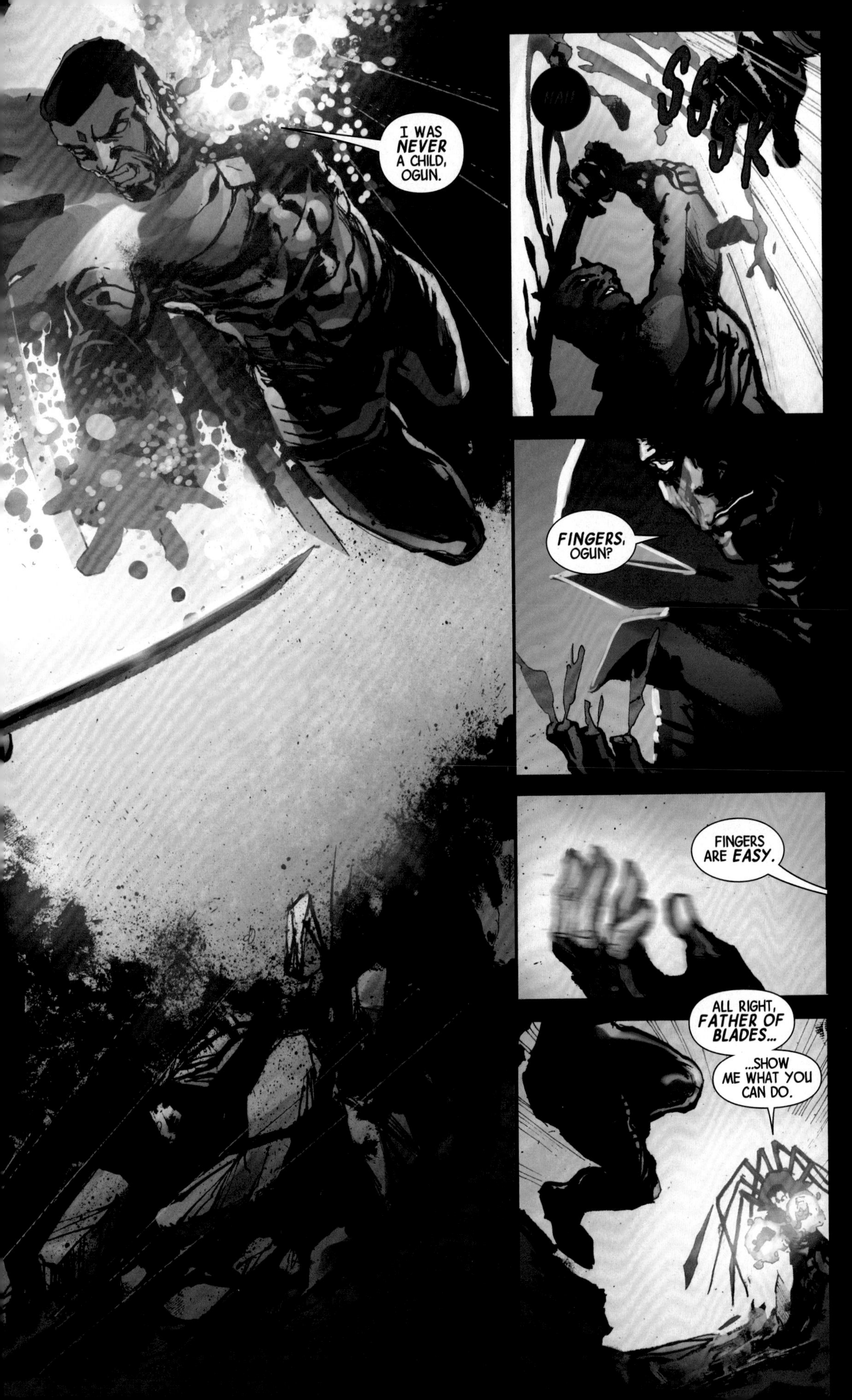
I WAS *NEVER* A CHILD, OGUN.
SSSK
FINGERS, OGUN?
FINGERS ARE *EASY.*
ALL RIGHT, *FATHER OF BLADES...*
...SHOW ME WHAT YOU CAN DO.

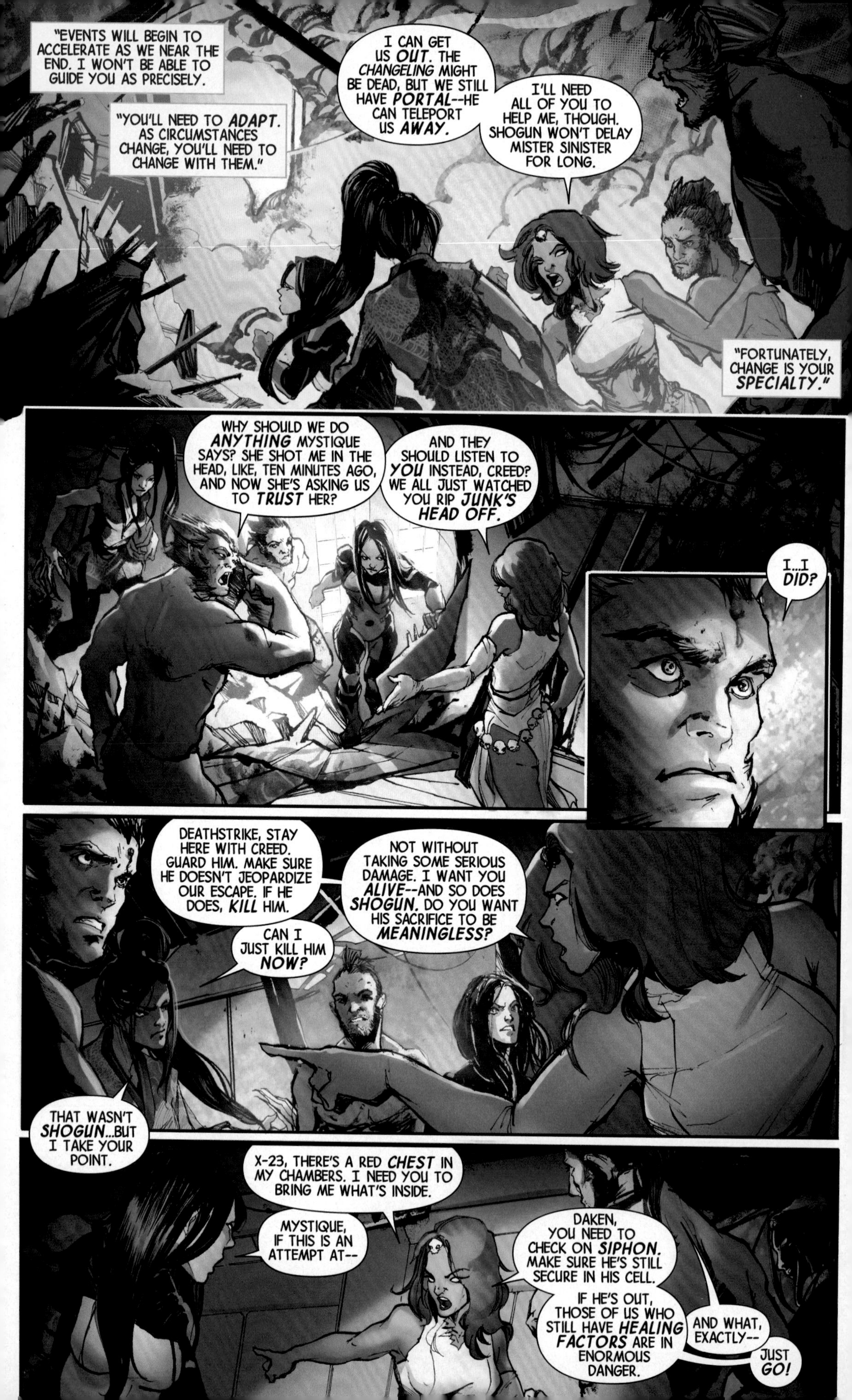
"EVENTS WILL BEGIN TO ACCELERATE AS WE NEAR THE END. I WON'T BE ABLE TO GUIDE YOU AS PRECISELY.
"YOU'LL NEED TO ADAPT. AS CIRCUMSTANCES CHANGE, YOU'LL NEED TO CHANGE WITH THEM."
I CAN GET US OUT. THE CHANGELING MIGHT BE DEAD, BUT WE STILL HAVE PORTAL--HE CAN TELEPORT US AWAY.
I'LL NEED ALL OF YOU TO HELP ME, THOUGH. SHOGUN WON'T DELAY MISTER SINISTER FOR LONG.
"FORTUNATELY, CHANGE IS YOUR SPECIALTY."
WHY SHOULD WE DO ANYTHING MYSTIQUE SAYS? SHE SHOT ME IN THE HEAD, LIKE, TEN MINUTES AGO, AND NOW SHE'S ASKING US TO TRUST HER?
AND THEY SHOULD LISTEN TO YOU INSTEAD, CREED? WE ALL JUST WATCHED YOU RIP JUNK'S HEAD OFF.
I...I DID?
DEATHSTRIKE, STAY HERE WITH CREED. GUARD HIM. MAKE SURE HE DOESN'T JEOPARDIZE OUR ESCAPE. IF HE DOES, KILL HIM.
CAN I JUST KILL HIM NOW?
NOT WITHOUT TAKING SOME SERIOUS DAMAGE. I WANT YOU ALIVE--AND SO DOES SHOGUN. DO YOU WANT HIS SACRIFICE TO BE MEANINGLESS?
THAT WASN'T SHOGUN...BUT I TAKE YOUR POINT.
X-23, THERE'S A RED CHEST IN MY CHAMBERS. I NEED YOU TO BRING ME WHAT'S INSIDE.
MYSTIQUE, IF THIS IS AN ATTEMPT AT--
DAKEN, YOU NEED TO CHECK ON SIPHON. MAKE SURE HE'S STILL SECURE IN HIS CELL.
IF HE'S OUT, THOSE OF US WHO STILL HAVE HEALING FACTORS ARE IN ENORMOUS DANGER.
AND WHAT, EXACTLY--
JUST GO!

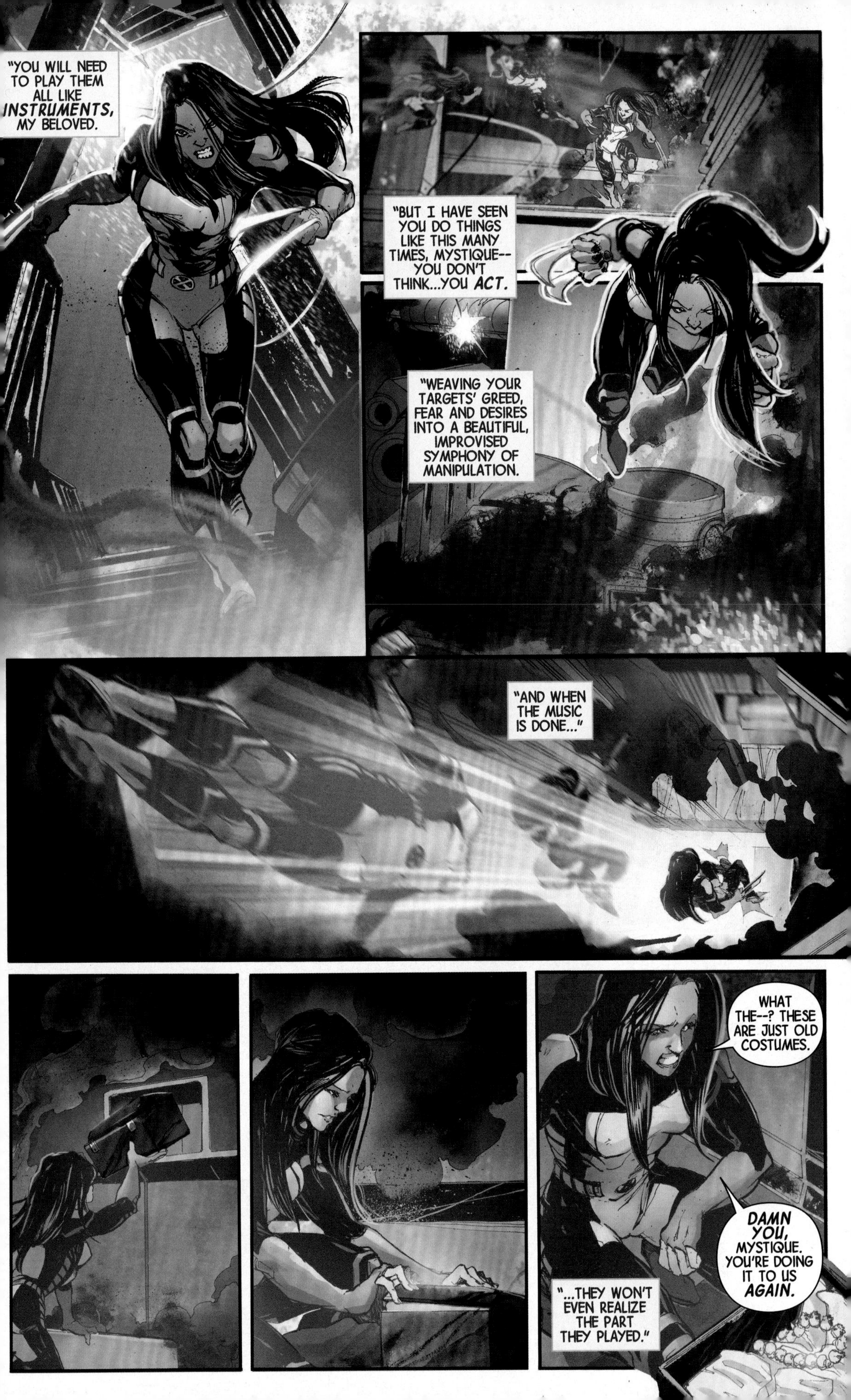
"YOU WILL NEED TO PLAY THEM ALL LIKE INSTRUMENTS, MY BELOVED.
"BUT I HAVE SEEN YOU DO THINGS LIKE THIS MANY TIMES, MYSTIQUE-- YOU DON'T THINK...YOU ACT.
"WEAVING YOUR TARGETS' GREED, FEAR AND DESIRES INTO A BEAUTIFUL, IMPROVISED SYMPHONY OF MANIPULATION.
"AND WHEN THE MUSIC IS DONE..."
WHAT THE--? THESE ARE JUST OLD COSTUMES.
DAMN YOU, MYSTIQUE. YOU'RE DOING IT TO US AGAIN.
"...THEY WON'T EVEN REALIZE THE PART THEY PLAYED."

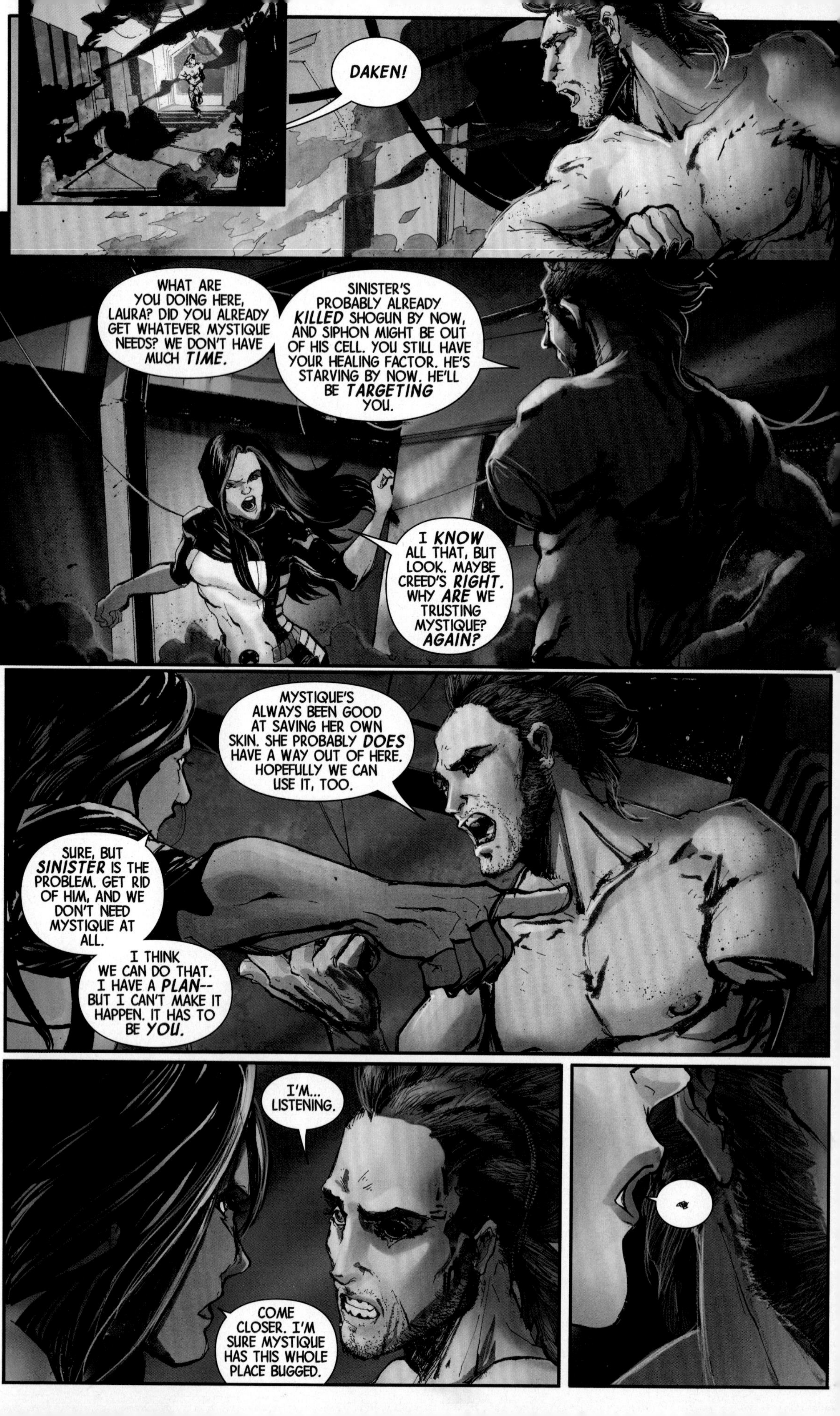
DAKEN!
WHAT ARE YOU DOING HERE, LAURA? DID YOU ALREADY GET WHATEVER MYSTIQUE NEEDS? WE DON'T HAVE MUCH TIME.
SINISTER'S PROBABLY ALREADY KILLED SHOGUN BY NOW, AND SIPHON MIGHT BE OUT OF HIS CELL. YOU STILL HAVE YOUR HEALING FACTOR. HE'S STARVING BY NOW. HE'LL BE TARGETING YOU.
I KNOW ALL THAT, BUT LOOK. MAYBE CREED'S RIGHT. WHY ARE WE TRUSTING MYSTIQUE? AGAIN?
MYSTIQUE'S ALWAYS BEEN GOOD AT SAVING HER OWN SKIN. SHE PROBABLY DOES HAVE A WAY OUT OF HERE. HOPEFULLY WE CAN USE IT, TOO.
SURE, BUT SINISTER IS THE PROBLEM. GET RID OF HIM, AND WE DON'T NEED MYSTIQUE AT ALL.
I THINK WE CAN DO THAT. I HAVE A PLAN-- BUT I CAN'T MAKE IT HAPPEN. IT HAS TO BE YOU.
I'M... LISTENING.
COME CLOSER. I'M SURE MYSTIQUE HAS THIS WHOLE PLACE BUGGED.

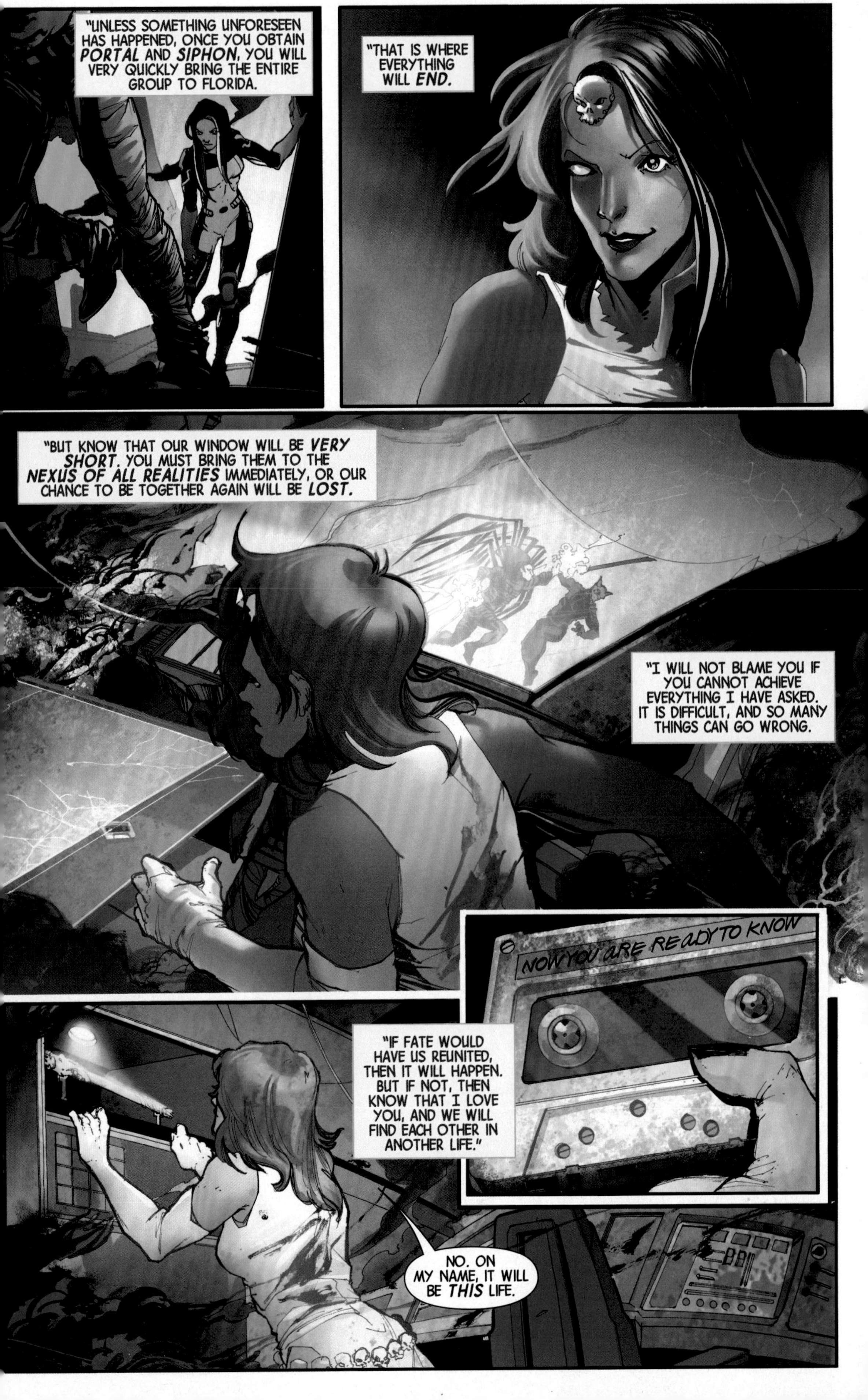
"UNLESS SOMETHING UNFORESEEN HAS HAPPENED, ONCE YOU OBTAIN PORTAL AND SIPHON, YOU WILL VERY QUICKLY BRING THE ENTIRE GROUP TO FLORIDA.
"THAT IS WHERE EVERYTHING WILL END.
"BUT KNOW THAT OUR WINDOW WILL BE VERY SHORT. YOU MUST BRING THEM TO THE NEXUS OF ALL REALITIES IMMEDIATELY, OR OUR CHANCE TO BE TOGETHER AGAIN WILL BE LOST.
"I WILL NOT BLAME YOU IF YOU CANNOT ACHIEVE EVERYTHING I HAVE ASKED. IT IS DIFFICULT, AND SO MANY THINGS CAN GO WRONG.
NOW YOU ARE READY TO KNOW
"IF FATE WOULD HAVE US REUNITED, THEN IT WILL HAPPEN. BUT IF NOT, THEN KNOW THAT I LOVE YOU, AND WE WILL FIND EACH OTHER IN ANOTHER LIFE."
NO. ON MY NAME, IT WILL BE THIS LIFE.

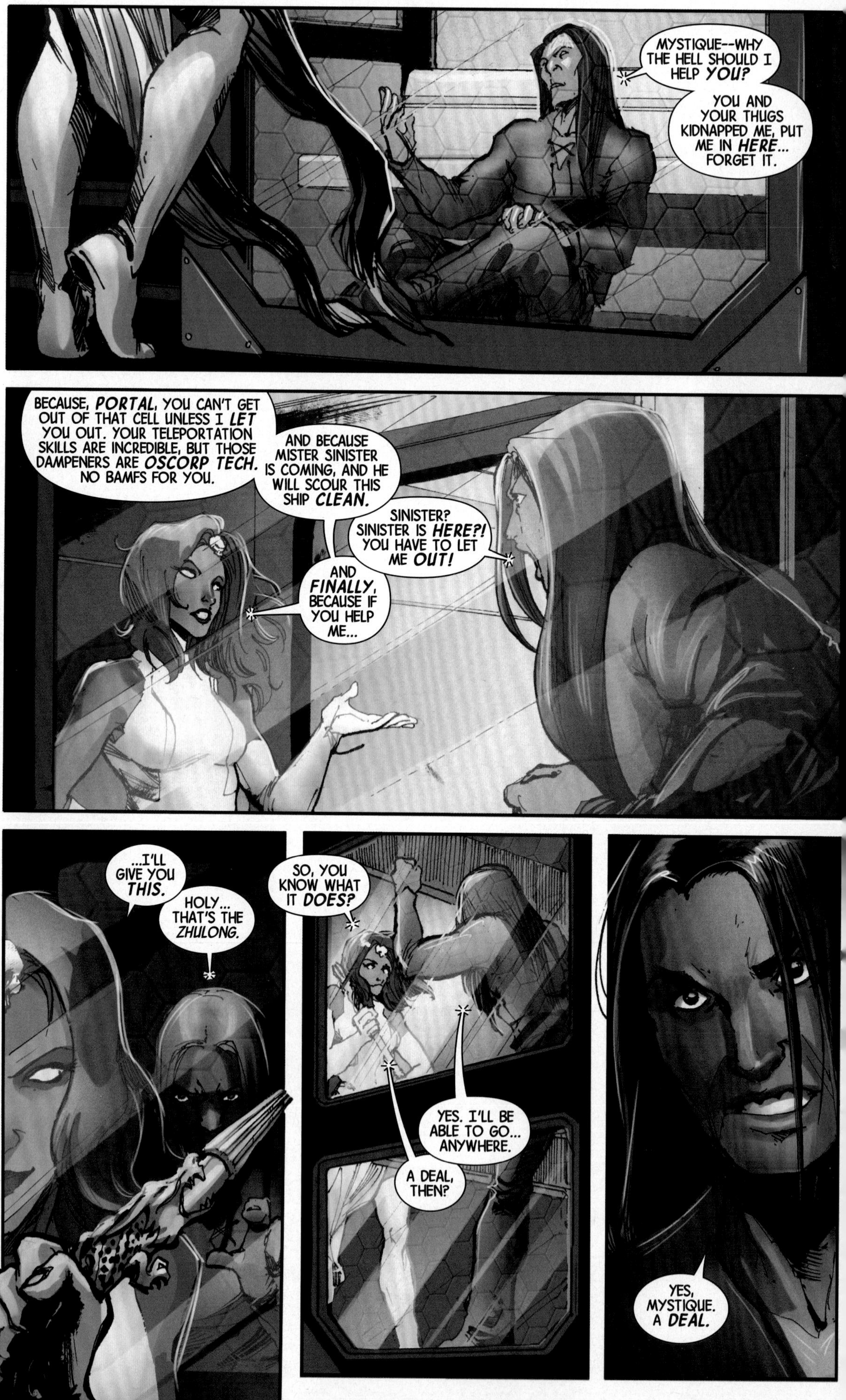
MYSTIQUE--WHY THE HELL SHOULD I HELP YOU?
YOU AND YOUR THUGS KIDNAPPED ME, PUT ME IN HERE... FORGET IT.
BECAUSE, PORTAL, YOU CAN'T GET OUT OF THAT CELL UNLESS I LET YOU OUT. YOUR TELEPORTATION SKILLS ARE INCREDIBLE, BUT THOSE DAMPENERS ARE OSCORP TECH. NO BAMFS FOR YOU.
AND BECAUSE MISTER SINISTER IS COMING, AND HE WILL SCOUR THIS SHIP CLEAN.
SINISTER? SINISTER IS HERE?! YOU HAVE TO LET ME OUT!
AND FINALLY, BECAUSE IF YOU HELP ME...
...I'LL GIVE YOU THIS.
HOLY... THAT'S THE ZHULONG.
SO, YOU KNOW WHAT IT DOES?
YES. I'LL BE ABLE TO GO... ANYWHERE.
A DEAL, THEN?
YES, MYSTIQUE. A DEAL.

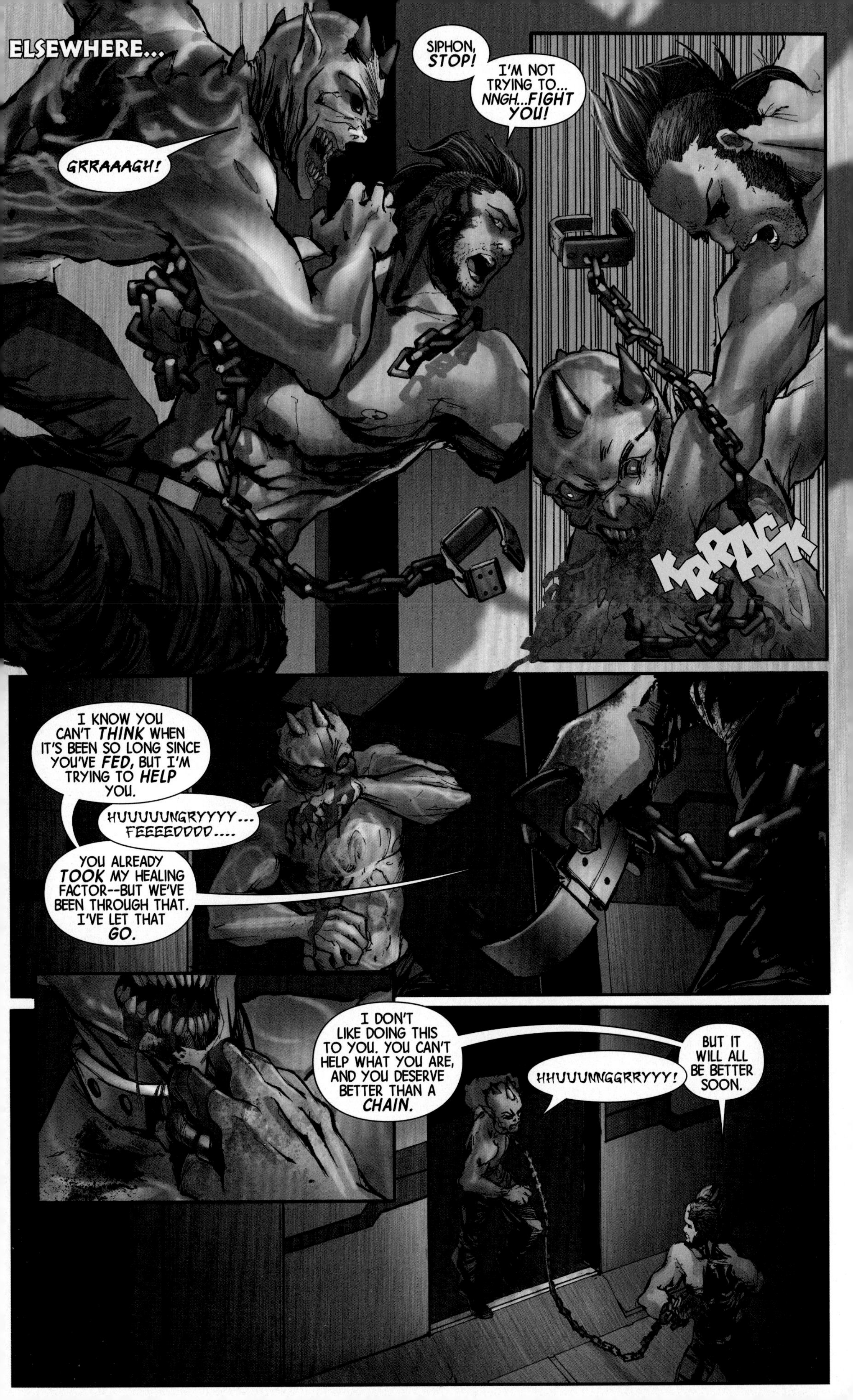
ELSEWHERE...
GRRAAAGH!
SIPHON, STOP!
I'M NOT TRYING TO... NNGH...FIGHT YOU!
KRRACK
I KNOW YOU CAN'T THINK WHEN IT'S BEEN SO LONG SINCE YOU'VE FED, BUT I'M TRYING TO HELP YOU.
HUUUUUNGRYYYY... FEEEEDDDD....
YOU ALREADY TOOK MY HEALING FACTOR--BUT WE'VE BEEN THROUGH THAT. I'VE LET THAT GO.
I DON'T LIKE DOING THIS TO YOU. YOU CAN'T HELP WHAT YOU ARE, AND YOU DESERVE BETTER THAN A CHAIN.
HHUUUNNGGRRYYY!
BUT IT WILL ALL BE BETTER SOON.

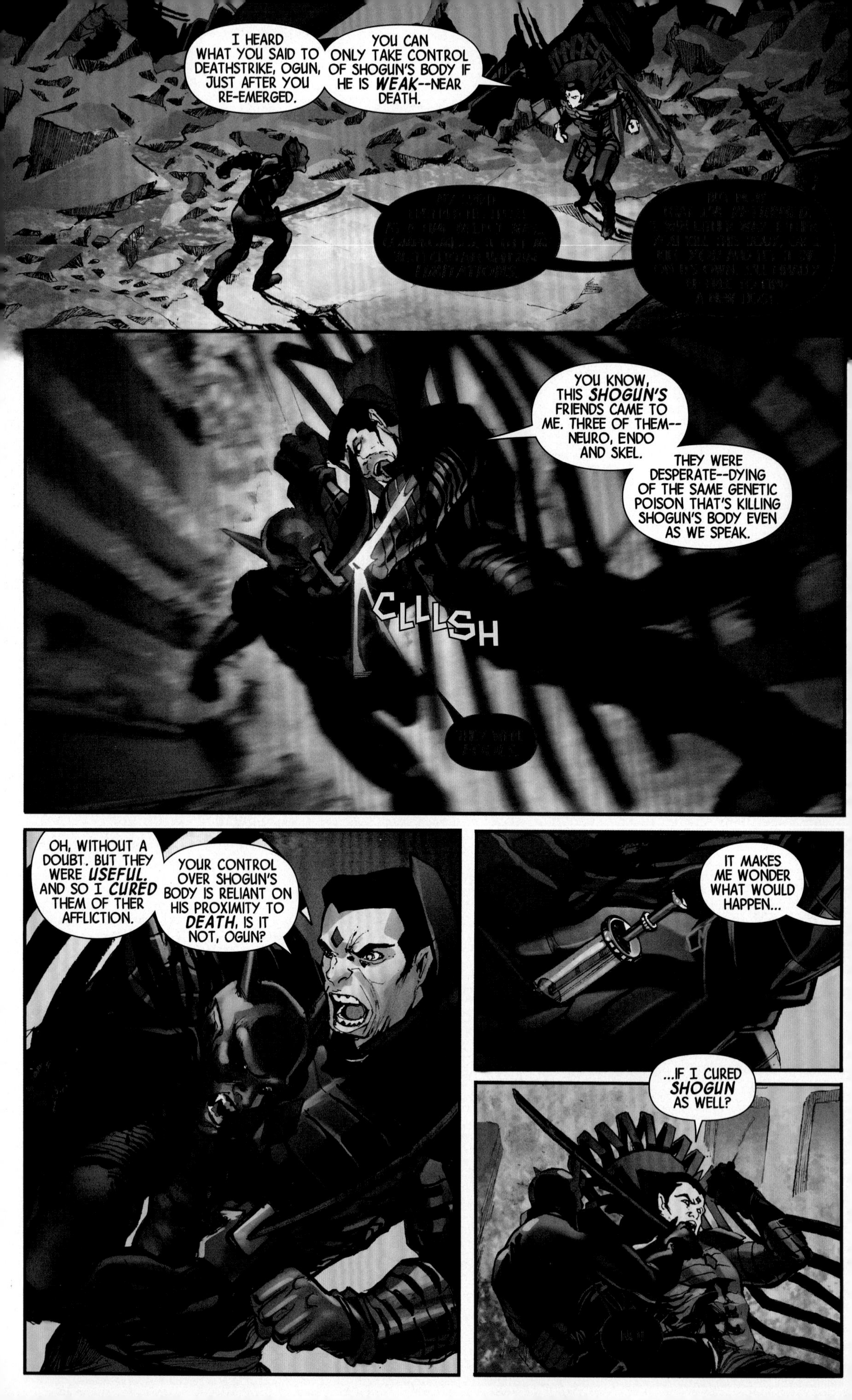

I HEARD WHAT YOU SAID TO DEATHSTRIKE, OGUN, JUST AFTER YOU RE-EMERGED.
YOU CAN ONLY TAKE CONTROL OF SHOGUN'S BODY IF HE IS WEAK--NEAR DEATH.
YOU KNOW, THIS SHOGUN'S FRIENDS CAME TO ME. THREE OF THEM--NEURO, ENDO AND SKEL.
THEY WERE DESPERATE--DYING OF THE SAME GENETIC POISON THAT'S KILLING SHOGUN'S BODY EVEN AS WE SPEAK.
CLLLLSH
OH, WITHOUT A DOUBT. BUT THEY WERE USEFUL. AND SO I CURED THEM OF THER AFFLICTION.
YOUR CONTROL OVER SHOGUN'S BODY IS RELIANT ON HIS PROXIMITY TO DEATH, IS IT NOT, OGUN?
IT MAKES ME WONDER WHAT WOULD HAPPEN...
...IF I CURED SHOGUN AS WELL?

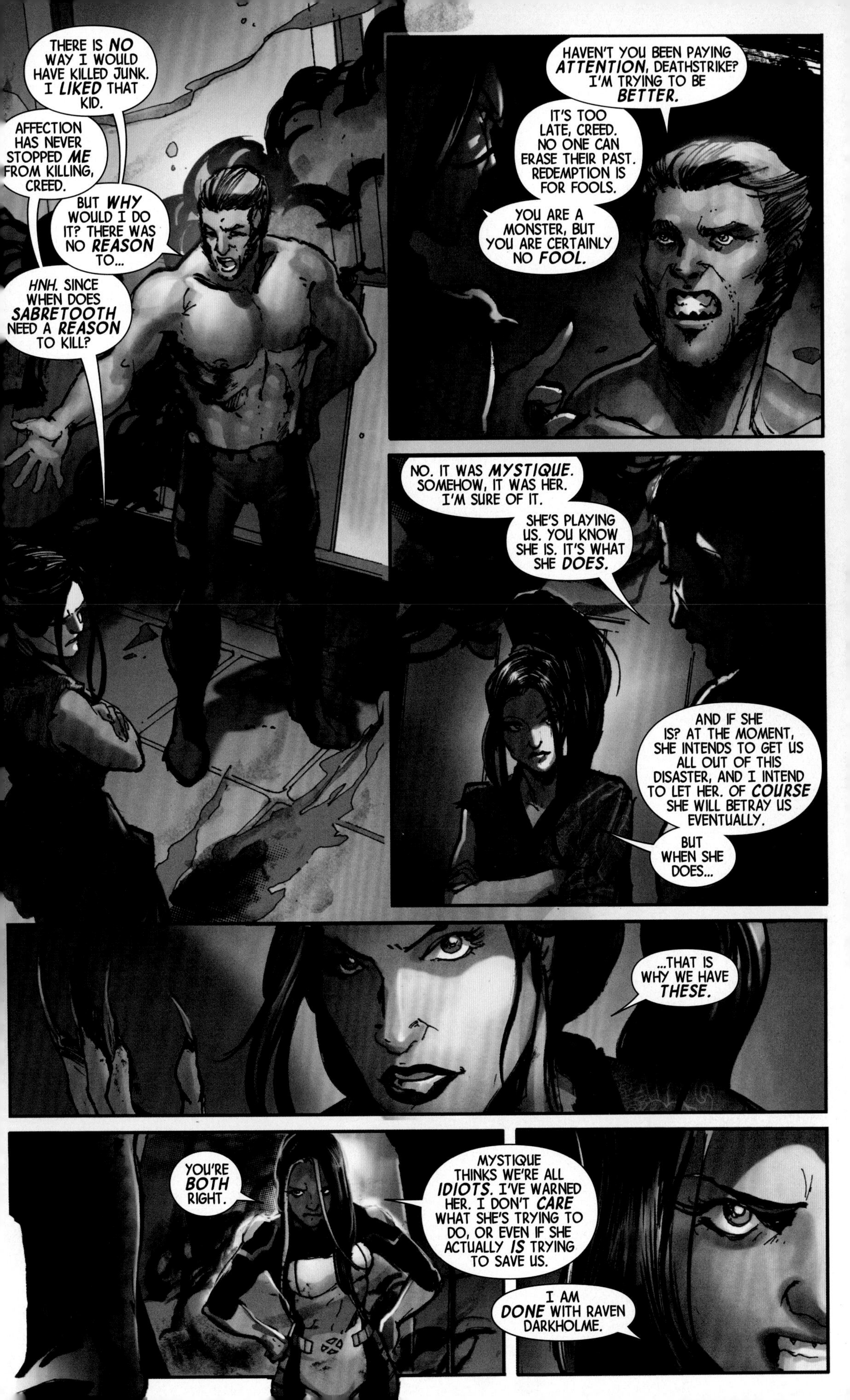

THERE IS NO WAY I WOULD HAVE KILLED JUNK. I LIKED THAT KID.
AFFECTION HAS NEVER STOPPED ME FROM KILLING, CREED.
BUT WHY WOULD I DO IT? THERE WAS NO REASON TO...
HNH. SINCE WHEN DOES SABRETOOTH NEED A REASON TO KILL?
HAVEN'T YOU BEEN PAYING ATTENTION, DEATHSTRIKE? I'M TRYING TO BE BETTER.
IT'S TOO LATE, CREED. NO ONE CAN ERASE THEIR PAST. REDEMPTION IS FOR FOOLS.
YOU ARE A MONSTER, BUT YOU ARE CERTAINLY NO FOOL.
NO. IT WAS MYSTIQUE. SOMEHOW, IT WAS HER. I'M SURE OF IT.
SHE'S PLAYING US. YOU KNOW SHE IS. IT'S WHAT SHE DOES.
AND IF SHE IS? AT THE MOMENT, SHE INTENDS TO GET US ALL OUT OF THIS DISASTER, AND I INTEND TO LET HER. OF COURSE SHE WILL BETRAY US EVENTUALLY.
BUT WHEN SHE DOES...
...THAT IS WHY WE HAVE THESE.
YOU'RE BOTH RIGHT.
MYSTIQUE THINKS WE'RE ALL IDIOTS. I'VE WARNED HER. I DON'T CARE WHAT SHE'S TRYING TO DO, OR EVEN IF SHE ACTUALLY IS TRYING TO SAVE US.
I AM DONE WITH RAVEN DARKHOLME.

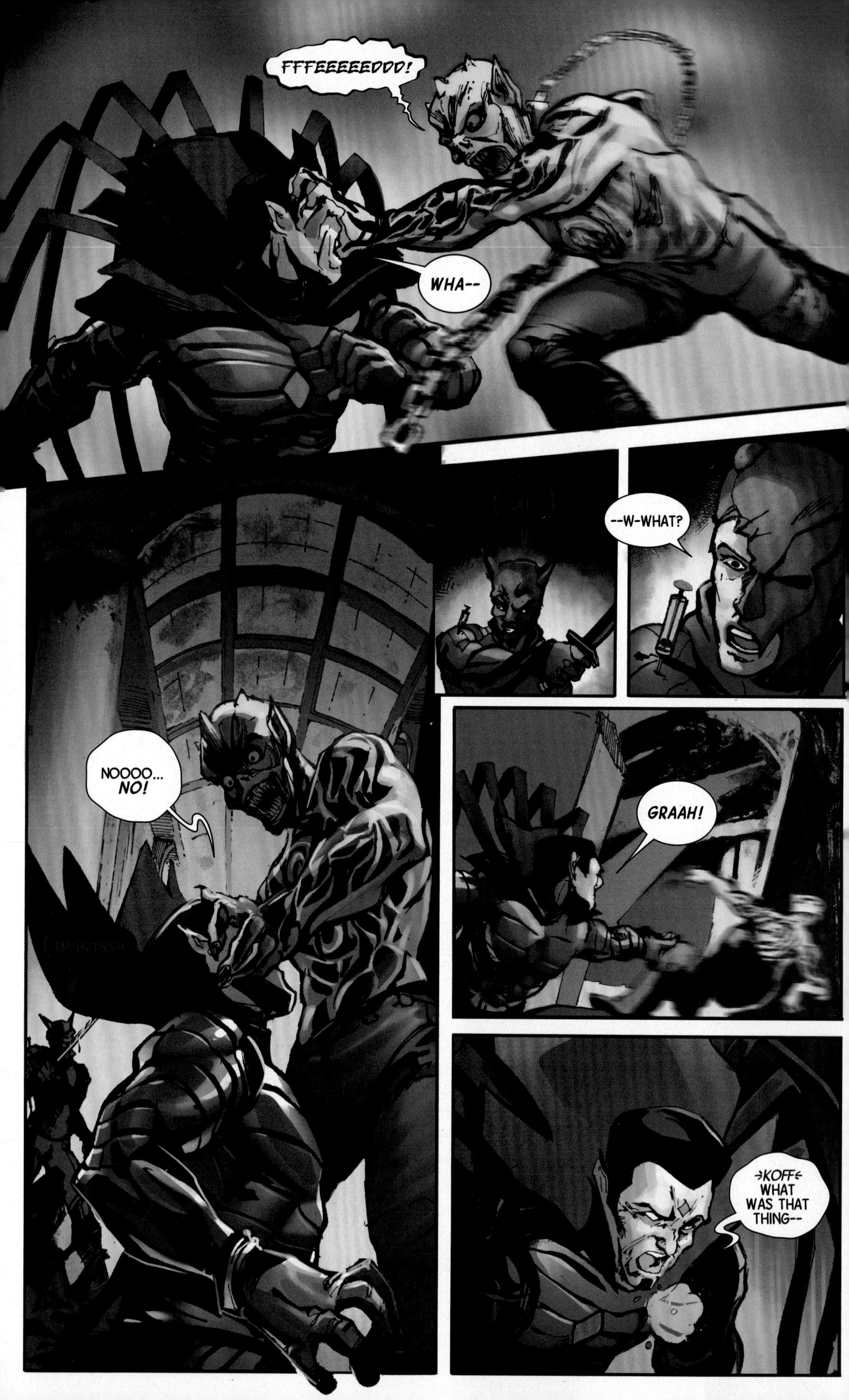
FFFEEEEEEDDD!
WHA--
--W-WHAT?
NOOOO...
NO!
GRAAH!
KOFF
WHAT
WAS THAT
THING--

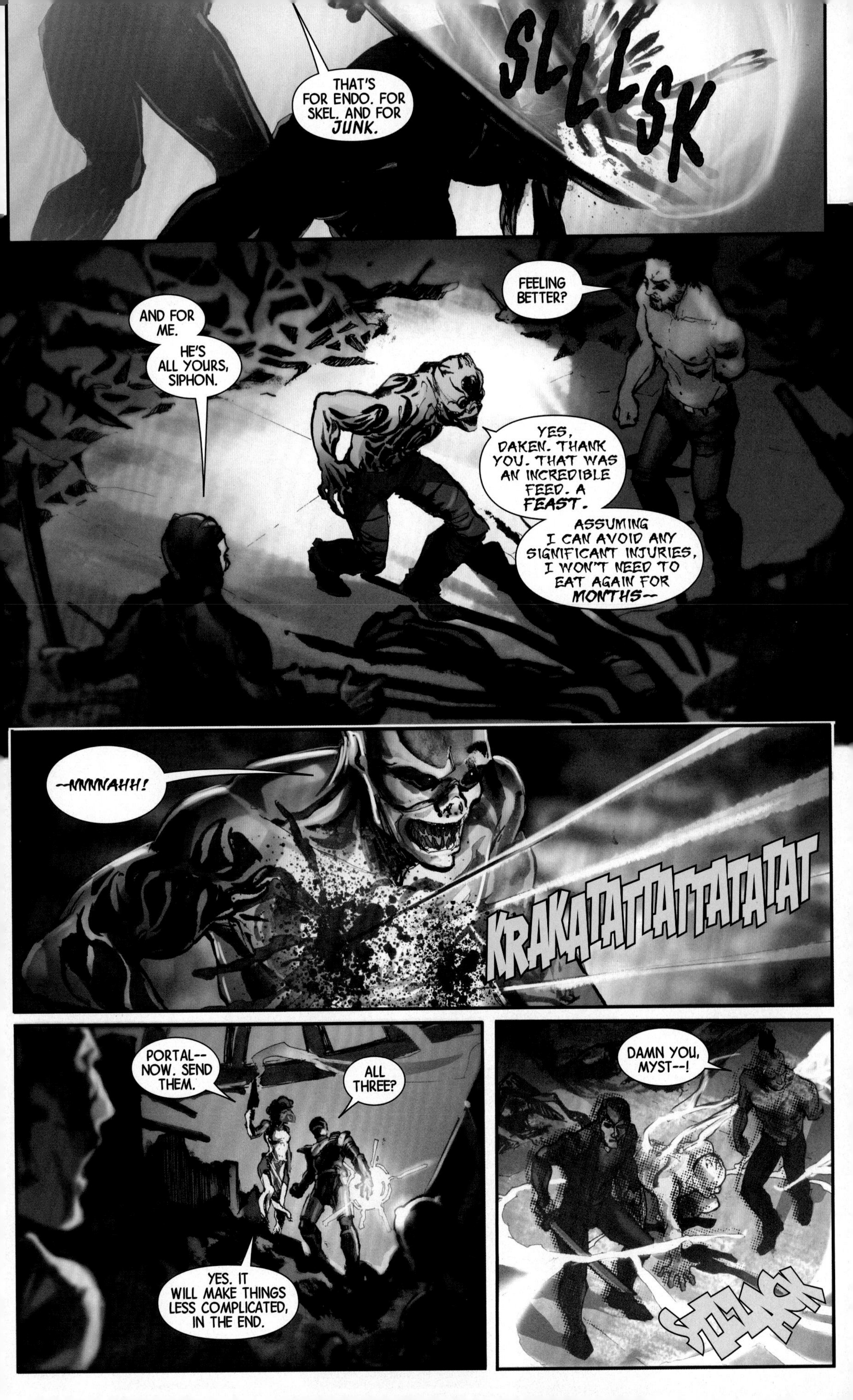
THAT'S FOR ENDO. FOR SKEL. AND FOR JUNK.
SLLLSK
FEELING BETTER?
AND FOR ME.
HE'S ALL YOURS, SIPHON.
YES, DAKEN. THANK YOU. THAT WAS AN INCREDIBLE FEED. A FEAST.
ASSUMING I CAN AVOID ANY SIGNIFICANT INJURIES, I WON'T NEED TO EAT AGAIN FOR MONTHS--
--NNNNAHH!
KRAKATATTATTATATAT
PORTAL-- NOW. SEND THEM.
ALL THREE?
YES. IT WILL MAKE THINGS LESS COMPLICATED, IN THE END.
DAMN YOU, MYST--!

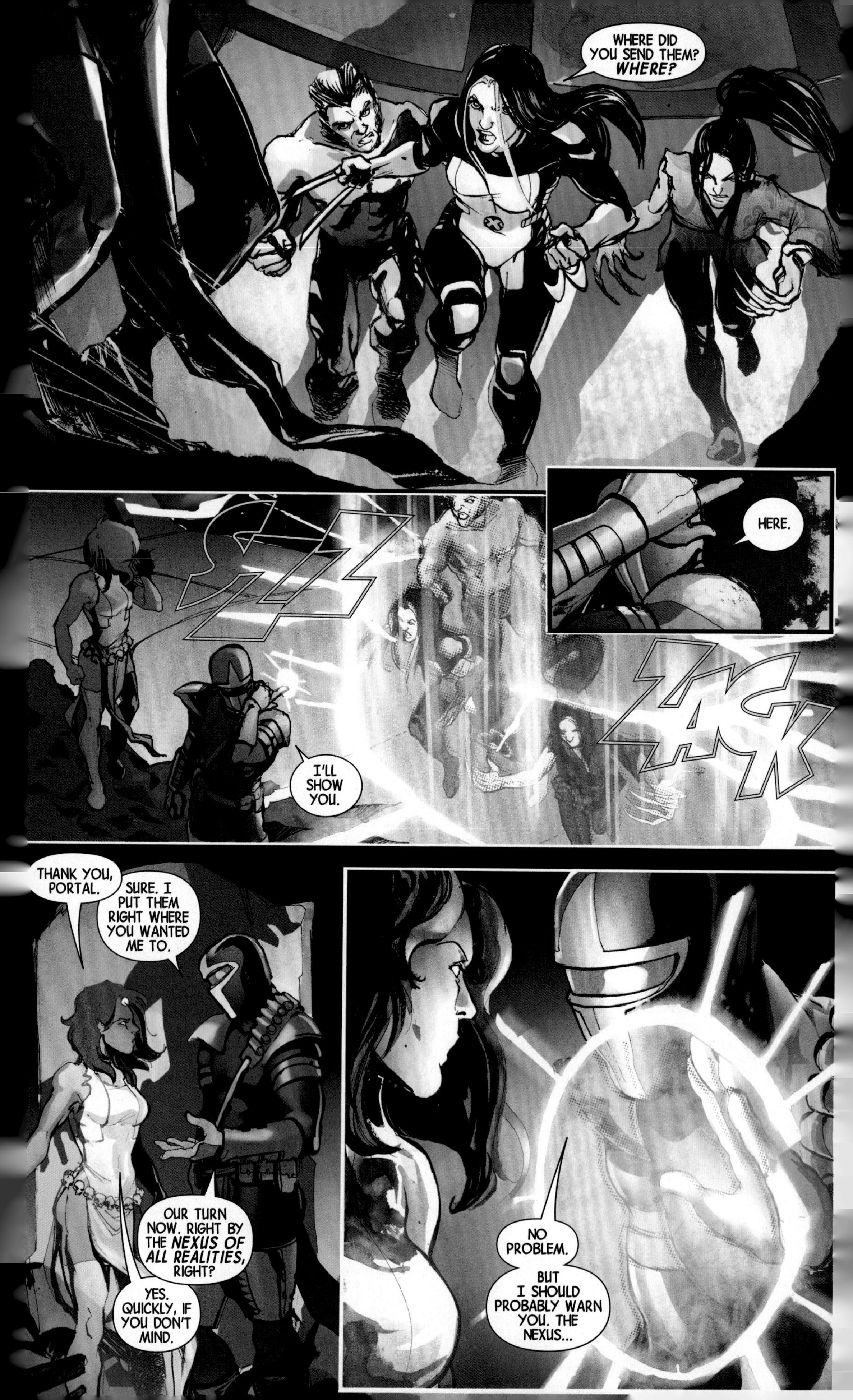
WHERE DID YOU SEND THEM? *WHERE?*
HERE.
SZZ
ZACK
I'LL SHOW YOU.
THANK YOU, PORTAL.
SURE. I PUT THEM RIGHT WHERE YOU WANTED ME TO.
OUR TURN NOW. RIGHT BY THE *NEXUS OF ALL REALITIES,* RIGHT?
YES. QUICKLY, IF YOU DON'T MIND.
NO PROBLEM.
BUT I SHOULD PROBABLY WARN YOU. THE NEXUS...

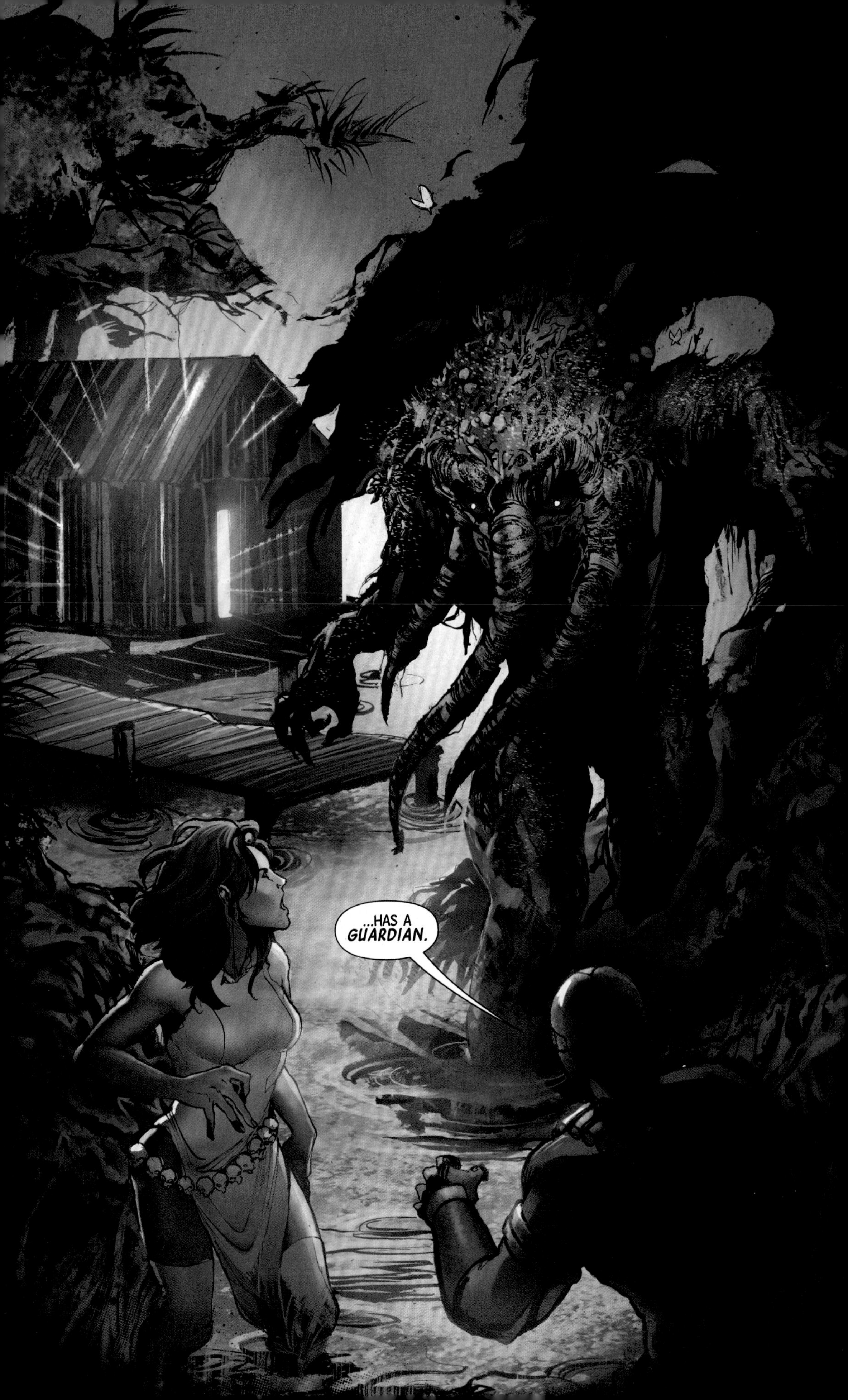
...HAS A GUARDIAN.

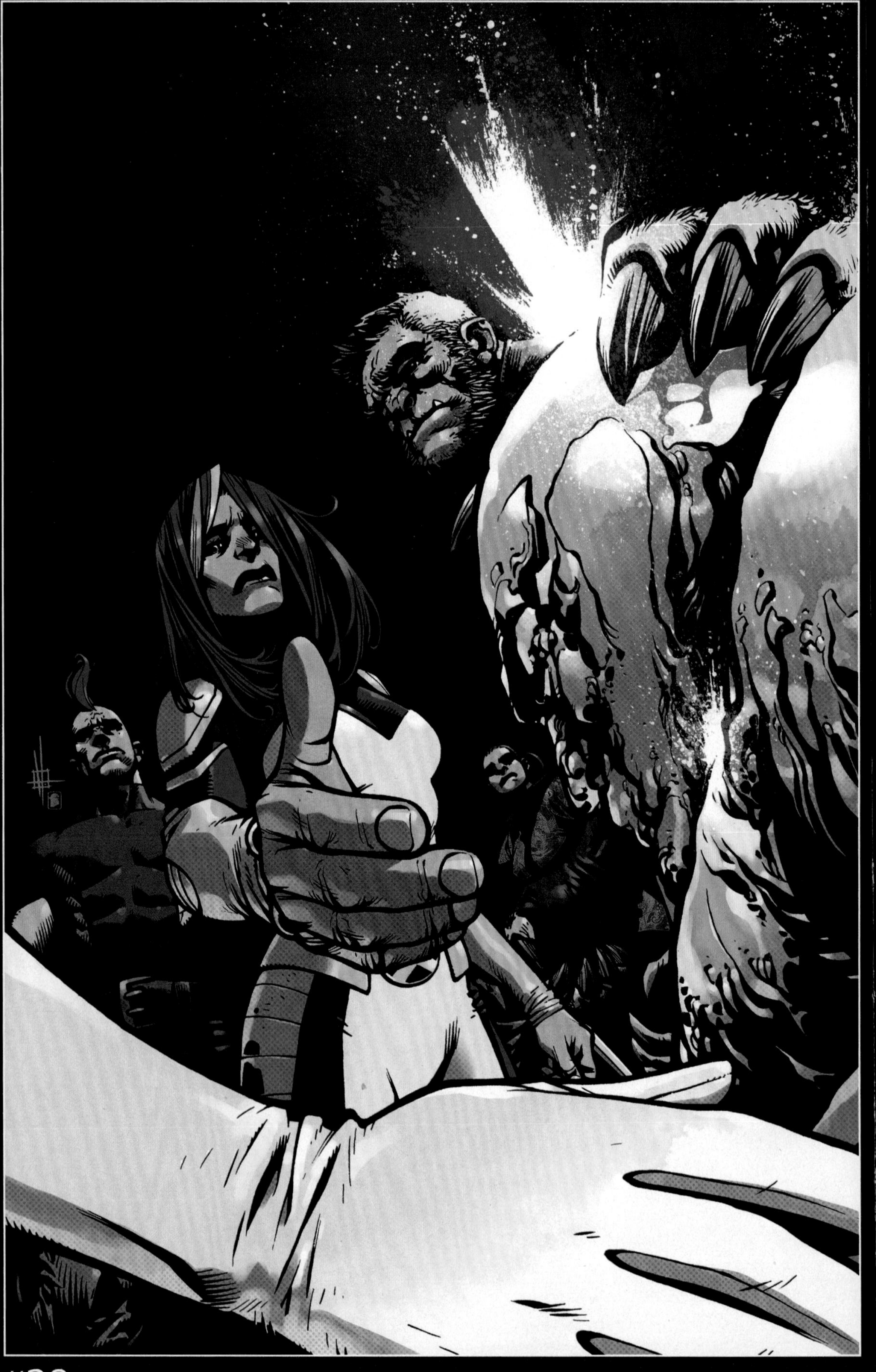

#20

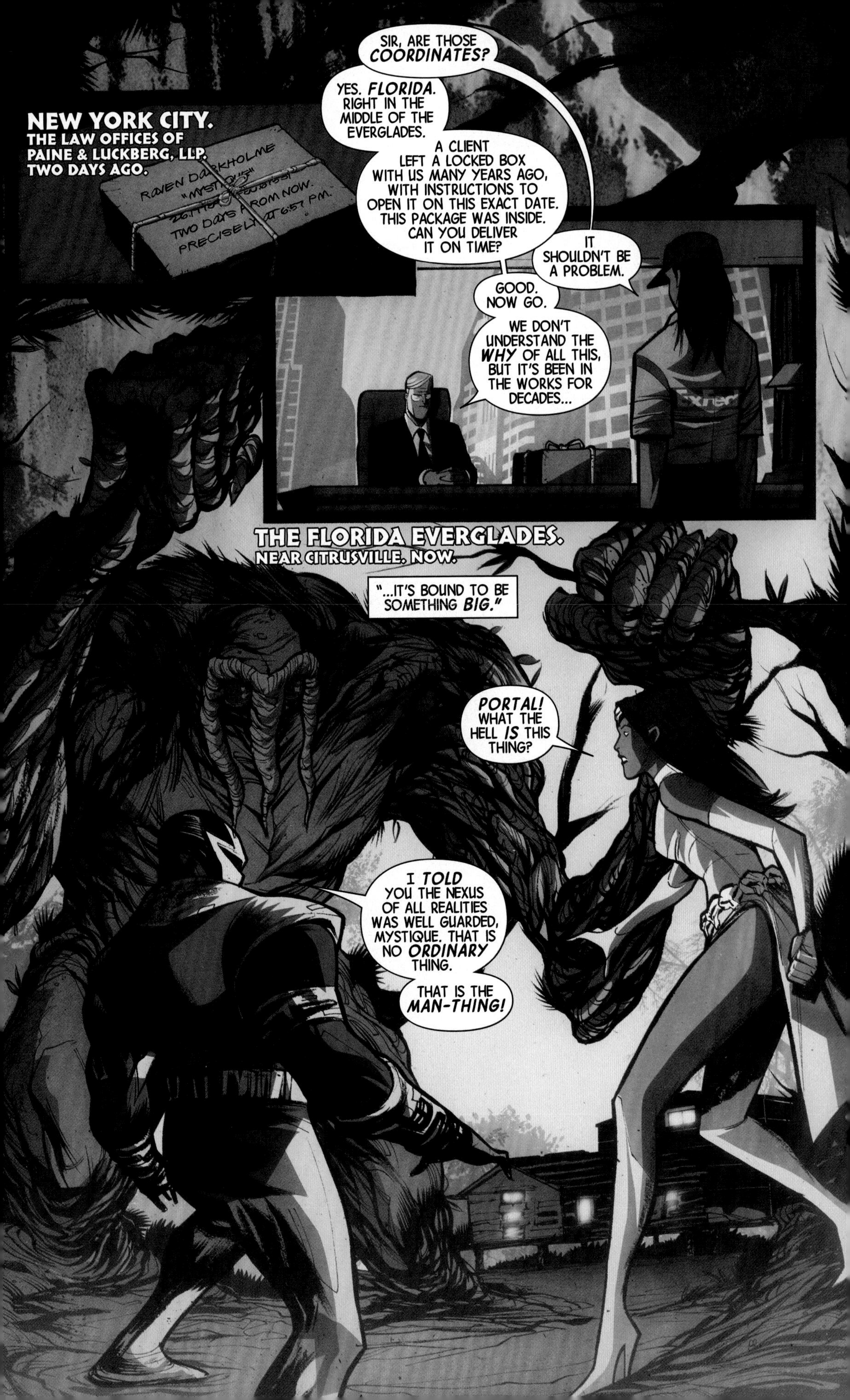
NEW YORK CITY.
THE LAW OFFICES OF PAINE & LUCKBERG, LLP. TWO DAYS AGO.
RAVEN DARKHOLME
SIR, ARE THOSE COORDINATES?
YES. FLORIDA. RIGHT IN THE MIDDLE OF THE EVERGLADES.
A CLIENT LEFT A LOCKED BOX WITH US MANY YEARS AGO, WITH INSTRUCTIONS TO OPEN IT ON THIS EXACT DATE. THIS PACKAGE WAS INSIDE. CAN YOU DELIVER IT ON TIME?
IT SHOULDN'T BE A PROBLEM.
GOOD. NOW GO.
WE DON'T UNDERSTAND THE WHY OF ALL THIS, BUT IT'S BEEN IN THE WORKS FOR DECADES...
THE FLORIDA EVERGLADES.
NEAR CITRUSVILLE. NOW.
"...IT'S BOUND TO BE SOMETHING BIG."
PORTAL! WHAT THE HELL IS THIS THING?
I TOLD YOU THE NEXUS OF ALL REALITIES WAS WELL GUARDED, MYSTIQUE. THAT IS NO ORDINARY THING.
THAT IS THE MAN-THING!

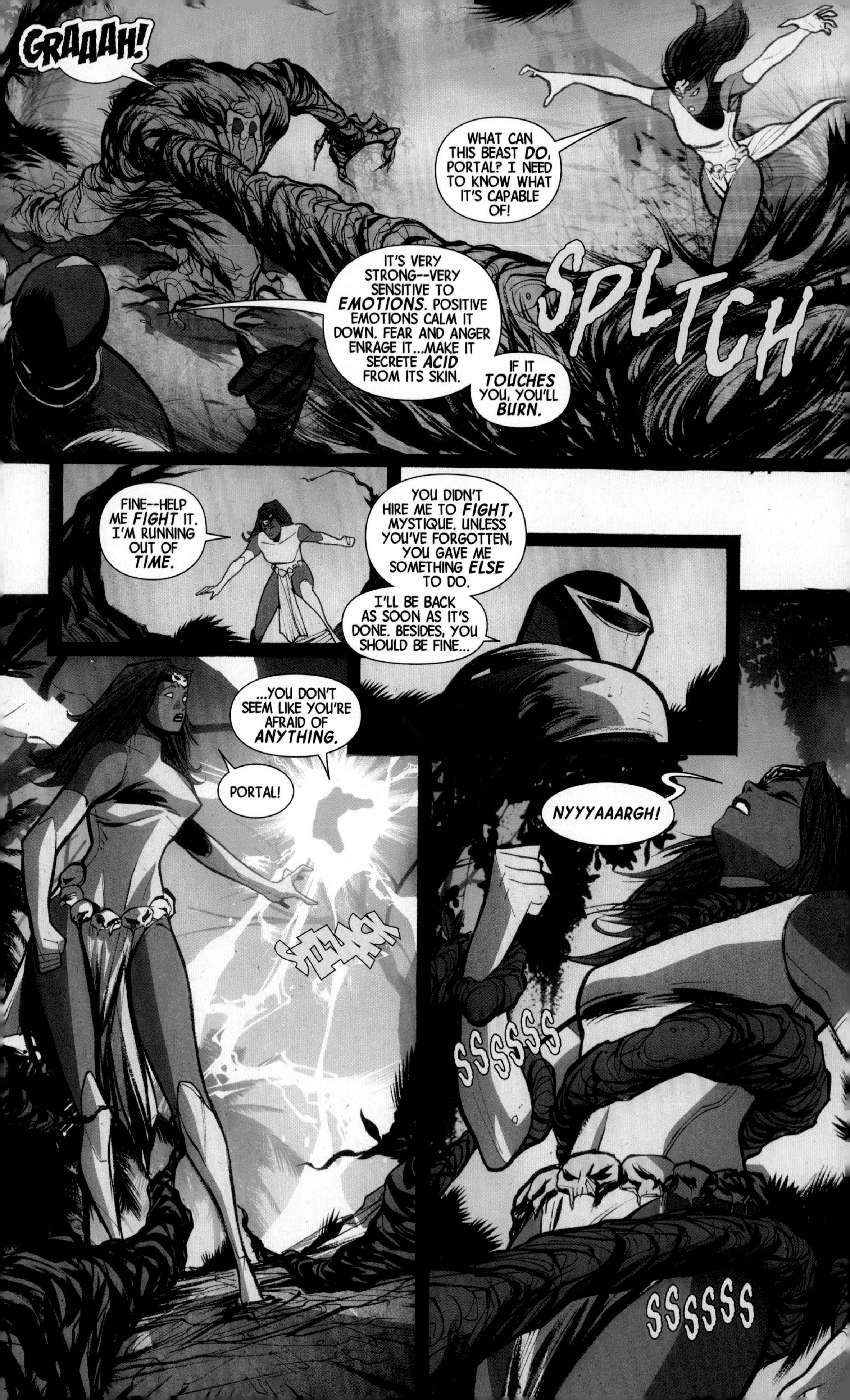
GRAAAH!
WHAT CAN THIS BEAST DO, PORTAL? I NEED TO KNOW WHAT IT'S CAPABLE OF!
IT'S VERY STRONG--VERY SENSITIVE TO EMOTIONS. POSITIVE EMOTIONS CALM IT DOWN. FEAR AND ANGER ENRAGE IT...MAKE IT SECRETE ACID FROM ITS SKIN.
IF IT TOUCHES YOU, YOU'LL BURN.
SPLTCH
FINE--HELP ME FIGHT IT. I'M RUNNING OUT OF TIME.
YOU DIDN'T HIRE ME TO FIGHT, MYSTIQUE. UNLESS YOU'VE FORGOTTEN, YOU GAVE ME SOMETHING ELSE TO DO.
I'LL BE BACK AS SOON AS IT'S DONE. BESIDES, YOU SHOULD BE FINE...
...YOU DON'T SEEM LIKE YOU'RE AFRAID OF ANYTHING.
PORTAL!
NYYYAAARGH!
SSSSSS
SSSSSS

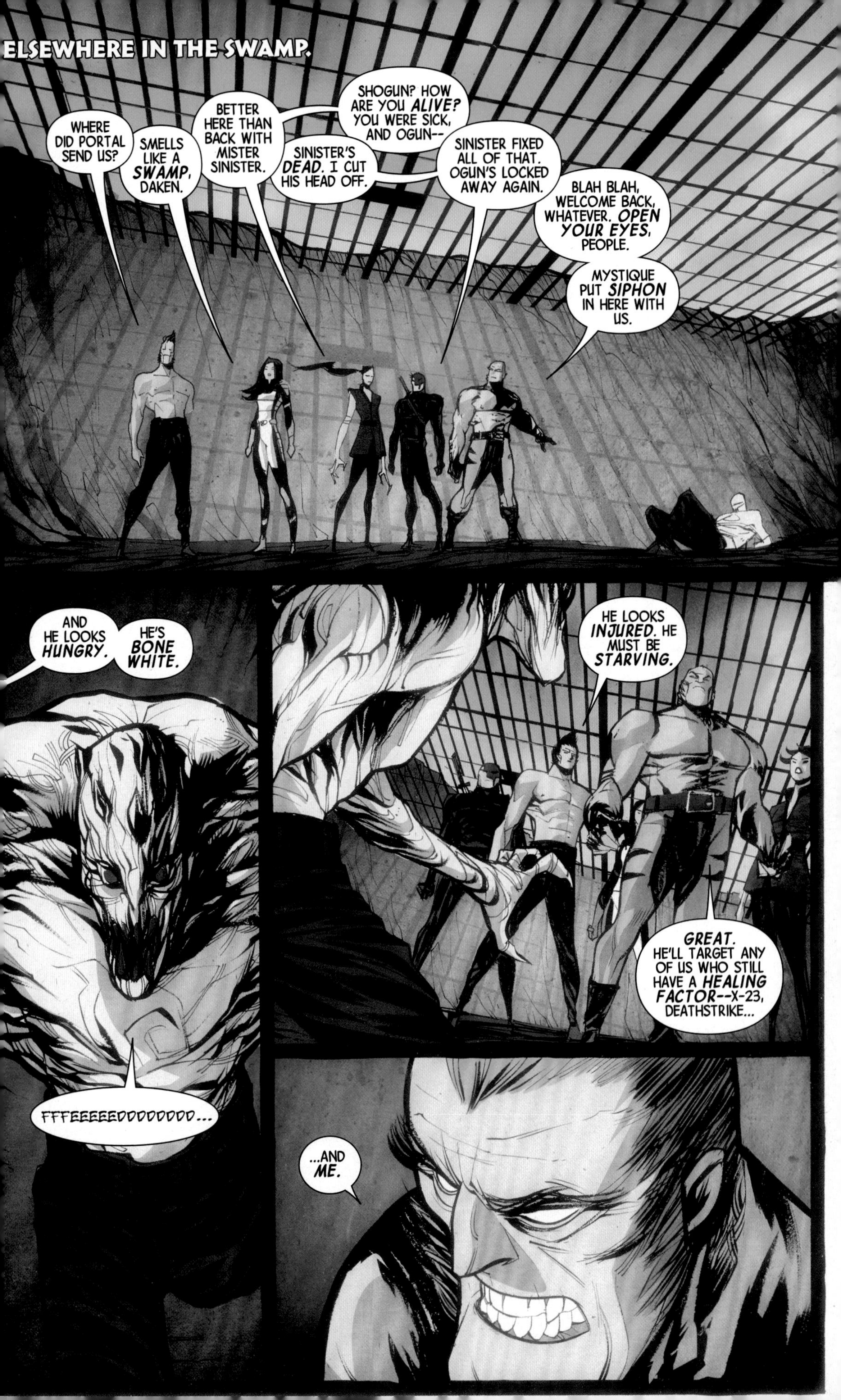
ELSEWHERE IN THE SWAMP.
WHERE DID PORTAL SEND US?
SMELLS LIKE A SWAMP, DAKEN.
BETTER HERE THAN BACK WITH MISTER SINISTER.
SHOGUN? HOW ARE YOU ALIVE? YOU WERE SICK, AND OGUN--
SINISTER'S DEAD. I CUT HIS HEAD OFF.
SINISTER FIXED ALL OF THAT. OGUN'S LOCKED AWAY AGAIN.
BLAH BLAH, WELCOME BACK, WHATEVER. OPEN YOUR EYES, PEOPLE.
MYSTIQUE PUT SIPHON IN HERE WITH US.
AND HE LOOKS HUNGRY.
HE'S BONE WHITE.
FFFEEEEEEDDDDDDDD...
HE LOOKS INJURED. HE MUST BE STARVING.
GREAT. HE'LL TARGET ANY OF US WHO STILL HAVE A HEALING FACTOR--X-23, DEATHSTRIKE...
...AND ME.

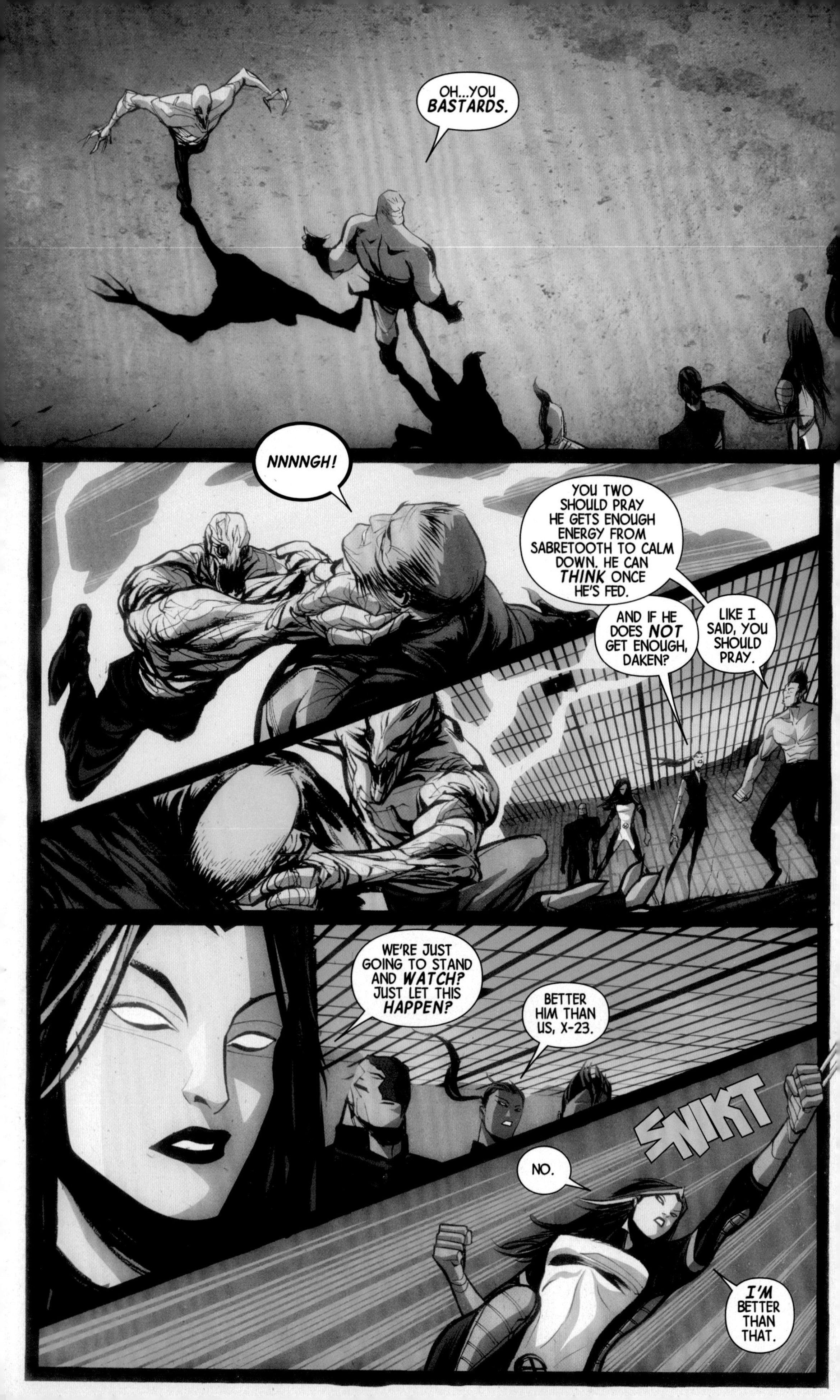

OH...YOU BASTARDS.
NNNNGH!
YOU TWO SHOULD PRAY HE GETS ENOUGH ENERGY FROM SABRETOOTH TO CALM DOWN. HE CAN THINK ONCE HE'S FED.
AND IF HE DOES NOT GET ENOUGH, DAKEN?
LIKE I SAID, YOU SHOULD PRAY.
WE'RE JUST GOING TO STAND AND WATCH? JUST LET THIS HAPPEN?
BETTER HIM THAN US, X-23.
SNIKT
NO.
I'M BETTER THAN THAT.

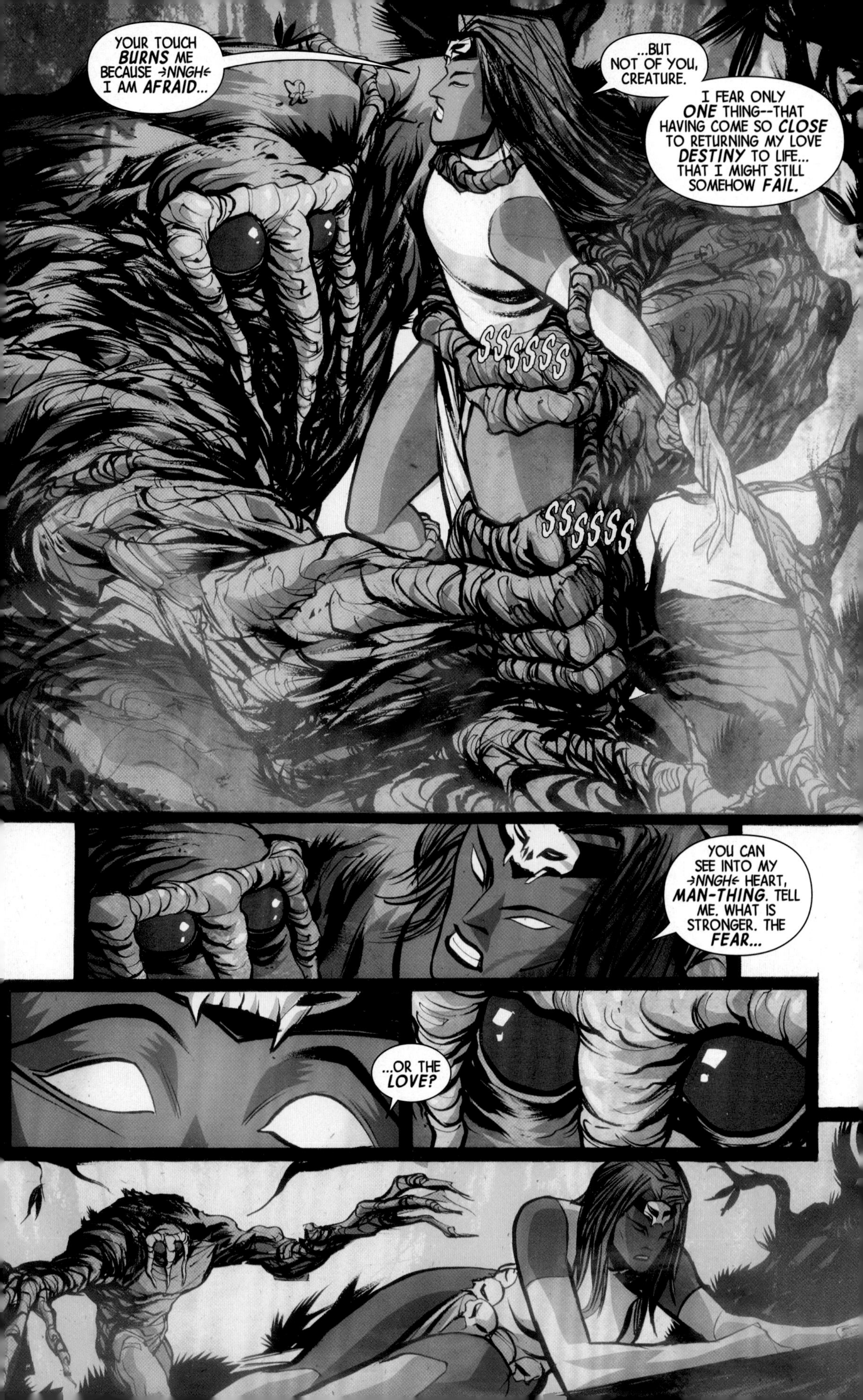
YOUR TOUCH BURNS ME BECAUSE →NNGH← I AM AFRAID...
...BUT NOT OF YOU, CREATURE.
I FEAR ONLY ONE THING--THAT HAVING COME SO CLOSE TO RETURNING MY LOVE DESTINY TO LIFE... THAT I MIGHT STILL SOMEHOW FAIL.
SSSSSS
SSSSSS
YOU CAN SEE INTO MY →NNGH← HEART, MAN-THING. TELL ME. WHAT IS STRONGER. THE FEAR...
...OR THE LOVE?

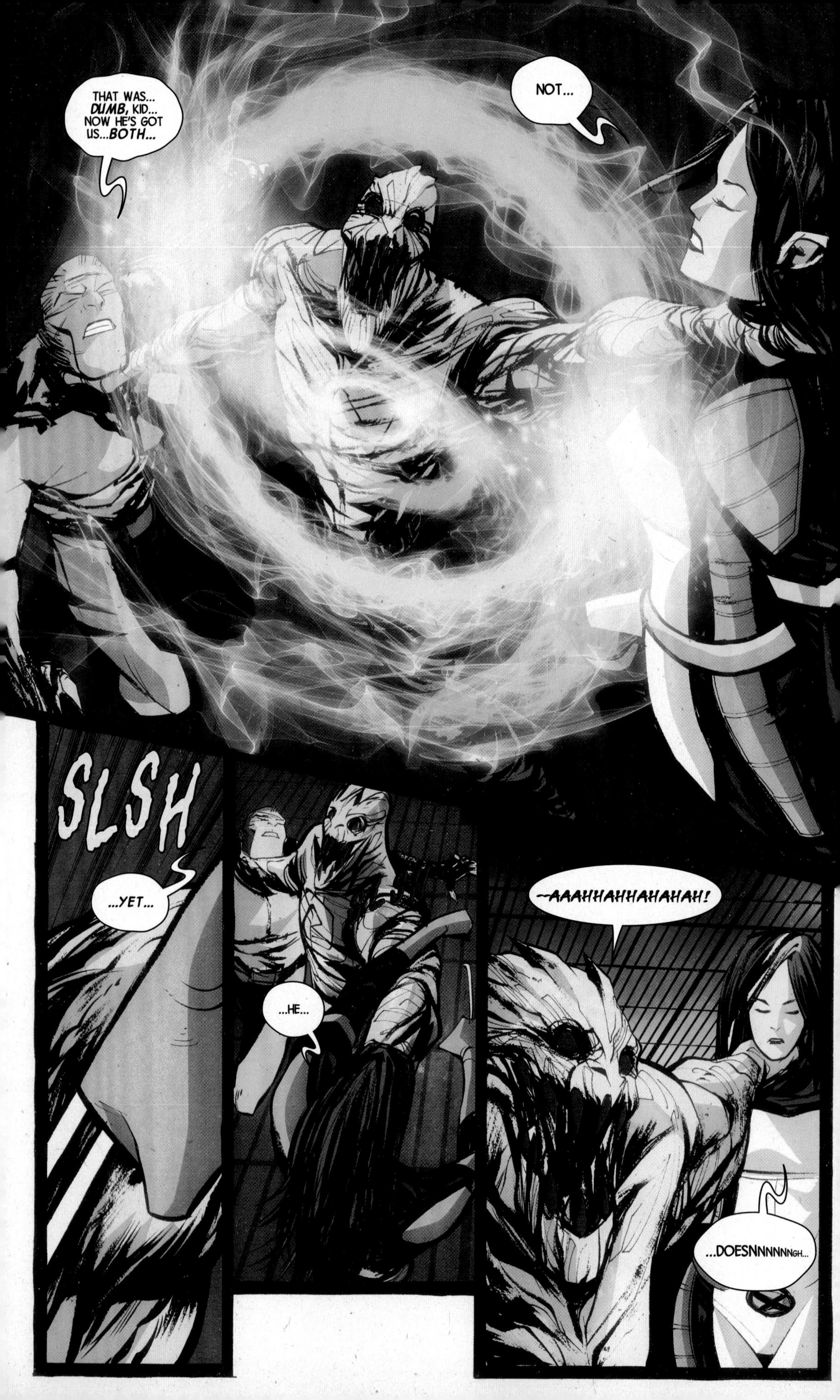
THAT WAS... DUMB, KID... NOW HE'S GOT US...BOTH...
NOT...
SLSH
...YET...
...HE...
--AAAHHAHHAHAHAH!
...DOESNNNNNNGH...

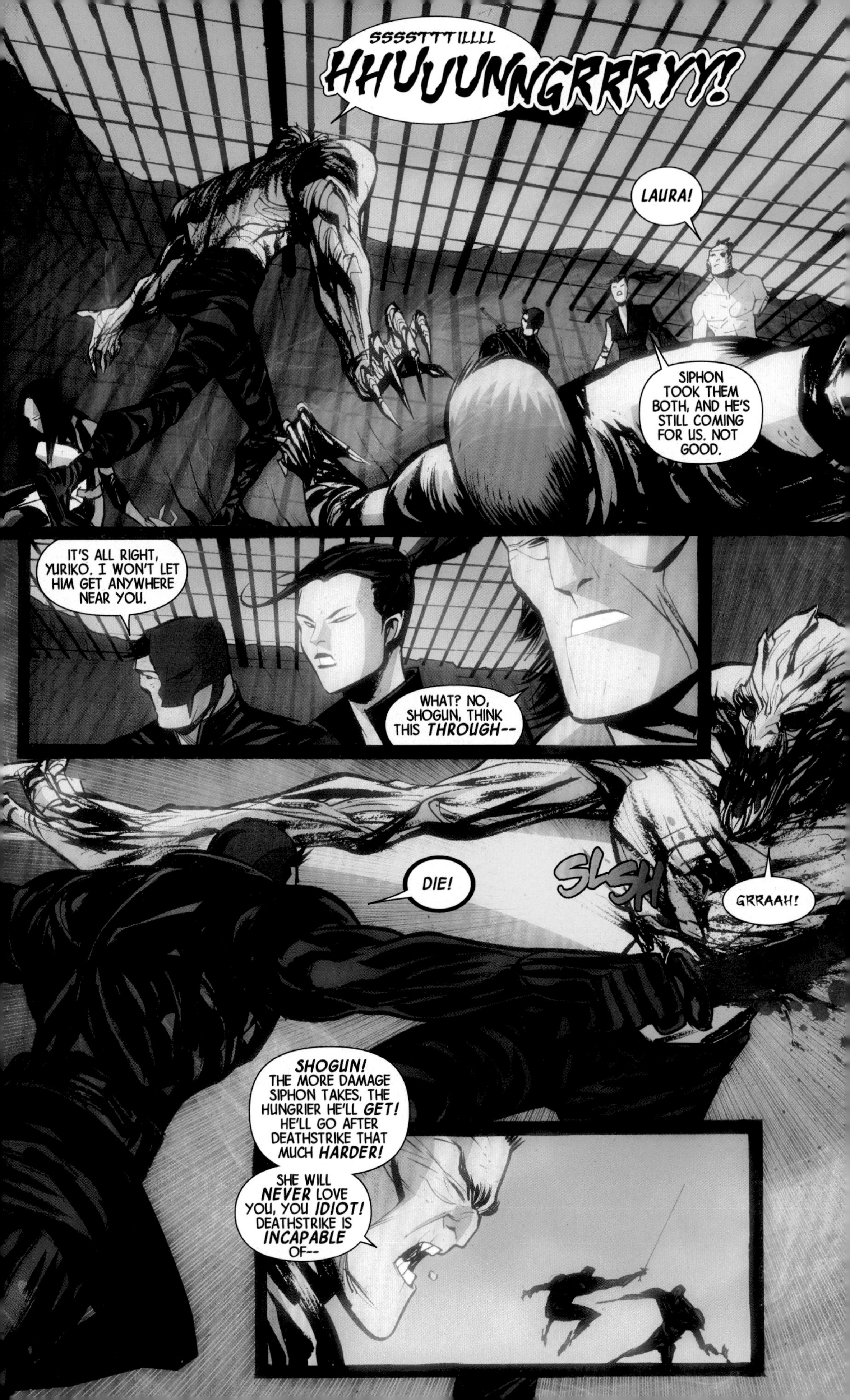
SSSSTTTTIIIII
HHUUUUNNGRRRYY!
LAURA!
SIPHON TOOK THEM BOTH, AND HE'S STILL COMING FOR US. NOT GOOD.
IT'S ALL RIGHT, YURIKO. I WON'T LET HIM GET ANYWHERE NEAR YOU.
WHAT? NO, SHOGUN, THINK THIS THROUGH--
DIE!
SLSH
GRRAAH!
SHOGUN! THE MORE DAMAGE SIPHON TAKES, THE HUNGRIER HE'LL GET! HE'LL GO AFTER DEATHSTRIKE THAT MUCH HARDER!
SHE WILL NEVER LOVE YOU, YOU IDIOT! DEATHSTRIKE IS INCAPABLE OF--

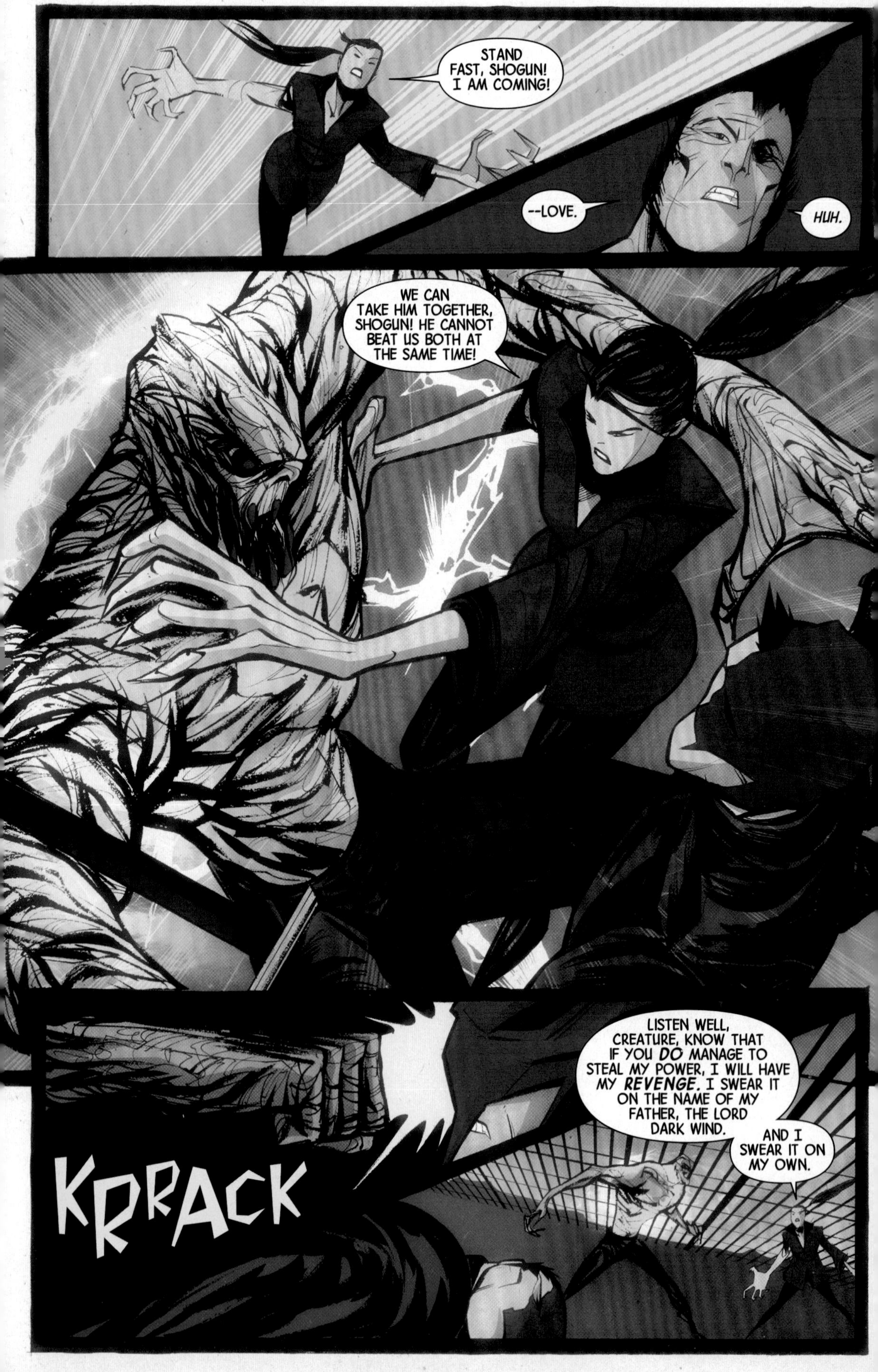
STAND FAST, SHOGUN! I AM COMING!
--LOVE.
HUH.
WE CAN TAKE HIM TOGETHER, SHOGUN! HE CANNOT BEAT US BOTH AT THE SAME TIME!
KRRACK
LISTEN WELL, CREATURE, KNOW THAT IF YOU DO MANAGE TO STEAL MY POWER, I WILL HAVE MY REVENGE. I SWEAR IT ON THE NAME OF MY FATHER, THE LORD DARK WIND.
AND I SWEAR IT ON MY OWN.

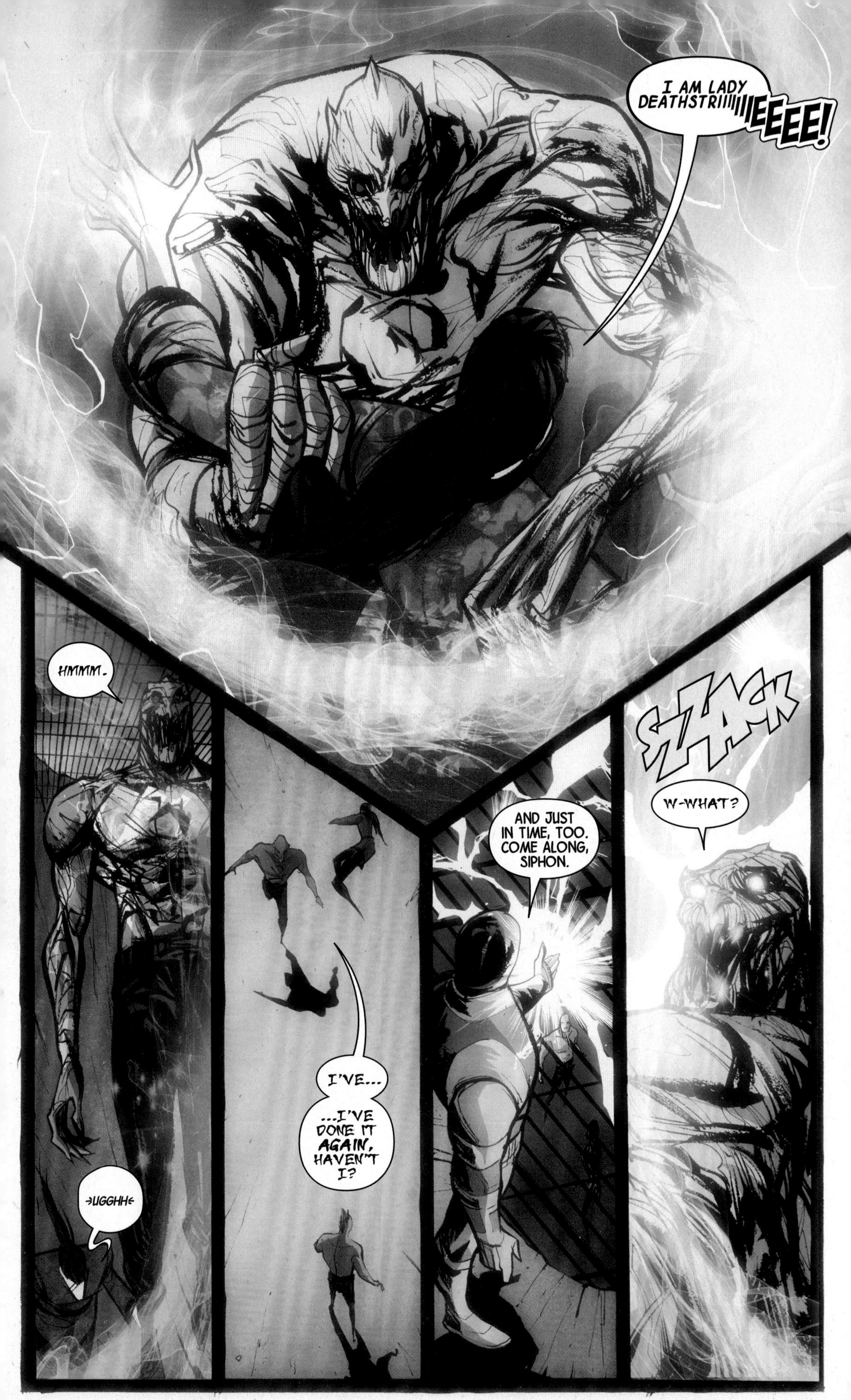
I AM LADY DEATHSTRIIIIIIIIEEEEE!
HMMM.
ÆUGGHH
I'VE...
...I'VE DONE IT AGAIN, HAVEN'T I?
AND JUST IN TIME, TOO. COME ALONG, SIPHON.
SZZACK
W-WHAT?

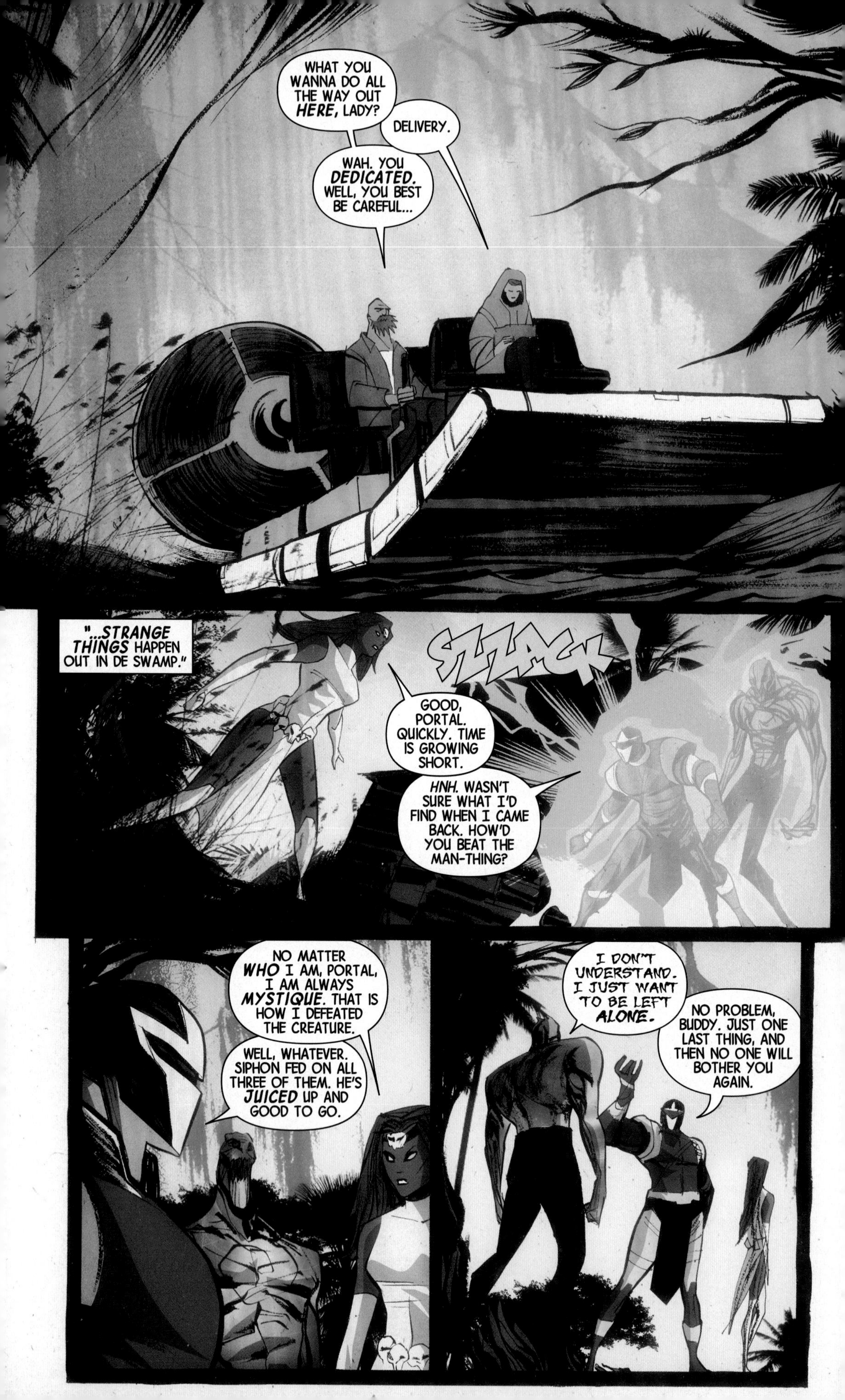
WHAT YOU WANNA DO ALL THE WAY OUT HERE, LADY?
DELIVERY.
WAH. YOU DEDICATED. WELL, YOU BEST BE CAREFUL...
"...STRANGE THINGS HAPPEN OUT IN DE SWAMP."
SZZACK
GOOD, PORTAL. QUICKLY. TIME IS GROWING SHORT.
HNH. WASN'T SURE WHAT I'D FIND WHEN I CAME BACK. HOW'D YOU BEAT THE MAN-THING?
NO MATTER WHO I AM, PORTAL, I AM ALWAYS MYSTIQUE. THAT IS HOW I DEFEATED THE CREATURE.
WELL, WHATEVER. SIPHON FED ON ALL THREE OF THEM. HE'S JUICED UP AND GOOD TO GO.
I DON'T UNDERSTAND. I JUST WANT TO BE LEFT ALONE.
NO PROBLEM, BUDDY. JUST ONE LAST THING, AND THEN NO ONE WILL BOTHER YOU AGAIN.

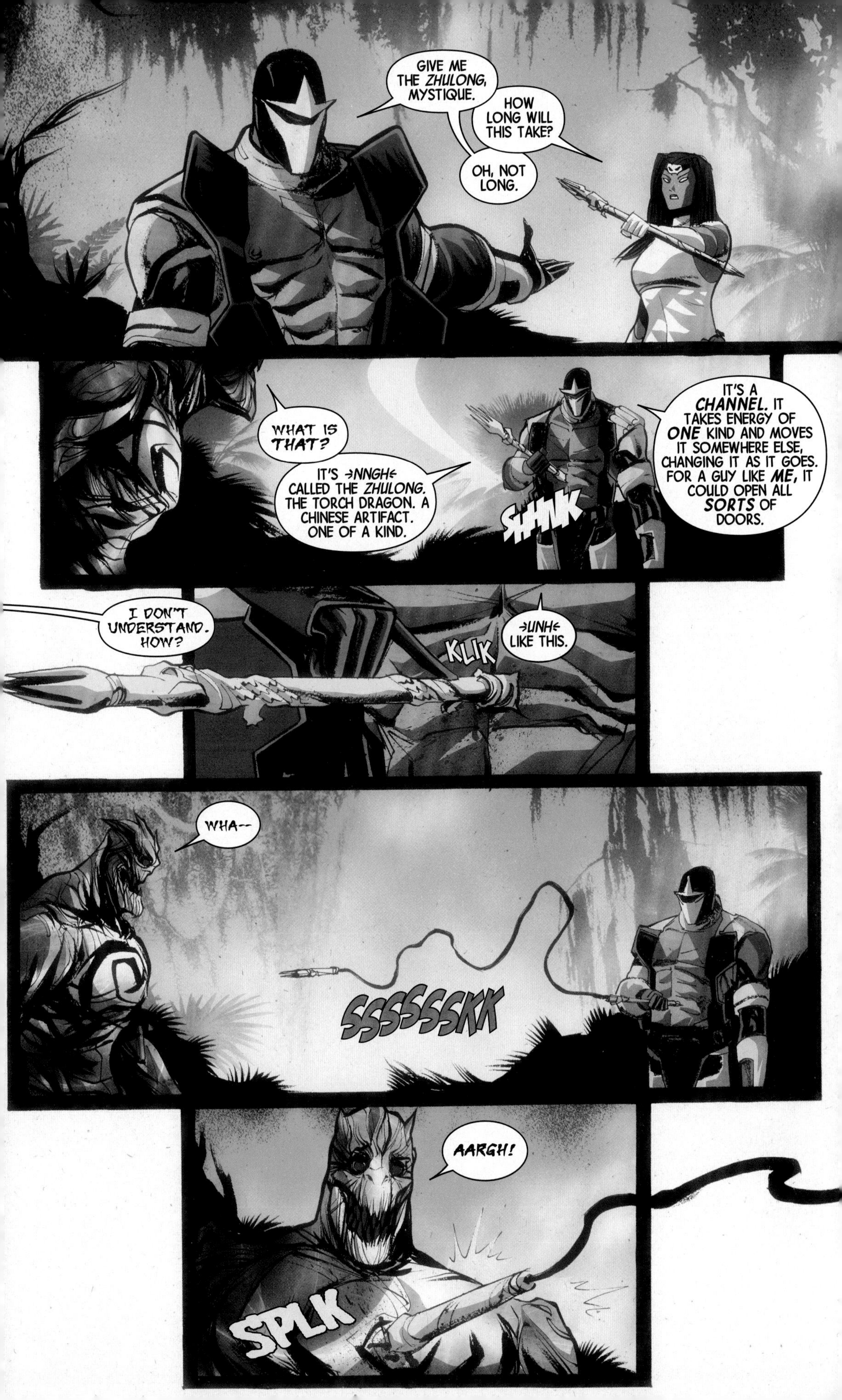

GIVE ME THE ZHULONG, MYSTIQUE.
HOW LONG WILL THIS TAKE?
OH, NOT LONG.
WHAT IS THAT?
IT'S ›NNGH‹ CALLED THE ZHULONG. THE TORCH DRAGON. A CHINESE ARTIFACT. ONE OF A KIND.
SHNK
IT'S A CHANNEL. IT TAKES ENERGY OF ONE KIND AND MOVES IT SOMEWHERE ELSE, CHANGING IT AS IT GOES. FOR A GUY LIKE ME, IT COULD OPEN ALL SORTS OF DOORS.
I DON'T UNDERSTAND. HOW?
KLIK
›UNH‹ LIKE THIS.
WHA--
SSSSSSKK
AARGH!
SPLK

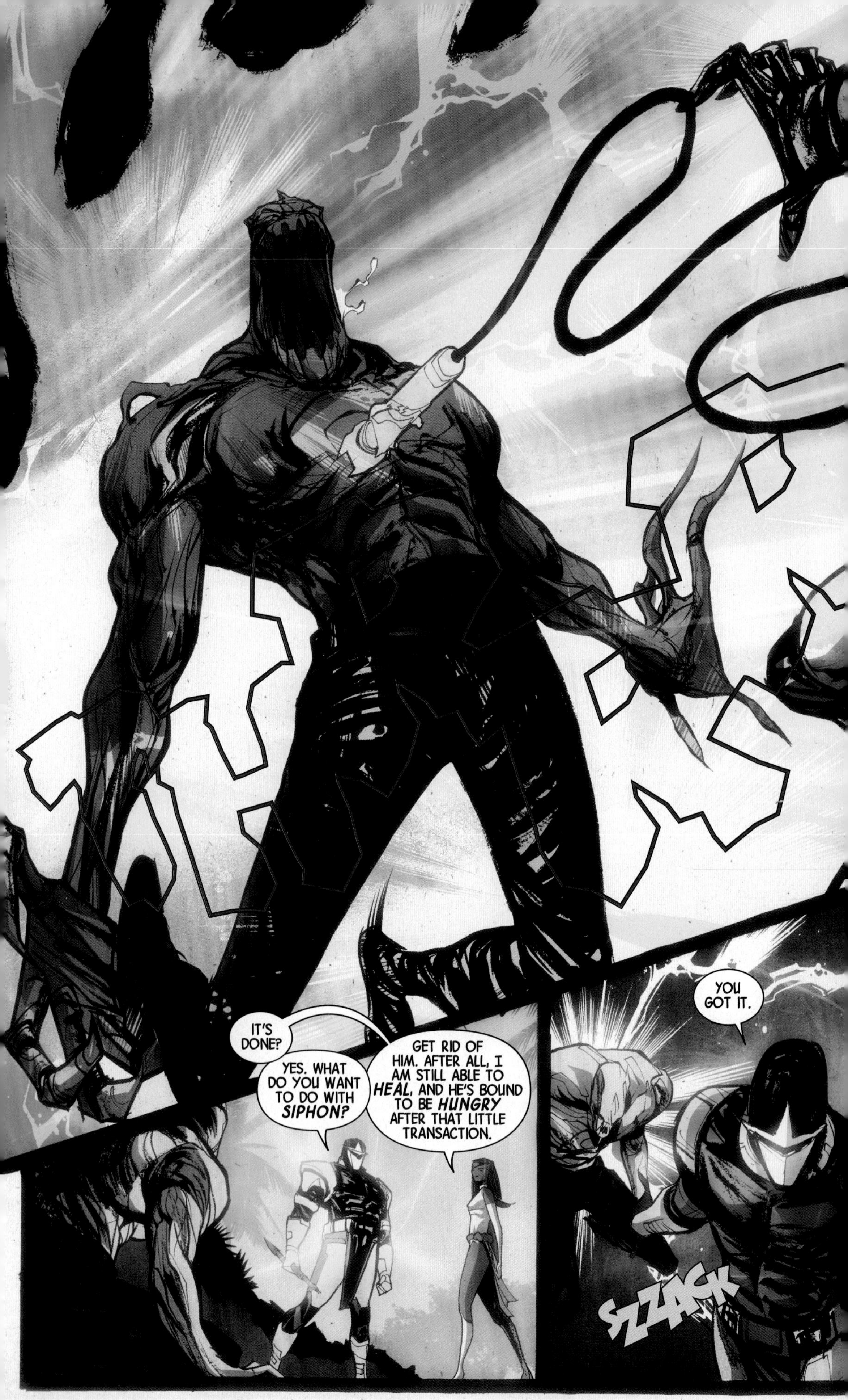
IT'S DONE?
YES. WHAT DO YOU WANT TO DO WITH SIPHON?
GET RID OF HIM. AFTER ALL, I AM STILL ABLE TO HEAL, AND HE'S BOUND TO BE HUNGRY AFTER THAT LITTLE TRANSACTION.
YOU GOT IT.
SZZACK

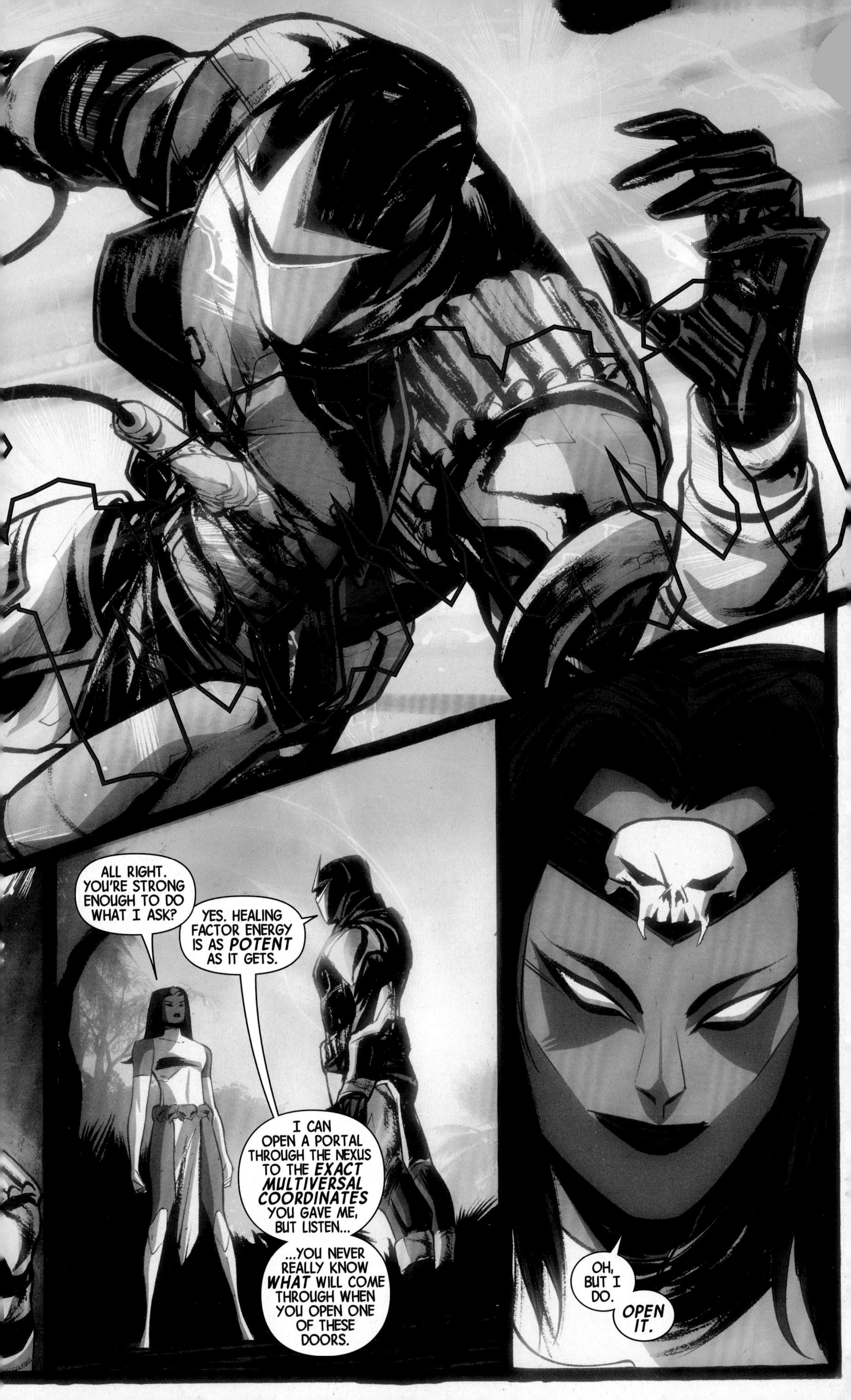
ALL RIGHT. YOU'RE STRONG ENOUGH TO DO WHAT I ASK?
YES. HEALING FACTOR ENERGY IS AS *POTENT* AS IT GETS.
I CAN OPEN A PORTAL THROUGH THE NEXUS TO THE *EXACT MULTIVERSAL COORDINATES* YOU GAVE ME, BUT LISTEN...
...YOU NEVER REALLY KNOW *WHAT* WILL COME THROUGH WHEN YOU OPEN ONE OF THESE DOORS.
OH, BUT I DO.
OPEN IT.

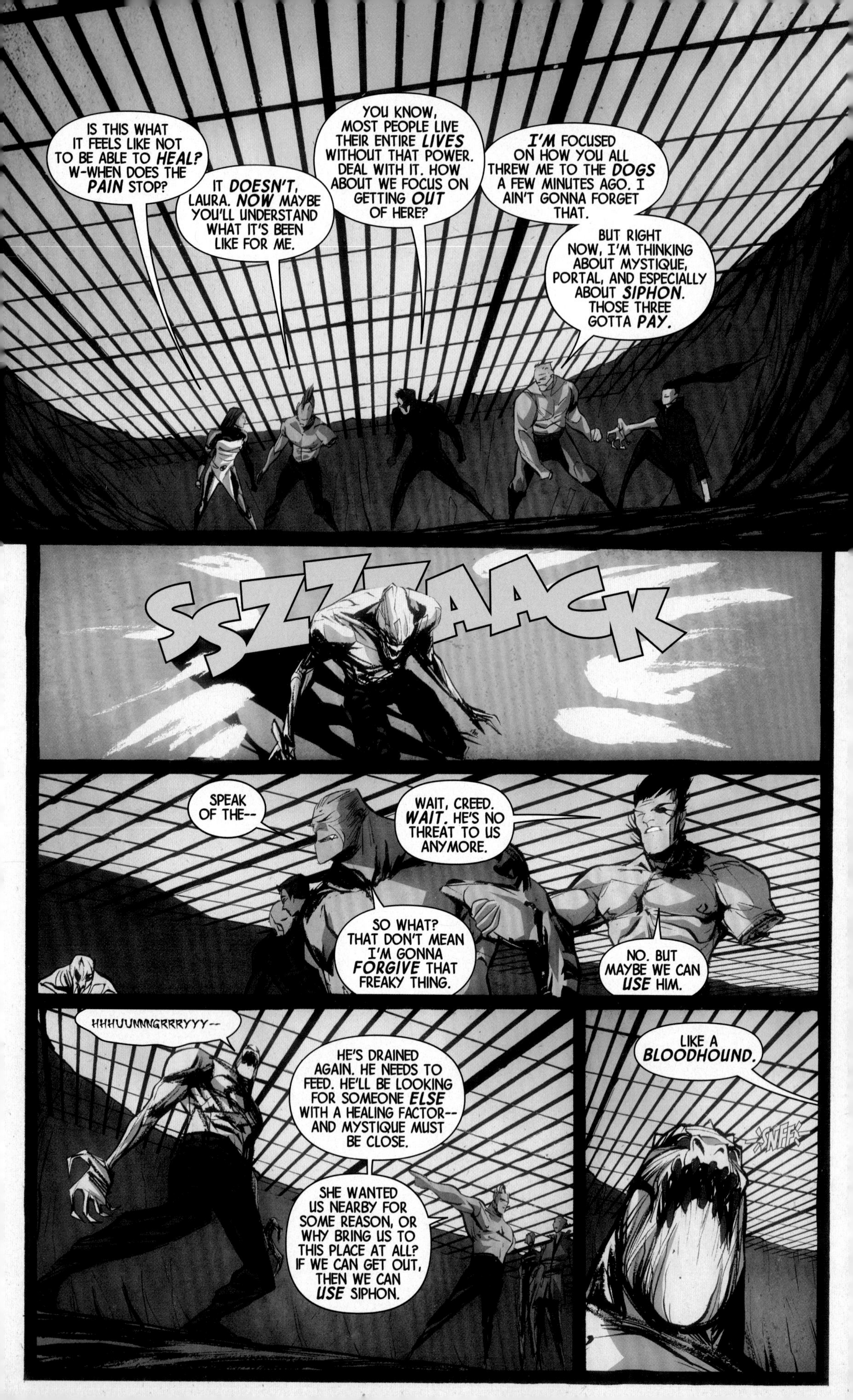
IS THIS WHAT IT FEELS LIKE NOT TO BE ABLE TO HEAL? W-WHEN DOES THE PAIN STOP?
IT DOESN'T, LAURA. NOW MAYBE YOU'LL UNDERSTAND WHAT IT'S BEEN LIKE FOR ME.
YOU KNOW, MOST PEOPLE LIVE THEIR ENTIRE LIVES WITHOUT THAT POWER. DEAL WITH IT. HOW ABOUT WE FOCUS ON GETTING OUT OF HERE?
I'M FOCUSED ON HOW YOU ALL THREW ME TO THE DOGS A FEW MINUTES AGO. I AIN'T GONNA FORGET THAT.
BUT RIGHT NOW, I'M THINKING ABOUT MYSTIQUE, PORTAL, AND ESPECIALLY ABOUT SIPHON. THOSE THREE GOTTA PAY.
SSZZZAACK
SPEAK OF THE--
WAIT, CREED. WAIT. HE'S NO THREAT TO US ANYMORE.
SO WHAT? THAT DON'T MEAN I'M GONNA FORGIVE THAT FREAKY THING.
NO. BUT MAYBE WE CAN USE HIM.
HHHUUMNNGRRRYYY--
HE'S DRAINED AGAIN. HE NEEDS TO FEED. HE'LL BE LOOKING FOR SOMEONE ELSE WITH A HEALING FACTOR-- AND MYSTIQUE MUST BE CLOSE.
SHE WANTED US NEARBY FOR SOME REASON, OR WHY BRING US TO THIS PLACE AT ALL? IF WE CAN GET OUT, THEN WE CAN USE SIPHON.
LIKE A BLOODHOUND.

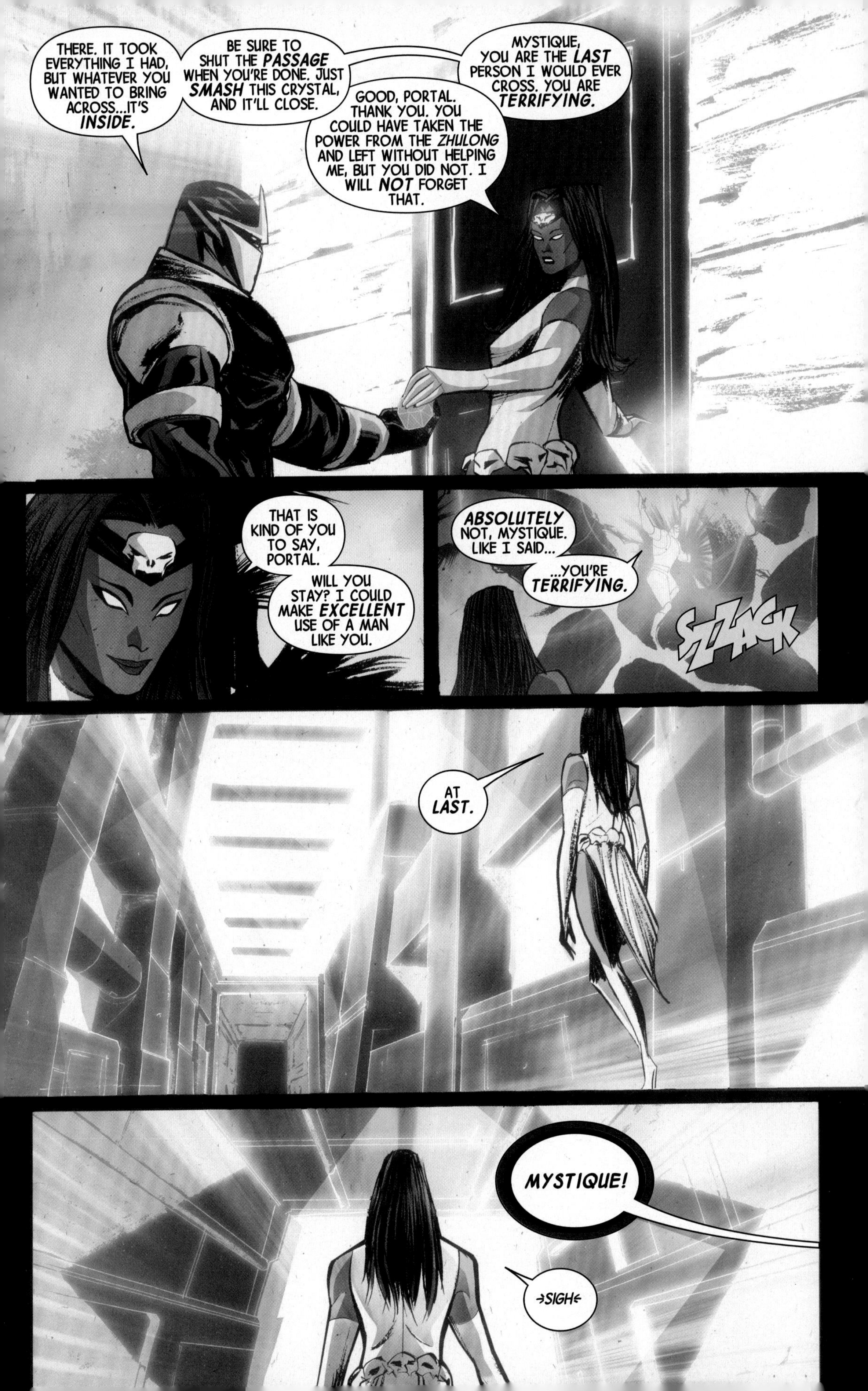
THERE. IT TOOK EVERYTHING I HAD, BUT WHATEVER YOU WANTED TO BRING ACROSS...IT'S INSIDE.
BE SURE TO SHUT THE PASSAGE WHEN YOU'RE DONE. JUST SMASH THIS CRYSTAL, AND IT'LL CLOSE.
MYSTIQUE, YOU ARE THE LAST PERSON I WOULD EVER CROSS. YOU ARE TERRIFYING.
GOOD, PORTAL. THANK YOU. YOU COULD HAVE TAKEN THE POWER FROM THE ZHULONG AND LEFT WITHOUT HELPING ME, BUT YOU DID NOT. I WILL NOT FORGET THAT.
THAT IS KIND OF YOU TO SAY, PORTAL.
WILL YOU STAY? I COULD MAKE EXCELLENT USE OF A MAN LIKE YOU.
ABSOLUTELY NOT, MYSTIQUE. LIKE I SAID...
...YOU'RE TERRIFYING.
SZZACK
AT LAST.
MYSTIQUE!
→SIGH←

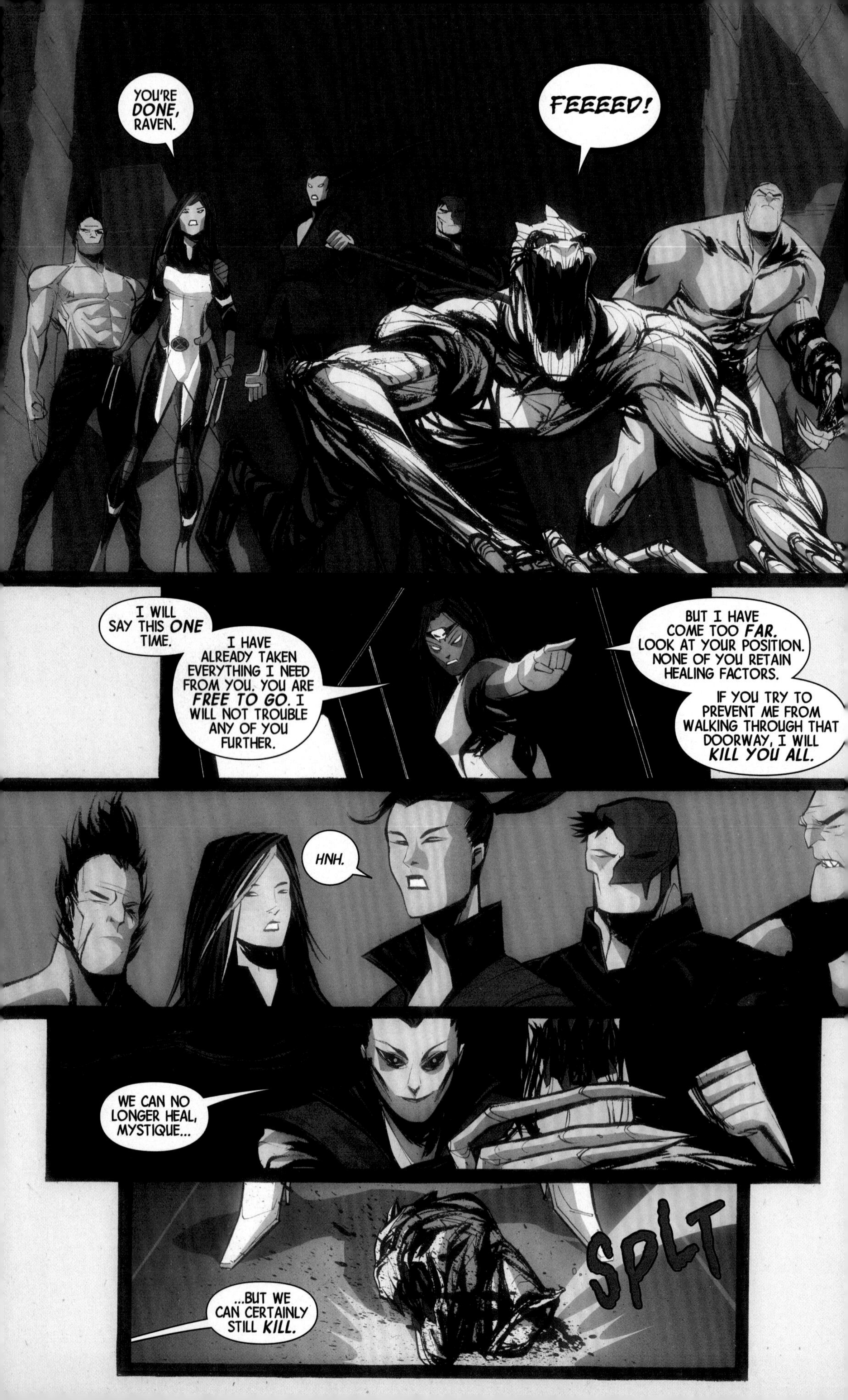

YOU'RE DONE, RAVEN.
FEEEED!
I WILL SAY THIS ONE TIME.
I HAVE ALREADY TAKEN EVERYTHING I NEED FROM YOU. YOU ARE FREE TO GO. I WILL NOT TROUBLE ANY OF YOU FURTHER.
BUT I HAVE COME TOO FAR. LOOK AT YOUR POSITION. NONE OF YOU RETAIN HEALING FACTORS.
IF YOU TRY TO PREVENT ME FROM WALKING THROUGH THAT DOORWAY, I WILL KILL YOU ALL.
HNH.
WE CAN NO LONGER HEAL, MYSTIQUE...
SPLT
...BUT WE CAN CERTAINLY STILL KILL.

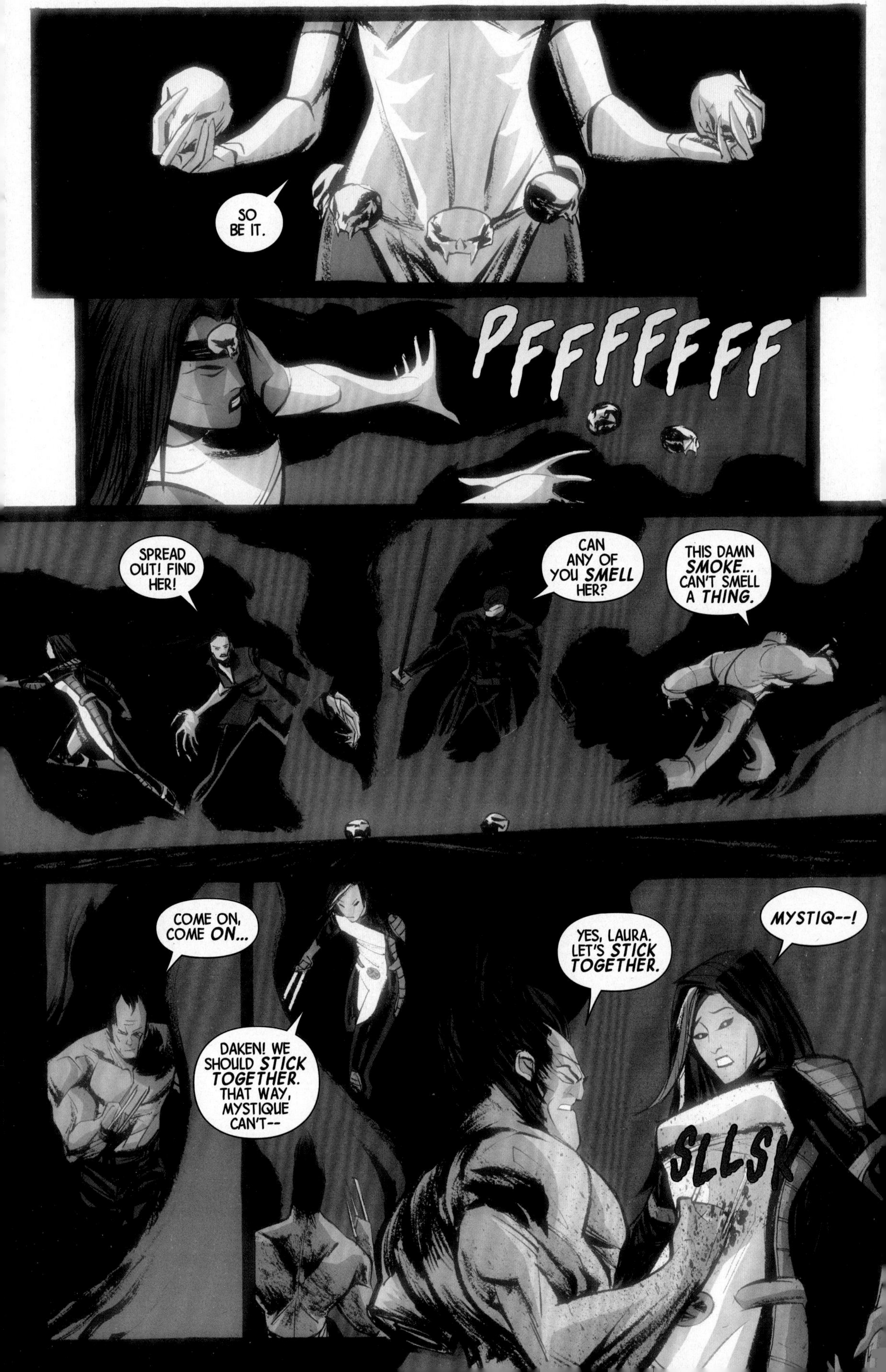
SO BE IT.
PFFFFFFF
SPREAD OUT! FIND HER!
CAN ANY OF YOU SMELL HER?
THIS DAMN SMOKE... CAN'T SMELL A THING.
COME ON, COME ON...
DAKEN! WE SHOULD STICK TOGETHER. THAT WAY, MYSTIQUE CAN'T--
YES, LAURA. LET'S STICK TOGETHER.
MYSTIQ--!
SLLSK

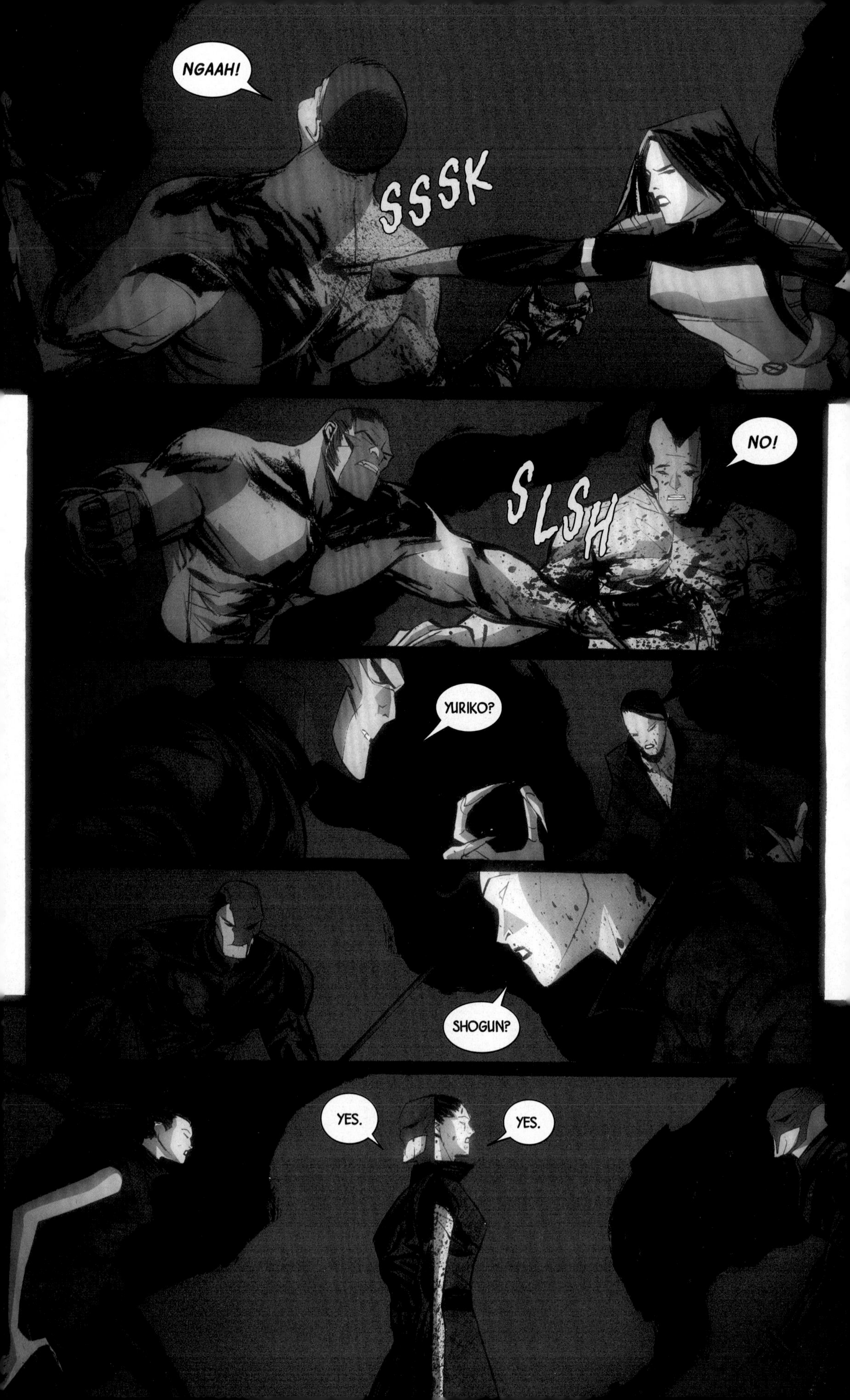
NGAAH!
SSSK
NO!
SLSH
YURIKO?
SHOGUN?
YES.
YES.

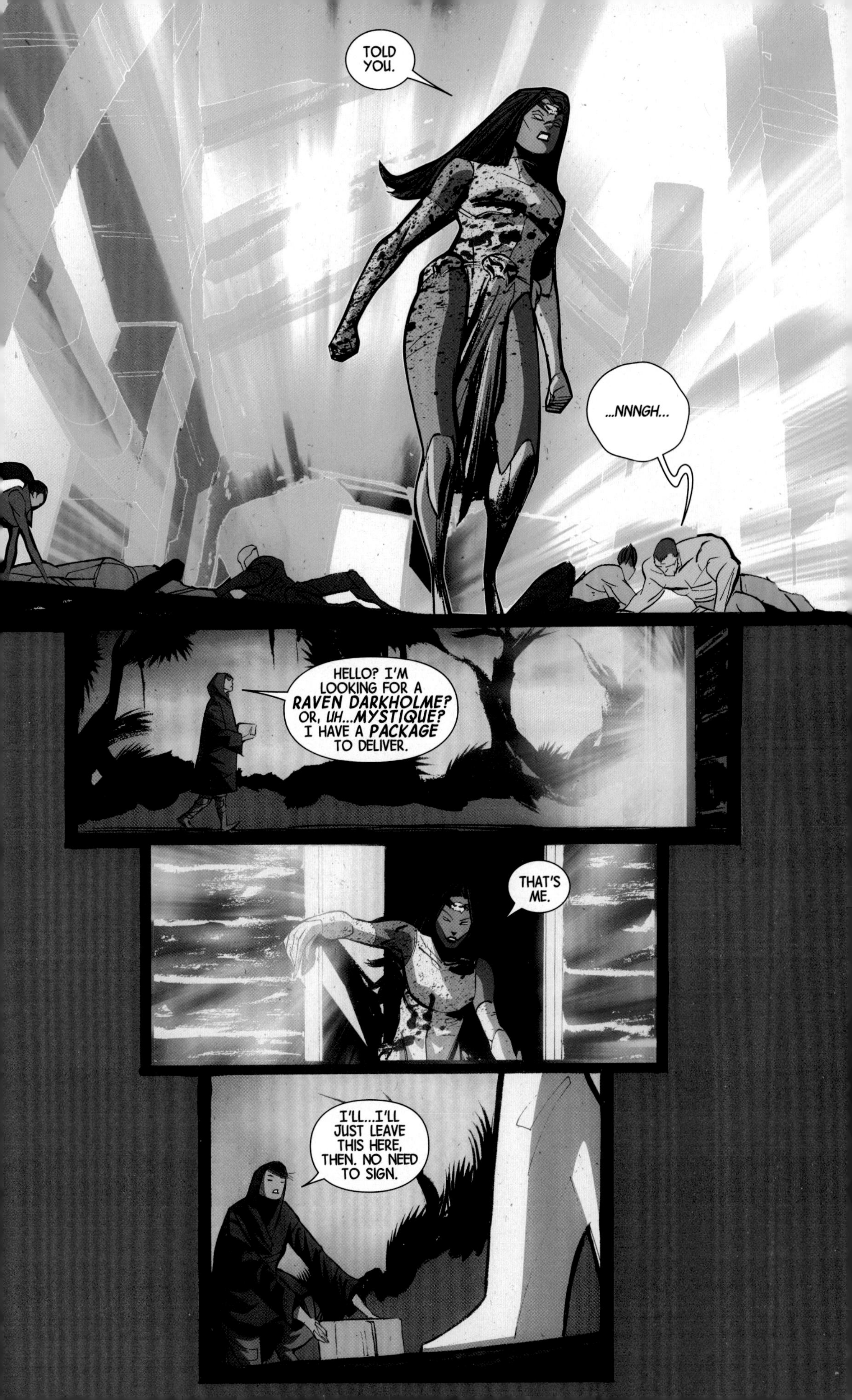
TOLD YOU.
...NNNGH...
HELLO? I'M LOOKING FOR A RAVEN DARKHOLME? OR, UH...MYSTIQUE? I HAVE A PACKAGE TO DELIVER.
THAT'S ME.
I'LL...I'LL JUST LEAVE THIS HERE, THEN. NO NEED TO SIGN.

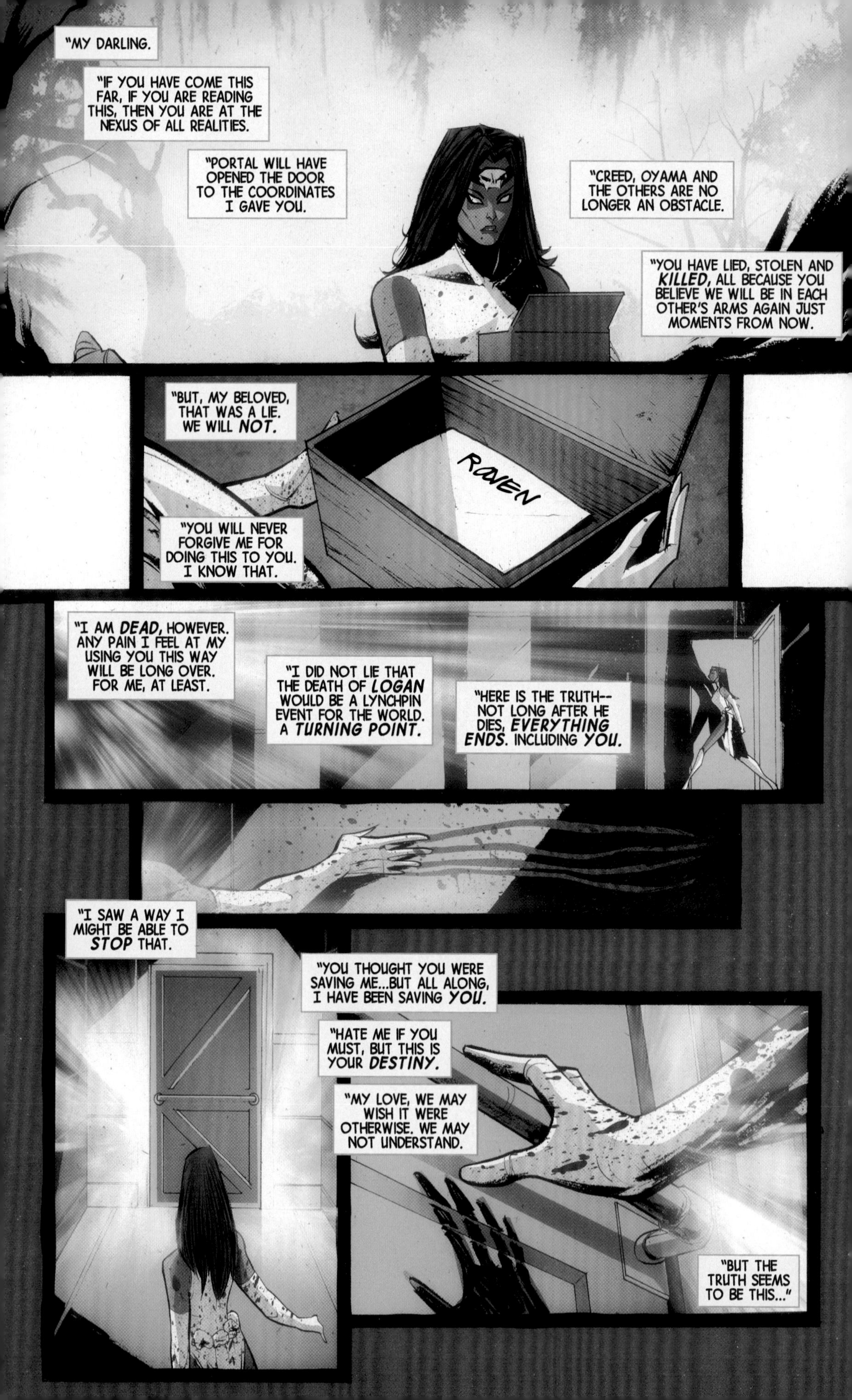
"MY DARLING.
"IF YOU HAVE COME THIS FAR, IF YOU ARE READING THIS, THEN YOU ARE AT THE NEXUS OF ALL REALITIES.
"PORTAL WILL HAVE OPENED THE DOOR TO THE COORDINATES I GAVE YOU.
"CREED, OYAMA AND THE OTHERS ARE NO LONGER AN OBSTACLE.
"YOU HAVE LIED, STOLEN AND KILLED, ALL BECAUSE YOU BELIEVE WE WILL BE IN EACH OTHER'S ARMS AGAIN JUST MOMENTS FROM NOW.
"BUT, MY BELOVED, THAT WAS A LIE. WE WILL NOT.
RAVEN
"YOU WILL NEVER FORGIVE ME FOR DOING THIS TO YOU. I KNOW THAT.
"I AM DEAD, HOWEVER. ANY PAIN I FEEL AT MY USING YOU THIS WAY WILL BE LONG OVER. FOR ME, AT LEAST.
"I DID NOT LIE THAT THE DEATH OF LOGAN WOULD BE A LYNCHPIN EVENT FOR THE WORLD. A TURNING POINT.
"HERE IS THE TRUTH-- NOT LONG AFTER HE DIES, EVERYTHING ENDS. INCLUDING YOU.
"I SAW A WAY I MIGHT BE ABLE TO STOP THAT.
"YOU THOUGHT YOU WERE SAVING ME...BUT ALL ALONG, I HAVE BEEN SAVING YOU.
"HATE ME IF YOU MUST, BUT THIS IS YOUR DESTINY.
"MY LOVE, WE MAY WISH IT WERE OTHERWISE. WE MAY NOT UNDERSTAND.
"BUT THE TRUTH SEEMS TO BE THIS..."

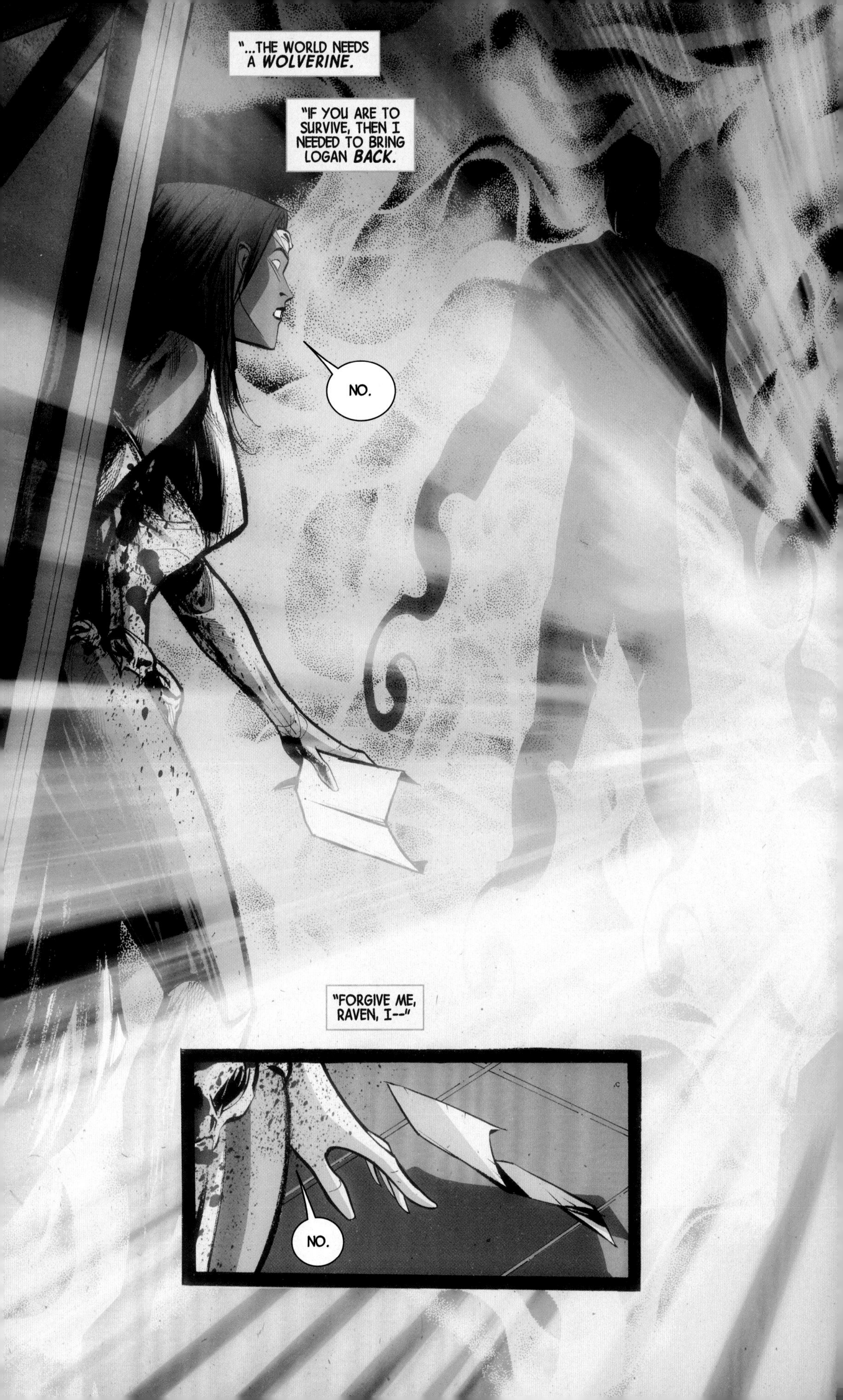
"...THE WORLD NEEDS A WOLVERINE.
"IF YOU ARE TO SURVIVE, THEN I NEEDED TO BRING LOGAN BACK.
NO.
"FORGIVE ME, RAVEN, I--"
NO.

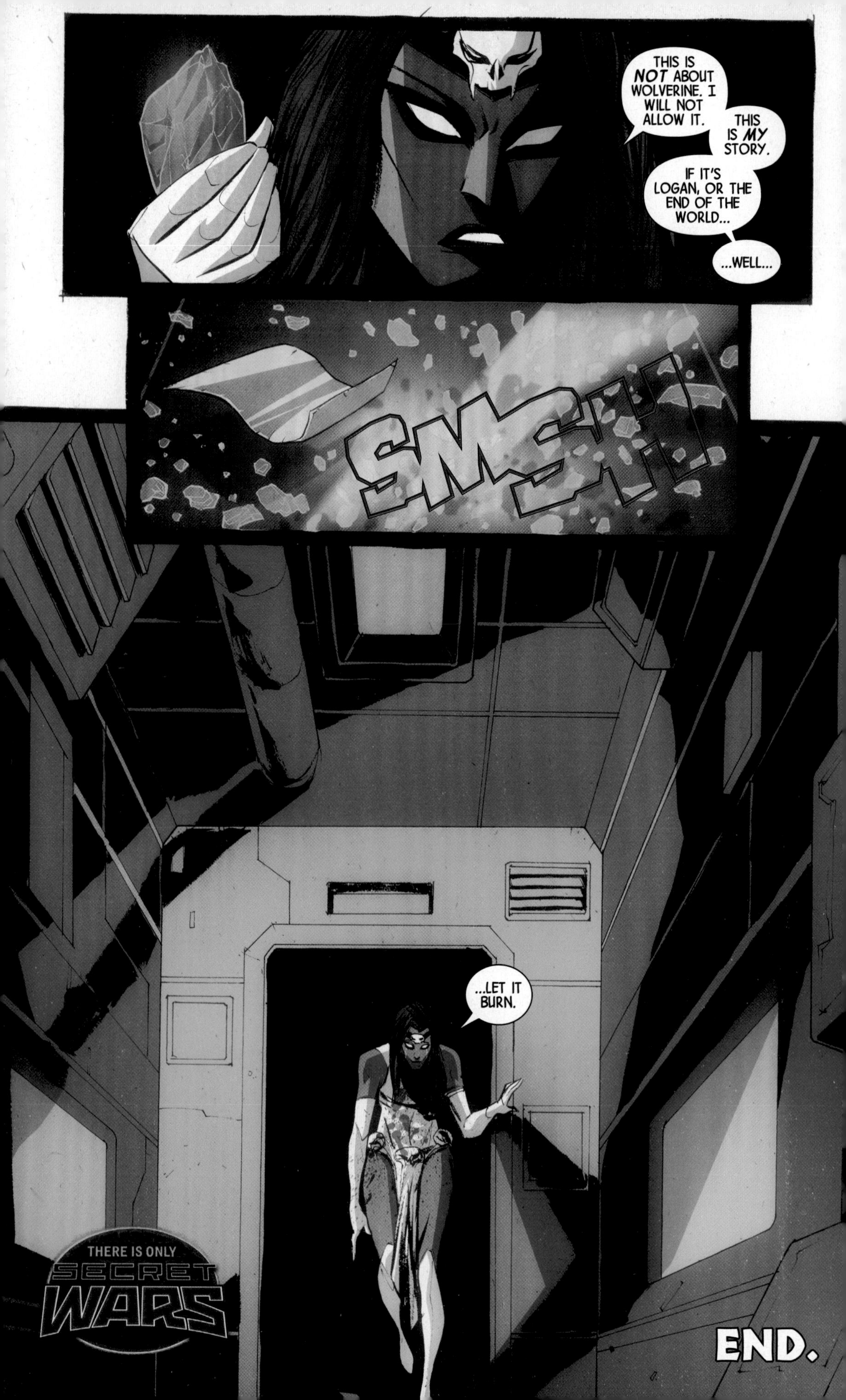
THIS IS NOT ABOUT WOLVERINE. I WILL NOT ALLOW IT.
THIS IS MY STORY.
IF IT'S LOGAN, OR THE END OF THE WORLD...
...WELL...
SMSH
...LET IT BURN.
THERE IS ONLY SECRET WARS
END.

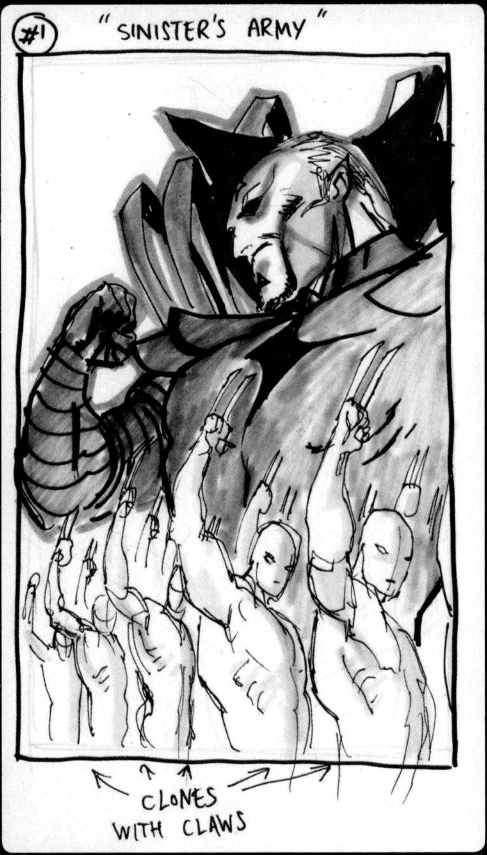
#1
"SINISTER'S ARMY"
CLONES WITH CLAWS

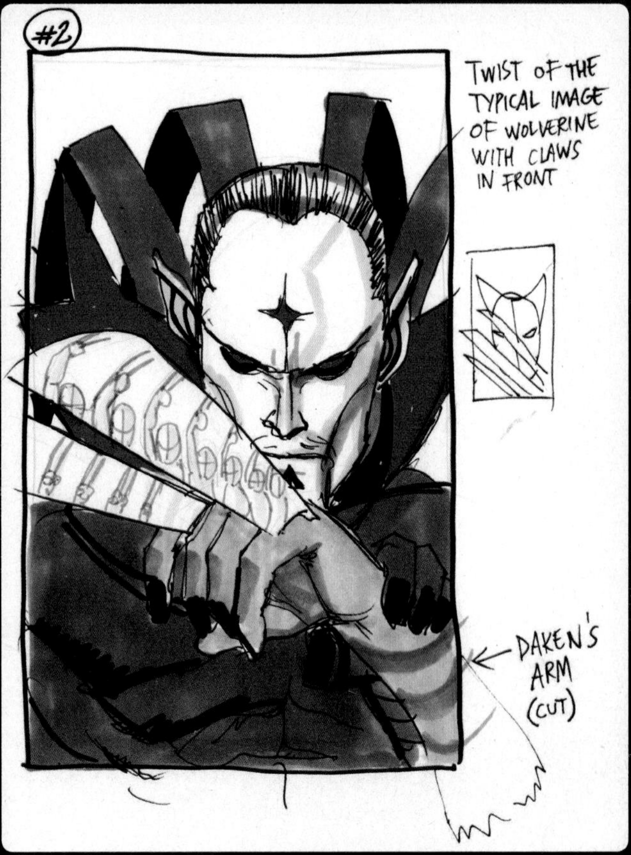
#2
TWIST OF THE TYPICAL IMAGE OF WOLVERINE WITH CLAWS IN FRONT
DAKEN'S ARM (CUT)

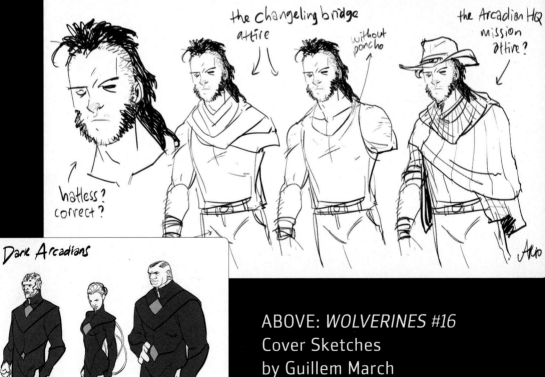

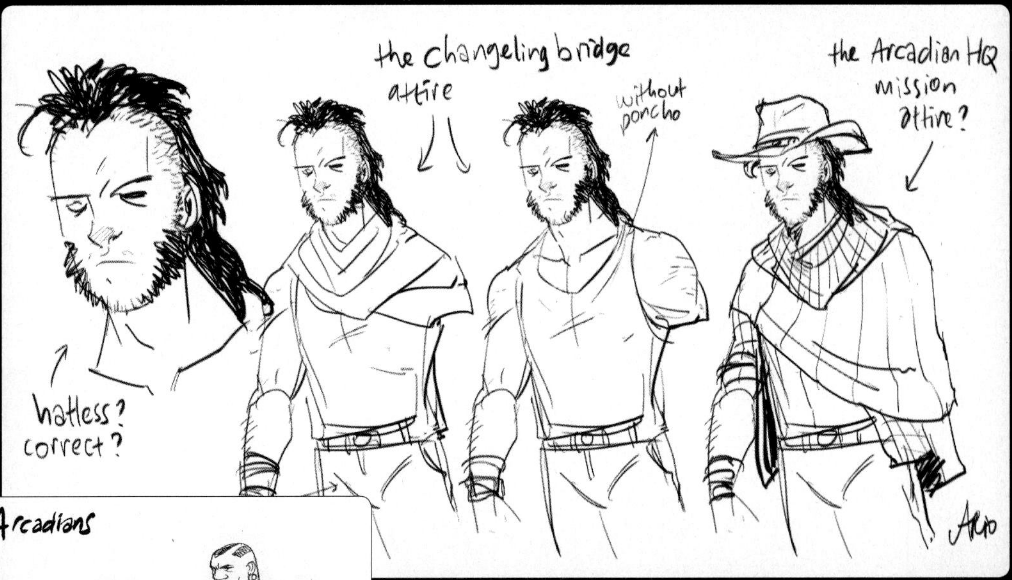
the changeling bridge attire
without poncho
the Arcadian HQ mission attire?
hatless? correct?
Ario

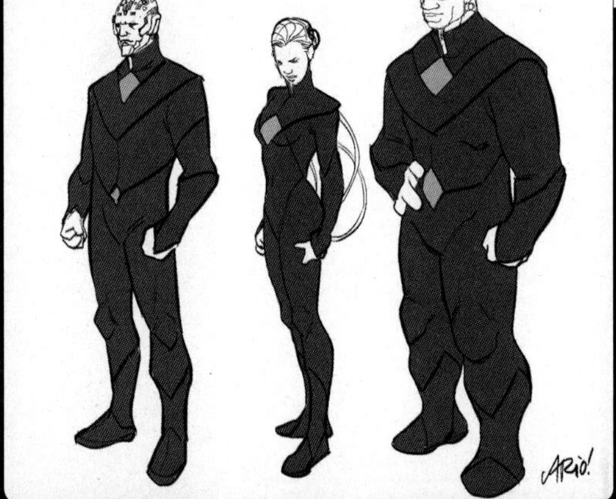
Dark Arcadians
Ario!

ABOVE: *WOLVERINES* #16
Cover Sketches
by Guillem March

BELOW:
Character Sketches
by Ario Anindito

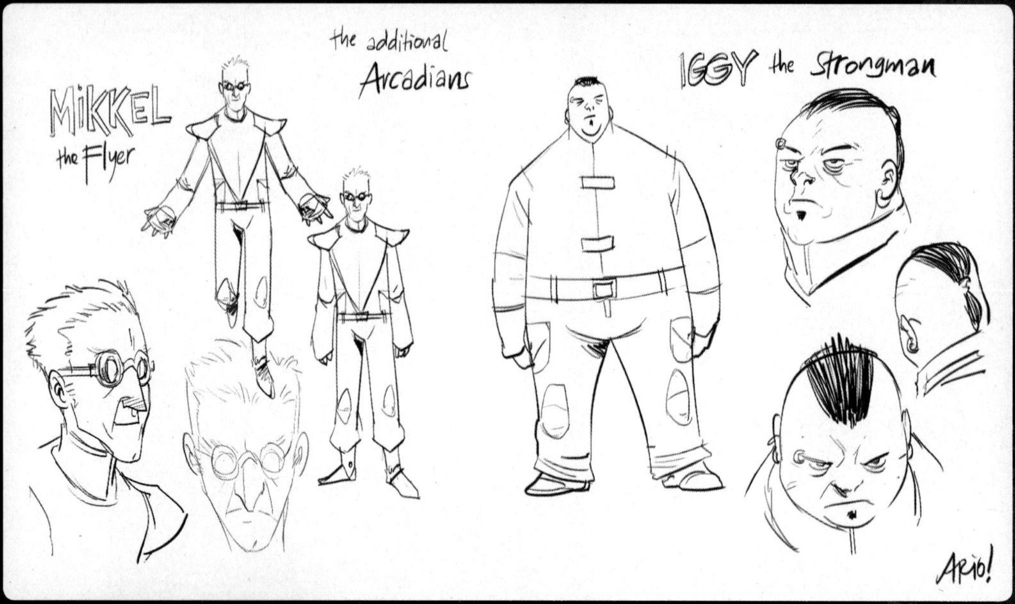
the additional
Arcadians
MiKKEL
the Flyer
IGGY the Strongman
Ario!

Character Sketches
by Ario Anindito

WOLVERINES #17-19
Cover Sketches
by Juan Doe

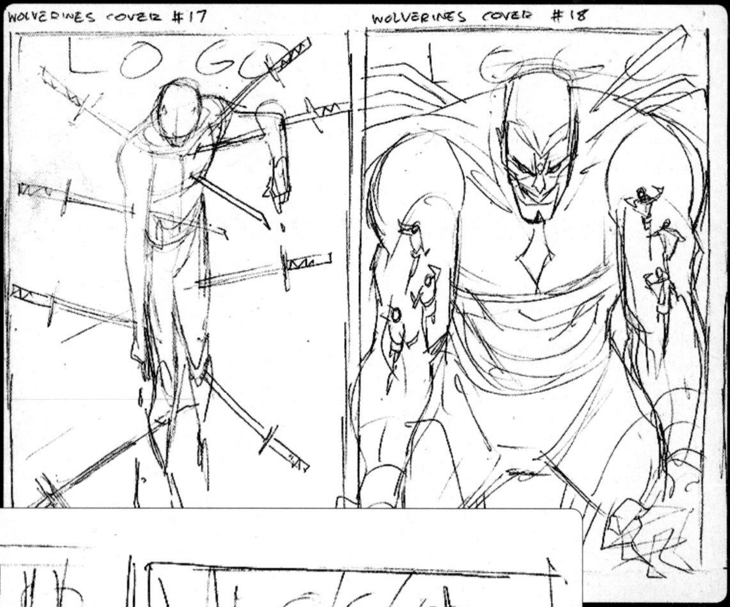
WOLVERINES COVER #17
WOLVERINES COVER #18
LOGO

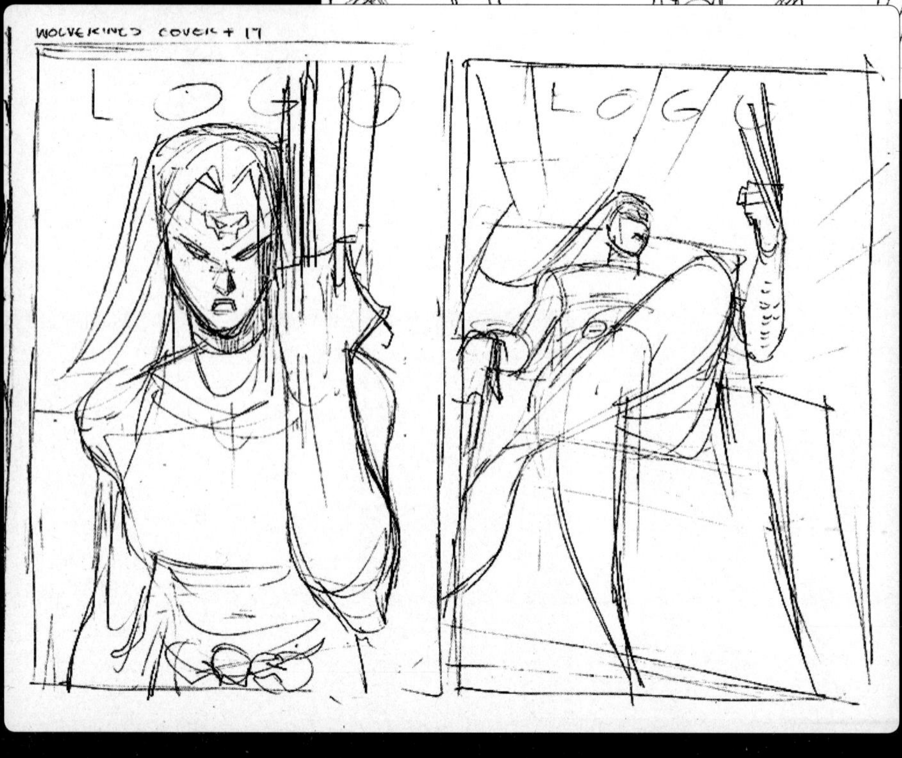
WOLVERINES COVER #17
LOGO
LOGO